ADAM KOK'S GRIQUAS

BOOKS IN THIS SERIES

ADAM KOK'S GRIQUAS

A study in the development of stratification in South Africa

ROBERT ROSS

CAMBRIDGE UNIVERSITY PRESS

CAMBRIDGE
LONDON · NEW YORK · MELBOURNE

Published by the Syndics of the Cambridge University Press
The Pitt Building, Trumpington Street, Cambridge CB2 1RP
Bentley House, 200 Euston Road, London NW1 2DB
32 East 57th Street, New York, NY 10022, USA
296 Beaconsfield Parade, Middle Park, Melbourne 3206, Australia

© Cambridge University Press 1976

First published 1976

Printed in Great Britain
by Redwood Burn Limited,
Trowbridge and Esher

Library of Congress Cataloguing in Publication Data
Ross, Robert, 1949—
Adam Kok's Griquas : a study in the development of
stratification in South Africa.
(African studies series ; 21)
Bibliography: p.
Includes index.
1. Griquas. 2. Kok, Adam, 1811—1875. I. Title.
II. Series.
DT764.G7R67   301.44'0968   75-43368
ISBN 0 521 21199 9

CONTENTS

PREFACE

This book is a micro-study, an attempt to illumine the history of southern Africa during the nineteenth century by focusing on the activities of one small group, who formed part of the mosaic of disparate but increasingly interrelated social units of the southern part of the continent. It is to be hoped that a view of that history looking outwards from Philippolis and Kokstad will provide a perspective rather different from those otherwise available. On the other hand, it is my hope that the story of the Griquas will prove interesting and, in a sad sort of way, enjoyable in its own right, so this work may be judged for its story-telling as well as for its purely academic value.

Nevertheless, this book is the product of extensive research, during the course of which I incurred many debts of gratitude, which I would like to acknowledge, if not fully repay, here. The Social Science Research Council and the Smuts Fund for Commonwealth Studies financed my research. Various aspects of my work as it progressed were presented to seminars of the Universities of Cambridge and Cape Town and of the Institute of Commonwealth Studies, London, and the participants in these meetings were most useful in directing me away from blind alleys into which I was heading, while the Thursday mornings at the ICS in Russell Square, in particular, did much to provide the context within which my ideas have developed.

I must also thank most heartily all those people who have given me hospitality in the course of a research project more peripatetic than most. A host of friends, friends of friends and casual acquaintances have from time to time allowed me to use their spare beds or their floors, and for this I am most grateful, as I am to the numerous people who have taken pity on a man standing by the side of the road with his thumb out.

Above all the loose society that gathered around the School of African Studies of the University of Cape Town made a long stay in a foreign country most enjoyable, and to them I owe my deep thanks. On a more formal level, the staff of the two dozen archives and libraries in which I worked were uniformly helpful. If I single out Miss Irene Fletcher of the London Missionary Society, it is because

vii

she inducted me into the ways of archives with the consideration for which she has been legendary among generations of students.

Various individuals require to be given special mention, although the customary absolution from responsibility for any errors in this work must of course apply. Professor Ronald Robinson, now of Balliol College, Oxford, fostered my original interest in South African history. Moreover, he suggested that I should work on the Griquas, once again giving evidence of his uncanny nose for an interesting problem. Dr Martin Legassick provided many of the first contours within which my work developed and has been a constant encouragement and stimulus ever since. My Ph.D. examiners, Professors Eric Stokes and Shula Marks, made what might have been a terrifying ordeal an immensely valuable one, while Anthony Atmore and my sister, Anne Stevens, read the typescript of this work and made many useful suggestions.

Various portions of chapter 8 have previously appeared in R. Ross, 'Grique government', *African Studies* 33 (1) (1974), 36–40, and in an article of mine in Robin Derricourt and C. C. Saunders (eds.), *Beyond the Cape Frontier, Studies in the History of the Transkei and Ciskei* (Cape Town, 1974), and are reprinted by permission of the Witwatersrand University Press, Johannesburg, and the Longman Group Ltd, respectively. In a similar vein, Hendrix von Aswegen of the Rand Afrikaans Uniwersiteit and Christopher Saunders of the University of Cape Town kindly allowed me to quote from their unpublished theses.

I owe special thanks to four people. Jeff Leeuwenburg not only drove me round South Africa and survived the two months' close proximity that this entailed but also used his great knowledge of the Griqua patois and culture to make a far better interviewer than I could ever have done. Moreover, he received and demolished many more of my ideas than was his due. John Iliffe's patient supervision and encouragement did as much as possible to overcome my own slapdash habits and make this work approach professional canons. Lastly, my parents' encouragement and concern have always been a great support and comfort to me, and to them I dedicate this book.

Leiden   R.R.

NOTE ON TERMINOLOGY

With two exceptions, the names of the various African peoples and areas follow those of the *Oxford History of South Africa* (eds. M. Wilson and L. M. Thompson (2 vols., Oxford, 1969, 1971), I, viii–ix), eliminating all prefixes and suffixes and keeping traditional spellings for areas but not for peoples – thus 'Mpondo' but 'Pondoland'.

The exceptions are: (1) where necessary, I have added the character representing the 'click' in the Khoisan languages, which was occasionally omitted by the *Oxford History* – thus, specifically, '!Kora' not 'Kora', and also ≠Kari and Tsuni-//Goam; (2) in order to stress that they were a Dutch-speaking people and therefore should be treated similarly to the Boers, I have anglicised the plural of the main subjects of this study – thus 'Griquas', not 'Griqua'.

Other terms present problems. The *Oxford History* distinguished between physical anthropological, linguistic and economic classifications, but as it is part of the argument of this thesis that the racial classifications used in the nineteenth century were of great importance in shaping its history, I have used the term 'whites' as opposed to 'caucasoids', 'speakers of Dutch' or 'farmers', because this represented more exactly the concept then in use. The difficulty is that three of the racial terms of the time, Bushman, Hottentot and Kaffir – or later words such as Native or Bantu – are generally considered offensive. In this book, they are therefore rendered as San, Khoikhoi (with Khoisan being used for those whose status between the two was indeterminate) and African, except in direct or implied quotations from original material.

Again, many people who are now classified as 'coloured' regard such a designation as insulting, and normally describe themselves as 'so-called coloured' or, more usually, in translation of colloquial Afrikaans, as 'brown people'. However, the first of these designations is unbearably clumsy and the second is unintelligible outside South Africa – and very widely within it. Therefore the term 'coloured' has been retained throughout this book, although it has always been put within inverted commas out of respect to those who dispute its value.

A further distinction is necessary, this time in the terminology used for whites. Following conventional historical usage, I have used the word Afrikaner to refer to all those self-designated whites who spoke Dutch as a main language, reserving the word Boer for those of them who were farmers, especially pastoralists, generally transhumant, and for those, such as the hunters and traders of the north, who were very closely connected with the farming community.

ABBREVIATIONS

South African Archives
The following refer to series in the Cape archives. They are expanded in the bibliography:
BW; CBG; CMK; CO; GH; GLW; GO; GR; GWLC; LG; NA; RLR; VC
The following refer to series in the Orange Free State archives. They are always preceded by (OVS) and are expanded in the bibliography:
AC; AKT; BR; GS; HC; IB; SC; VR
The following refer to series in the Natal archives. They are always preceded by (Natal) and are expanded in the bibliography:
GH; PP; SNA

Other

AS   Assistant Secretary

ASLG   Assistant Secretary to the Lieutenant Governor

AYB for SAH   *Archives Year Book for South African History*

Bas. Rec.   G. M. Theal (ed.), *Basutoland Records* (3 vols., Cape Town, 1883)

BPP   This refers to a House of Commons Parliamentary Paper and is followed by the command number and the date of the session. The titles of the various papers are given in the bibliography.

CC   Civil Commissioner

CPP   This refers to a South African Parliamentary Paper, mainly from the Cape Province. It is always followed by an initial to describe the authoriser of the Paper (A = published by order of the Cape House of Assembly, G = published by order of the Cape Government, SC = the report of a Select Committee of the Cape House of Assembly, UG = published by order of the Union Government). They are always followed by the command number and the session date. The full titles may be seen in the bibliography.

Friend   *Friend of the Sovereignty* (after March 1854, *Friend of the Free State*) and *Bloemfontein Gazette*

JAH   *Journal of African History*

KCL   Killie Campbell Library, Durban

LMS   London Missionary Society. When followed by figures, as 11/3/C, these refer to the box number, the jacket number and the folder letter of the South African In Letters in the LMS archives.

OHSA   M. Wilson and L. M. Thompson (eds.) *The Oxford History of South Africa* (2 vols., Oxford, 1969, 1971)

PEMS   Paris Evangelical Missionary Society

RCC   *Records of the Cape Colony*, edited by G. M. Theal (36 vols., London, 1897–1910)

SAAR   Union of South Africa, Archives Commission, *South African Archival Records*

SAJS   *South African Journal of Science*

USPG   United Society for the Propagation of the Gospel, usually followed by a file number from the archives.

WMMS   Wesleyan Methodist Missionary Society. Usually refers to a box in the archives of the WMMS.

GLOSSARY

baaskap: domination
bywoner: white sharecropper
canteen: grog shop
commando: small military expedition, usually mounted
dorp: small town or village
erf (plural *erven*): plot of urban ground
fontein: spring
gebied: area, jurisdiction
karosse: skin blankets
kloof: ravine
knegt: servant
laager: fortified camp
land(d)rost: district magistrate
maatschappy: company/community
muid: a measure of volume, about a hectalitre
Nagmaal: The Lord's Supper, which in Afrikaaner communities generally served
    as the main social gathering for the surrounding population
opgaaf: annual poll tax
raad: council
rix dollar: Cape colonial currency (1 rix dollar = 7½p approx.)
schafmeester: shepherd
smous: pedlar
trek: migrate, travel
tronk: prison
veld: grazing, pasture
veldkornet: elected local leader, who acted both as the lowest rung in the admin-
    istration and as the military commander of the burghers of his *wyk*
volksraad: national council
voorlaier: muzzle-loading gun
voorloper: forerunner, but also literally as the boy who guided the leading oxen
    of a wagon team
wyk: district

xiii

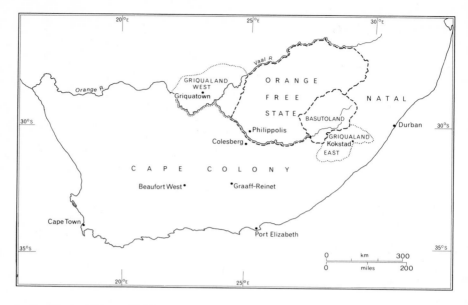

1 Southern Africa *c* 1850

CHAPTER 1

INTRODUCTION

This is a tragedy, *sensu stricto*. It describes the growth, the aspirations, the flourishing, the decline and the final collapse of the Griqua Captaincies of Philippolis and Kokstad, during the evolution of nineteenth-century South Africa. The Griquas were descendants of early Boer frontiersmen; of the remnants of Khoisan tribes — hunters, gatherers and pastoralists; of escaped slaves from the wine and wheat farms of the south-west Cape; of free blacks from the colony who could find no acceptable place for themselves in it; and of African tribesmen, detached from their tribes by war or by choice. They formed a community which attempted to discover what their role in South Africa was, or if there was none, to create one for themselves. In the end they could not do this. Philippolis is today distinguished from the other *dorps* of the Orange Free State only by the street pattern which the Griquas gave it, not by any of its inhabitants. In Kokstad the tomb and statue of Adam Kok are prominent features. The Griqua church dominates the centre of the town, but its worshippers have been driven to the edge. Far more of the descendants of the old Griquas are spread around the towns of the four provinces of South Africa, but their sense of community has gone, and many now forget their heritage. Their community, indeed, disappeared with their independence, for annexation signified the failure of their attempts to gain acceptance into the society of the Cape Colony as a respectable, Christian, prosperous people. In the ambiguity inherent in their aspirations lay the dynamic of their history.

The reasons which have been advanced for their failure are various. To contemporary colonists, they were nothing but a bunch of lazy good-for-nothings who acquired successively two of the finest tracts of South Africa for farming by a combination of force and fraud, but were too indolent to make anything of them. The president of the Orange Free State once wrote of the Griquas as 'an indolent people, neither understanding nor caring for the value of land, which nearly half a century has proved they were and still are incapable of improving in any way, or of otherwise bettering their condition'.[1] Prejudice and self-interest evidently have much to do with such a description, but it has often been echoed by historians, who have generally ignored other aspects of Griqua history: the development of a stable political system among the Griquas and its working by at least three politicians of considerable ability; the trading trips which the Griquas made through Botswana deep into central Africa, which did much to open the road to the north; the prosperity acquired from the flocks of merino sheep; and the spectacular cutting of a road over Ongeluks Nek, at one of the highest points of the Drakensberg. The place of the Griquas in the history of South Africa must be seen within these wider horizons.[2]

Nevertheless, the Griquas failed. The poles of the argument as to why they failed, as represented by those who sympathised with them and recognised their potential, come on the one hand from a missionary and on the other from two committed left-wing historians of South Africa. John Mackenzie, who was fleetingly in Philippolis just before the Griquas left it, wrote that 'their only fault was their features'.[3] Conversely, according to H. J. and R. E. Simons, 'the Griquas were destroyed because the colonists coveted their land'.[4] In a very bald sense, both of these contentions are true, but neither could be unless the other was. It would not have been a fault to look like a Griqua unless this signified possession of some resource, in this case primarily land, which was sought by colonists who could use their political and economic power to wrest it from the Griquas. Conversely, the colonists coveted the land of the Griquas only because they would not accept that the Griquas were as entitled to it as they were. To understand Griqua history, it is therefore necessary to comprehend, as far as possible, the development of racial stratification within nineteenth-century South Africa as a whole.

It would be impossible to describe the history of southern Africa before the beginning of the nineteenth century in any unified way. There were a variety of histories, of all those people who have lived between the Zambesi and the Cape of Good Hope. Many of these histories are shadowy, and are likely to remain so, although the increasing pace of archaeological research is making more and more of the remote and not so remote past of southern Africa intelligible.[5] On the other hand, it would be a bad history — which, unfortunately, is far from unusual — to write of any section of the South African population during the twentieth as if it existed in isolation from the others. It can be argued that the despised proposition that South African history begins with van Riebeck is true, even if it remains false to consider that it should therefore concern itself only with self-designated 'whites', for their history is incomprehensible without an understanding of their dealing with their fellow South Africans (in the widest sense).[6] Even before the advent of industrialisation the society that emanated from Cape Town spread out to bring almost all the inhabitants of the region into a single over-arching system of relationships. In so doing, it began the process by which all the diverse social groups of the area were reduced from independence to a position of subordination.

This expansion was driven on by a single segment of colonial society, distinguished from the others by its wealth and by its pigmentation. South African economic and political science has tended in recent years to concentrate on the interrelationships between ethnic and economic stratification, between 'race' and 'class'.[7] The subject is at the core of the controversies which enmesh and invigorate — or enervate — South African intellectual effort. But any attempt to elevate either pole of the dichotomy to paramountcy and to declare the other irrelevant must prove vain. If there were now, and always had been, economic equality between the various racial groups, with consequent parity in terms of power, then there would be nothing to argue about. Conversely, if racial criteria played no part in the identification of class patterns, then South African society and the arguments about it would have taken very different forms from those they currently do. Rather, the dichotomy is false, stemming mainly from an insufficient understanding of the dynamics of class. Following E. P. Thompson, class should be defined as 'an historical phenomenon . . . not . . . as a "structure" or even as a "category" but as something which in fact happens (and can be shown to have happened) in human relationships'. Above all, 'the notion of class entails the notion of historical relationship'. Therefore,

> class happens when some men, as a result of common experience (inherited or shared), feel and articulate the identity of their interests as between themselves, and as against other men whose interests are different from (and usually opposed to) theirs. The class experience is largely determined by the productive relations into which men are born — or enter involuntarily. Class consciousness is the way in which these experiences are handled in cultural terms: embodied in traditions, value-systems, ideas, and institutional forms.[8]

When such concepts are applied to South Africa, it is apparent that there has long been a ruling class, which originated among the officials of the Dutch East India Company and the farmers of the south-west Cape and has incorporated more and more social groups as the South African economy has expanded and diversified. However, the 'cultural terms' within which this class has operated have become primarily racial, and the criteria for incorporation almost entirely so. Without exception those who have ruled have been categorised as white, and they have been prepared to share both the semblance and the substance of power only with those of the same putative ancestry. Therefore there has been a long process of consolidation of the great racial blocks which form the categories into which all South Africans are now divided. Men are legislated into four main

3

blocks, and many see themselves as living in a land split into two unequal sections, the white and the black. But this is a phenomenon of relatively recent growth, associated with the spread of the white-dominated commercial and industrial economy. To give two examples, Martin Legassick rightly criticises Sheila Patterson for considering it strange that the white frontiersmen of the early nineteenth century should ally themselves with an Xhosa chief. At that time, argues Legassick, 'enemies and friends were not divided into rigid static categories; non-whites were not regarded implacably as enemies'.[9] Again, the Bantu speakers were always prepared to accept Khoisan into their midst.[10] Only during the nineteenth century was the concept of race, in its modern sense, imposed.

Clearly, major processes of South African history resulted from the imposition of the concept of race. As individuals and groups came to be incorporated into the wider circles of South African economic life, they found themselves assigned to categories according to the preconceptions of those who controlled the political economy of the country. It was as though a centrifuge was operating, by which the old alignments were broken down and new ones formed, much larger in scale than the local or tribal communities which had preceded them, but much less ambiguous. Many forms of diversity within the non-European society were destroyed, particularly when these seemed to conflict with the interests of the dominant settler group. Thus the gradual expansion of the white-held land within the country and the gradual depression of Africans and coloureds into a situation where they are little more than agricultural and urban proletariat stems from this process, which was determined by the white ruling class. As the dominant force within South African society it has been able to determine the main patterns of development, so that those who have entered into the white-controlled orbit have had their position within that society determined for them, on the basis, primarily, of their racial origin. Where the aspirations of those entering the society conflicted strongly with the expectations of the whites as to the position of that group, then there was naturally a struggle, but in all cases the victory went in time to the far greater coercive power of the settler, the mining capitalist, the farmer and the industrialist.

This was a long-term process. The particular cultural terms by which classes define themselves take time to develop, and are always changing. Nevertheless, by the mid-nineteenth century at the latest, a set of criteria for inclusion in the ruling class of South Africa had been delineated. In order to be fully accepted into the nascent ruling group of South African society, it was necessary to possess the characteristics in the left-hand column of the following table:[11]

white	black
rich	poor

landed	landless
Christian	non-Christian
literate	illiterate
within the money economy	purely within the subsistence economy
free-born	slave (or ex-slave)
farmer/merchant	artisan
self-employed (ideally)	employed by another

Various points have to be made about such a classification. First, pigmentation is the most visible of the characteristics. Someone can tell relatively easily whether another is black or white, while to discover the extent of his property or his religion is a more lengthy procedure. Therefore there is a very definite tendency for the fact of colour to become dominant in assessing social relations. Conclusions that have been jumped to in this way are difficult to undermine.[12] Secondly, the criteria do not of themselves generate each other. There was no reason why a black ex-slave artisan should not have been Christian, literate or even rich. Certainly, he would have been within the money economy. On the other hand, until political measures were taken to end the problem they were said to have created, during the middle of this century, there was always a substantial number of people who were considered white but who were poor, landless *bywoners*, at best semi-literate and relying for their subsistence on the herds they ran and the land they farmed for others or, later, on the most menial urban occupations.

During the mid-nineteenth century, moreover, three major forces tended to confuse the criteria. First, there were present among the ruling group elements who attempted to liberate various of the subordinate groups from the bondage of slavery, of heathenism, of illiteracy and, to a certain degree, of poverty. Foremost among these were the Christian missionaries, who generally considered that the adoption of Christianity entailed the social advancement of the formerly pagan, but there were others, often in influential positions in government or in the press, who made similar attempts to upset the distinctions of society. It was because they were shaking the foundations of the world which others were attempting to build that such men as Dr John Philip, John Fairbairn of the *South African Commercial Advertiser*, even Sir Andries Stockenström, were held in such opprobrium. Moreover, the successes of missionary endeavour often found that the society into which they hoped to gain access was hostile to them. The prejudice against the 'Christian native' and in favour of the 'raw blanket Kaffir' arose because the former threatened the bases of the social organisation which the white ruling class hoped to establish in a way that the latter could never do. Secondly, there was the threat posed by those groups, frequently under mission influence, who had been able to gain sufficient land to set up efficient peasant farms, which were always disliked by sections of the white community, as they undercut agricultural prices, occupied land that the whites coveted and deprived the whites of labour which they thought should have been under their control. If only in a small way, these two groups created counter-cultures within the interstices of white society which challenged that society, by depriving it of control over a portion of the major resources of pre-industrial South Africa, land and labour, and by negating the taxonomy by which it ordered its social relations. Thirdly there were several groups which were able to set themselves up beyond the boundary of white settlement and which attempted to fulfil the requirements for acceptance into that society as it expanded over them. Individuals and family groups who had come into contact with the ways of life in the Cape Colony, but who were not accepted by the colony, moved north and north-east into areas which were within the orbit of the colony and its economic system but which were not as yet dominated by its social order. Often, of course, these people were half-caste children of white farmers but equally they included ex-slaves and various Khoisan bands which had seen the advantages of a connection with the colonial economy. In time, these groups became sedentary, settling around the supplies of water that are vital to human existence in the interior of southern Africa. As the white population expanded, however, it continually required a greater area of land on which to run its flocks and herds.[13] Thus it began to exert pressure on these settlers on its border, who had the choice of either moving farther into the interior, where they would clash with the powerful and thickly settled African tribes, Xhosa, Sotho, Tswana or Herero, or staying put and trying to maintain themselves against the expansion of white settlement. Moreover, because of the leapfrogging of the southern Orange Free State, the Transkei and Basutoland by the movements associated with the Great Trek of the 1830s, these communities, which had once been beyond the boundaries of colonial society, now found that they were locked within its social networks, and subject to pressures to accept its criteria of status.

In these ways, and in others, South Africa came to contain within itself sizeable elements which challenged the system of hierarchy that its ruling class wished to impose. They were anomalous, as are the uncomfortable facts by which, in one theory, scientists are persuaded to alter the basic assumptions of their disciplines.[14] However, unlike scientific facts, which can only be ignored, social relationships are not given, but may be altered by the actions of men, alone or in concert. The communal deeds of sectors of the white ruling class throughout the nineteenth century, whether encased in legislation or stemming from the individual actions of its members, may frequently be seen as attempts, which ultimately were successful, to maintain the paradigms of social relationships by which they wished their world to be governed.

The particular processes by which these alignments were established have not, as yet, been fully investigated by historians. Nevertheless, certain of the most obvious lines of conflict need to be distinguished before a full description is given of the ways in which such processes determined the plot of the main drama with which this book is concerned, that of the Griquas of Philippolis and Kokstad. Thus, at times, definite legislative and executive decisions were made to limit or to remove opportunities for those in subordinate positions to acquire the attributes of their superiors. For instance, when colonial officials were licensing the first mission stations, they were careful to forbid the teaching of writing to natives. They were only to be allowed to read, because then they would have access to Scripture.[15] Even at this early date, moreover, the belief was current that the Moravian mission at Genadendaal locked up Khoi labour that would be better employed on white farms. Significantly, it was held by a representative of one of the richest families in South Africa, which has built its wealth on progressive farming and on its corner on the meat market.[16] Again, at the end of the nineteenth century, there was a possibility that a Malay leader might be elected as a member of the Cape House of Assembly. This was so abhorrent to the sitting members that they swiftly changed the election rules in such a way as to forestall this eventuality.[17]

More generally, however, the conflict was over the concrete economic advantages of access to opportunities, to credit, to labour and, above all, to land. Land, of course, was not scarce in South Africa. The deserts of the Karroo and Namaqualand have remained thinly populated even now. However, productive land which is fertile, well watered and within reach of a market has always been scarce, especially as white farming systems have seldom been intensive. That which there is has always been worth struggling for.

At times the methods of conflict were blatant. For instance, the Bastard community at de Tuin in the deserts of Boersmanland was under pressure throughout the middle of the nineteenth century from trekboers who moved into the area in their seasonal migrations from the Roggeveld. The consequences for the Bastards was described as follows, on the basis of reports from their missionary:

> The Boers drove their cattle into the free grazing land in order to spare the grass on the lands they had leased, sat down at the springs which the Bastards had opened up, brought their sick cattle among those of the Bastards, followed them with their immense herds whithersoever they might retreat, in short pestered them in every conceivable manner in order to drive them forth from the neighbourhood.[18]

After representations to the government in Cape Town had failed, the Bastard community was forced to trek away north, re-siting itself at Rehoboth near Windhoek and leaving the trekboers in control of their grass and their water.

In areas of the country that were closer to the eyes of the magistrates and the missionaries, the mechanisms by which the lines of hierarchy were preserved and established were subtler. There was rarely the blatant use of power by the whites, at least in the earlier period, but rather assumptions as to the worth of blacks were made. Thus, in the eastern Cape, and around the Kat River settlement, the Khoisan found it very difficult to get the credit they needed to set up as independent farmers, above all in wool. On one occasion, for instance, it was announced at an auction that any 'Hottentots' would have to pay for any purchases they might make immediately and in cash because they were not trusted not to default. Whites, of course, were allowed several months to pay.[19] More than this, however, the Kat River settlement suffered from continual overcrowding, as the sheep farmers of the eastern Province pressed on the lands of the Khoi and were occasionally allocated land within the area originally designated for 'coloured' occupation. At the same time, the settlement came to be used as a 'dumping' ground for discharged members of the Cape Corps, a coloured force, and for squatters from the various municipalities throughout the eastern Cape. In consequence the pressure on land within the settlement, which had only been formed in the 1820s and which suffered heavily from the various frontier wars, became acute. This was particularly so in that part of the settlement that was primarily pastoral, especially as administrative fiat caused a number of Africans, who had been clients of the Khoi and were mainly Mfengu, to be expelled. Finally, during the frontier war of 1850, many of the inhabitants joined the Xhosa and, on being defeated, their lands were distrained and handed over to the colonists.[20]

Similar processes seem to have been common throughout southern Africa. Indeed, it is clear that the transition from 'tribesman' to 'proletarian', whether urban or rural, which has been the general lot of the mass of South Africa's population, was frequently not made at a single leap. Increasingly there is evidence that within this process there was a phase during which a significant proportion of the black population became, for a time, independent peasant producers of substantial wealth. In Natal, for instance, it has been shown 'that during the 1860s most Africans were able to pay their taxes by selling off surplus grain or cattle'. By the end of the century, they could no longer hope to do so.[21] In the eastern Cape, too, there was a period of considerable peasant prosperity.[22] Mfengu, Thembu and other Africans are recorded as producing substantial agricultural surpluses for sale in the Witteberg Reserve of Herschel District ('the granary of both the Northern Districts and the Free State') and in the districts of

8

Peddie, Victoria East, Queenstown, Kingwilliamstown, Stutterheim, Bedford, Glen Grey and Keiskama Hoek. Even in the Orange Free State and the Transvaal there were many Africans who rented land from white farmers and, giving half their produce to the owner of the farm, became quite rich enough never to have to labour for him or for any other white man.

Nevertheless, these peasantries failed, because they had been built on inherently unstable foundations and because they never had the power to alter that base for a better. Rather those who did have the power made it impossible for them to continue, by a series of legislative acts and by the operation of the market. Fundamentally, the Africans never had enough land. The Reserves were initially perhaps just large enough to support their population, but as numbers increased they could only do so at a reduced level, and even then the soil was quickly exhausted. Moreover, this was intentional. Of the Glen Grey Act, which was passed at the end of the century and finally regularised the position of the peasantry in the Cape Province, it was said that:

> The intention was to locate then resident natives on these surveyed allotments, and to make no provision for the natural increase of the population, the surplus to find work elsewhere, so that . . . during the coming generations a limited number will be agriculturalists, i.e. native farmers — and the rest will have to go out and work.[23]

Similarly, when in 1913 the Natives' Lands Act was applied to the Transvaal and the Orange Free State, the effect was to crush the wealthier Africans who had been farming on halves and building up capital in various forms.[24] That way of life was simply ruled out of order.

It was not only through the Acts of legislators and the shortage of land that peasantries suffered. As Bundy has argued forcibly, it is necessary to look to the power of 'the trader in whose hands were concentrated the several economic functions of purchaser of agricultural produce, purveyor of manufactured goods and supplier of credit', the want of access to markets, especially after the building of a railway system which almost completely avoided the reserves and the lack of either private or public investment in peasant agriculture.[25] It is, indeed, almost surprising that the peasantries lasted as long as they did.

The place of the Griquas within such a schema is clear, although the rest of this study will be devoted to describing the particular features of their history. To the deculturated individuals who had been forced into the region of the Orange River valley by the beginning of the nineteenth century, five models of existence were open. Some definition is needed here. The models in question were in the minds of the actors. They consisted of the sets of alternative systems of life from which they could choose that which seemed most appropriate. They

9

were whole patterns of life, which it was difficult or impossible to blend together. One could not be a commercial farmer and a cattle raider, although one could move from one status to the other.[26]

The possibilities were, first, that a man could remain as a hunting and gathering 'bushman', or, secondly, that he would remain within the colonial orbit either as an independent operator in some such sphere as transport riding or as a farm labourer. Thirdly, there was still, at least until the 1870s, the possibility of a nomadic, herding and raiding life, based on such natural fortresses as the Orange River bush. Fourthly, it was possible for communities to set themselves the main purpose of living as an aristocracy over various Bantu tribes, as, for instance, Jonker Afrikaner and his followers managed with regard to the Herero, and the Griquas of Griquatown failed in respect of the Sotho-Tswana who lived north of them.[27] Fifthly, and this was the model adopted by the Griquas of Philippolis, there was the Christian, commercial mode of existence. The reference group for such a system was undoubtedly the trekboers, from whom the Griquas had been excluded by virtue of their colour and their illegitimacy. They adopted three of the main characteristics of this group.

First, they partook of the material advantages of the Cape Colony. They were concerned to build up an income derived from commercial activities, integrated into the Cape economy. Initially they sold as many cattle as they could spare and acted as intermediaries in the ivory trade with the interior. When the opportunity arose, they responded quickly to the possibility of building up considerable herds of merino sheep. They bred horses in large numbers for sale to Boer or Sotho. In the years of their prosperity, their wealth was translated into such commodities as wagons, European clothing and European-style housing. Such expenditure was obviously a claim for respectability, so that observers might argue that they were the equals of the Afrikaner farmers among whom, by this time, they lived. Secondly, they began to accept Christianity, not necessarily as a system of belief — it is always difficult, in view of the available evidence, to penetrate the inner cosmologies, or even social thoughts, of the Griquas — but rather as an integral part of the communal life which they had chosen. The reasons for this are obvious. It had been, in large part, their exclusion from the communion of the Dutch Reformed Church that had signalled their outcasting from white society.[28] The reassertion of Christian brotherhood through the missions was a claim to reacceptance by that society. Thirdly, they needed political autonomy, and the membership of a community which could withstand the pressures which were put on landholders and farmers in a frontier situation. There thus developed the Griqua Captaincies,[29] which were coalitions of men and family groupings with such desires, their political structure being a peculiar style of democratic oligarchy under the leadership of the Kok and Waterboer families.

The models of existence which have been outlined here are obviously ideal types rather than the actual style of life of all the individuals who fell into the various polities which were directed by them. On the other hand, the political struggles within and between the Griqua Captaincies were fought above all between the various conceptions of the type of community which the Griquas were to be. This is true for the Hartenaar revolts against the old *Kaptyns*, around 1816, for the Bergenaar rebellion which absorbed the political energies of the Griquas throughout the 1820s and led directly to the founding of Philippolis, and for the succession crisis in that town between 1835 and 1837. In both Griquatown and Philippolis, however, the Christian, commercial mode of existence finally triumphed. Conversely, individuals and family groups could migrate from one community to another, along the length of the Orange River, and so move from one particular social style to another which was better represented elsewhere. Thus the Khoikhoi who came up to Philippolis from the Kat River during the late 1830s were doing so to achieve independence, but also to become part of a settled, primarily agricultural community, in which the material possessions which they had enjoyed in the Kat River would still be available.[30] Similarly, those who moved from Griqualand to the Orange River, or, like the Witboois to Namaqualand, were looking for a freer marauding and dominating style of existence, which they could not hope to enjoy under the established rule of Andries Waterboer.[31]

It can be seen that the model of life adopted by the Griquas was not compatible with the direction given to South African society by its dominant class. The Griquas aimed at independence, at respectability, perhaps at incorporation into the white ruling group. These aspirations obviously came into conflict with the pressure towards racial homogeneity which has pervaded South Africa from the mid-nineteenth century on. Independent, wealthy, landowning 'coloured' communities did not fit into its taxonomy. The importance of this may perhaps be demonstrated by analogy with the New World, where, among the reasons given for the different racial situations which pertained in Brazil and the southern States of the USA, was the fact that the white population of Brazil was so small that it needed mulattoes to act as artisans and so forth, in the middle reaches of the economy. In the south, in contrast, such functions could be performed by the non-slave-owning whites, and the blacks were thus much more strictly maintained in a position of subordination. They had no 'bridge' by which they could cross the chasm between the races. In South Africa, the Griquas constituted part of the construction force building that bridge. As they failed to move across the chasm, there could be little hope that any sizeable community thereafter could do so.[32] In their attempts to leap the gap between the dominant conceptions of society and their own view of their place within it lies the motor and the tragedy of the Griquas' history.

CHAPTER 2

THE EARLY HISTORY OF THE GRIQUAS

In 1815, a representative of the London Missionary Society, the Rev. John Campbell, was visiting a community of 'coloured' people north of the Orange River who called themselves the Bastards.[1] He objected to this appellation and, as they wished to maintain cordial relations with him and his society, 'on consulting among themselves, they found the majority were descended from a person of the name of Griqua, and they resolved hereafter to be called Griquas'.[2] In fact, no such person seems ever to have existed. Rather the term referred to a Khoikhoin tribe, the Chariguriqua,[3] which had lived about a hundred miles north of Cape Town.

Like most of the other Khoikhoin cattle and sheep herding tribes of the coastal plains, the Chariguriqua social organisation disintegrated during the eighteenth century. From the first arrival of Europeans at the Cape, Khoisan had been in commercial relations with them, particularly around Table Bay, but with the establishment of European farmers, the Khoi came increasingly under pressure. Khoi economic organisation seems to have required extensive seasonal movements of stock to cope with mineral deficiencies of the pasture,[4] so that with permanent settlements of wine and wheat the Boers would have quickly made their mode of life impossible. Already by 1705, there were 'Hottentots' working as travelling harvesters in the Stellenbosch district.[5] At the same time, the perennial shortage of draught oxen in the Cape forced the Government and the settlers to trade continually with the Khoi beyond its borders. At its best, this trade was unequal. In a well conducted expedition north of the Oliphants River in 1705, the *landdrost* of Stellenbosch bartered '33 oxen for 33 pounds of tobacco and 33 bunches of copper beads, together with some glass ones and pipes'.[6] At its worst the intercourse degenerated into armed robbery. On the same journey, Starrenburg was told that a kraal had no cattle because 'a certain Freeman . . . had come to their kraal a few years previously, accompanied by some others, and without any parley fired on it from all sides, chased out the Hottentots, and took away all their cattle'.[7] In addition to this the epidemics of smallpox that ravaged the Cape in 1713 and again in 1755 killed many Khoi, destroying the viability of many Khoi tribes. This process was speeded by the breaking of the patron—client relations that the tribes had had with the San hunter-gatherers. As the herders lost their wealth in stock and in numbers, the clients seem to have claimed their independence, which naturally led to further depletions of the herds and power of their erstwhile patrons.[8] Thus most Khoi were forced either to become stockless hunters, gatherers and cattle raiders in the hills or to take service with the farmers.[9] Most often they succumbed to the opiates of a broken people, alcohol, dagga, and a sexual laxity that contrasted with the rigid morality of their tribal life.[10] Many became bondsmen of the colonists, although, at least in the west, they maintained their Khoi identity until, with emancipation, there was no chance of their becoming slaves.[11]

Some groups managed to preserve their unity, or even managed to manufacture a new one. In the eastern Cape, there developed a policy on a larger scale than previous Khoi units, based on the skilful manipulation of trading relations between white, Khoi and Xhosa and on the powerful, if enigmatic, personality of Captain Ruyter, who had once been a farm servant in the Roggeveld.[12] In the west, it was possible to move north, preserving some measure of unity. The tribes that Wikar met on the middle Orange River have been identified with those Van Riebeck encountered in the vicinity of Table Mountain a century earlier,[13] and the traditions of both !Kora and Nama tell of a move to the north during the mid-eighteenth century.[14]

In addition to the displacement caused by the destruction of Khoisan social organisation, the expanding white colony produced a large number of men and women who had no place within it, not only Khoisan but also slaves who had escaped from their bondage in the metropolitan areas of the colony and those known as 'Bastaard—Hottentots'. These last were considered by the whites to be of mixed origin, having either one slave or one white ancestor. In fact, however, the term denoted a social rather than a genetic status.[15] The Bastards were those who could not claim to be Christian, but who were integrated into the colonial cash economy other than as tied farm-labourers or as slaves. They were transport riders, day-labourers, craftsmen and, most frequently, small farmers, living without title to their lands beyond the current frontier of white expansion. Initially they were privileged above other non-Christians, but they were the most vulnerable, for they alone had a status which was valuable to them and possessions as well as labour worth contesting. Thus during the eighteenth century they were under pressure from the white trekboers, whose immense families and traditions of independence were swiftly exhausting the available land and water supplies. The Bastards were forced to move either towards the east, to the Xhosa frontier, or north from the mountain valleys beyond Cape Town, through the arid lands of the Karroo and Namaqualand up to the Orange River. Lichtenstein described what was no doubt a typical instance:

Many Hottentot families of this description had established themselves in the Lower Bokkeveld,[16] when the increasing population of the colony occasioned new researches to be made after lands capable of cultivation; and the white children of the colonists did not hesitate to make use of the right of the strongest to drive their half yellow relations out of the places where they had fixed their abodes. These Bastard Hottentots were then obliged to seek an asylum in more remote parts, till at length, driven from the Sack River,[17] as they had been from the Bokkeveld, nothing remained for them but to retreat to the Orange River.[18]

George Thompson also described in detail the predicament which these individuals had to face, when he wrote:

It is a great hardship to this class of people that they have been systematically prevented from acquiring landed property in the Colony. In consequence of this, they are generally driven entirely beyond the boundary, and tempted to become outlaws and robbers; for if any of them occupy and improve a vacant spot within the limit, they are always liable to be dispossessed by some boor obtaining a grant of it from the Government, who thus reaps the fruit of all their improvements and industry.[19]

The processes at work are perhaps best illustrated by the history of the Kok family, which was able to unite both the Khoikhoi and the Bastard strains under itself. The founder of the family, Adam Kok I, was a slave who gained his freedom in a lawful manner and moved to the area of the Piquetberg, a hundred miles north of Cape Town, around the middle of the eighteenth century. Despite being described as a 'Hottentot', he was granted grazing rights by the Dutch Government for the farm Stinkfontein between 1751 and 1760,[20] and the burgher rights that the family somewhat mysteriously acquired at the same time were long of use to them. In this area Kok came into contact with the remnants of the Chariguriqua, and, according to one rather dubious tradition, married the chief's daughter.[21] Certainly, Adam had a large progeny and came into possession of considerable herds of stock, so that many adherents attached themselves to the clan as it moved north from the Piquetberg into Little Namaqualand. Adam I died in 1795, but had already been succeeded as 'patriarch' by his son, Cornelis I. By this time the family had grown very considerably and was already spreading up the Orange River into the area which was to become Griqualand West. By 1804, for instance, Solomon Kok (Cornelis's son) was engaged in ivory trading among the Tswana from a base in Witwater near Griquatown.[22] Cornelis himself considered that the prosperity of his family burgeoned from the time at which they settled in Griqualand West, even though he himself spent most of his life further west, in Little Namaqualand, where he owned at least five farms and five thousand sheep.[23]

Griqualand West was classic frontier country. It lay on the southern border of Bantu-speaking Africa, for its rainfall was insufficient to allow settled agriculture without irrigation, and had therefore long been an area of interaction between Khoikhoi and the southern Tswana tribes who formed the outliers of the Bantu culture.[24] Because its position was marginal and because it possessed springs around which small villages could be set up, a community of Bastards developed there, consisting of men who had drifted up from the colony in much the same way as the Koks. Indeed, although the Koks were the largest and richest family in the settlement, they were by no means the only powerful one. The adherents of Barend Barends (mainly of Bastard origin) were very important, while there were many other clans who were attached only loosely to either of these groups.[25] The society was organised on a loose clan structure, for ties of kinship and of clientage remained paramount. Only the development of a wider political organisation could cut across these to produce a more unified entity capable of acting in a concerted fashion. Even this, which began to arise in the first two decades of the nineteenth century, had to rely for its authority on the familial links which had been established by the Koks and the Barends.

It was, however, around the mission church that this organisation developed. Marais has convincingly demolished the myth, promulgated by such apologists as John Philip, that the Griquas were nothing but naked savages until the arrival of the missionaries, to whom is due all Griqua progress,[26] but the missionaries certainly acted as a catalyst towards political centralisation. The circumstances were right, for the Orange valley was becoming more and more crowded, and there was need for regulation of the allocation of water and grazing rights. The Bastards also considered that some degree of cohesion would give them more coercive power over the San (Bushmen) and the !Kora whom they were attempting to reduce to dependent status, as stock herds and so forth. From 1805 onwards, magistrates who were all members or close adherents of the Kok or the Barends families were appointed. The missionaries, Anderson and Kramer, who had the backing of the colonial Government, acted as a central focus, and performed various administrative duties.[27] Some few years later, Barend Barends and Adam Kok II, who was the son and successor of Cornelis as patriarch, were appointed as joint *Kaptyns* over the nascent polity, and the functions of previous lawmen atrophied. As against this, the institutions of the church remained active, particularly as a native agency was set up, whereby Griquas acted as preachers in the settlements away from the missionaries. This proved of great importance in furthering the process of acculturation. !Kora, San and Tswana were brought under the aegis of the Bastard *Kaptyns* in this way, so that when Campbell, on

15

his visit to Klaarwater, the main settlement, in 1813, codified a set of laws for the community, he was able to insist on the legal equality of all its members, of whatever origin. Simultaneously, as has been shown, the name Griqua, which had egalitarian overtones, was adopted and Klaarwater (the recognised centre of the new polity) was consequently renamed Griquatown.[28]

Throughout this period of early political formation, both permeating and eroding the power which Adam Kok II and Barend Barends were building up were three developments which run as themes throughout Griqua history. First there was the effect of the expansion of the colonial economy into Transorangia. Griqua society could be delineated as coterminous with involvement in the trading net which spread out from Cape Town, for the particular features that distinguished them from the as yet unassimilated !Kora and San were the direct consequence of such interaction; firearms, ammunition and wagons. Similarly the mode of existence that was developing under the influence of the missionaries was directly imitative of colonial mores. The trade that developed was twofold. In part the Griquas were able to sell of their own surplus stock, above all draught oxen, of which there was a dearth in the colony.[29] In this sense the Griquas were no more than an extension of the trekboer economy. On the other hand, the Griquas began to encroach on the pre-existing patterns of trade on the High Veld which had been based on Delagoa bay. Tlhaping, Rolong and Ngwaketse, from the northern Cape and southern Botswana, who had previously sent their ivory northwards, now began to come within the orbit of Griqua hunters and traders, who made considerable killings as middlemen.[30] The two activities were somewhat contradictory, for many of the cattle sold had previously been lifted from the Tswana tribes, so that the products of hunting and trading progressively took over from cattle as the main export of the Griqua economy, at any rate for a time.

The income that was so gained went, in large measure, on firearms and ammunition. The trade was largely contraband, and it is consequently difficult to gauge its extent, but by the early 1820s the Griquas were estimated to be in possession of 500 muskets, a considerable number when none of their competitors was so equipped.[31] The advantage gained was not only political, for aside from increased efficiency in elephant hunting, game could be cropped more easily for food, so that domestic herds could be built up much more swiftly. For the rest, Griqua income was spent in part on agricultural equipment, ploughs, wagons, tar and so forth, and in part on clothes and other trappings of civilisation to demonstrate the wealth of individuals, and on goods which, by dispersal, would enhance the status and adherents of the purchaser, primarily such commodities as tea, coffee and sugar which could be dispensed as hospitality. These were obtained initially through occasional visits to Cape Town,[32] but later through the fair at Beaufort West, although this signally failed to meet Griqua wants, as traders were not acquainted with their needs.[33] All in all, the Griqua involvement in such economic exchanges was considerable and ramified throughout the period.

The second process leading towards the erosion of the old *Kaptyns'* authority was the continuation of immigration into Griqualand. The old kin ties that had maintained the cohesion of the original grouping evidently no longer operated in this case. Indeed, occasional pressure from the colonial Government and their own reluctance to allow the diminution of their power caused the Griqua authorities to make token attempts to reduce this flow, so that the threat of extradition caused escaping slaves to keep clear of the Griqua settlements.[34] However, growing pressure on land in the northern districts of the western Cape pushed many Bastards north. John Melvill, for a time Government agent among the Griquas, described one recently arrived community of these families which he was attempting to persuade to return south. Nine families had come, apparently in a single party, from the Roggeveld to the Orange River, where they joined with two others who had moved from the same area five or six years earlier, and with one man who left considerable debts behind in the Nieuwveld.[35] In other cases it is not possible to be other than anecdotal. A few examples drawn from later sources may be given. Andries van Rooy claimed to have been born on the Oliphants River in 1798, but was on the Kuruman River by 1804.[36] Arie Samuels came from around Beaufort West about 1820.[37] He had been preceded by Carel Kruger, who was forced out of the Warm Bokkeveld by the actions of the *landrost* of Tulbagh.[38] A considerable community of de Vries and Bezuidenhouts, who had come under the influence of the short-lived mission on the Zak River came from Roggeveld about 1820,[39] at about the same time as Jan Pienaar (probably the one known as Gamga) moved from the Kamiesberg.[40]

The third development in this period was the beginnings of mission Christianity among the Griquas. William Anderson, one of the first LMS missionaries in South Africa, arrived north of the river in 1801, and after a few years was able to found a settled community at Klaarwater, later to become Griquatown. Compared to many other missionaries he was working in a fruitful field, for many of his flock, especially recent immigrants from the colony, were only too glad to be associated with a Christian minister. In this way they could assert the status which had been denied to them further south. A willing congregation was quickly forthcoming.[41] Thus the ideas as to the conduct of human affairs that were typical of mission Christianity, such as frugality, monogamy, individuality and settled agriculture, were introduced into the community. Some Griquas learnt to read and write under the mission's tutelage, and in time would use their skill in government. Both Andries Waterboer, the *Kaptyn* of Griquatown from

1820, and Hendrick Hendricks, who for 25 years conducted the business of Philippolis from his position as Secretary, were taught by the early missionaries at Klaarwater. Christianity thus became in some senses a badge of Griquadom, at once an inherent part of Griqua identity and a prime means of acculturation.

The speed with which the Griquas accepted Christianity was remarkable. Perhaps it was not always sincere. Robert Moffat, a good evangelical missionary and a scathing critic of spiritual inadequacy, was very doubtful when he wrote that among the Griquas

> something honourable is attached to the name Christian. By being baptised, their external conditions are bettered. Persecution, confiscation, imprisonment and death, which were the harbingers of the ancient believers, are unknown here. Here is nothing to deter, on the contrary everything to stimulate them to become Christians. When members under such circumstances are received under a mere profession, manifested by a redundancy of tears and unconnected, inexplicable confession of their faith in the Gospel, it is contrary to reason and experience for a missionary to appeal to such converts as letters known and read of all men, adorning the doctrine they profess with a holy life and unblameable conversation.[42]

Maybe these factors operated in many cases, but given the nature of the evidence they would be hard to discern. At times they become evident. Jan Bloem once asked the Berlin society to send him a missionary. He reported that he had considered where God resided. Was he, he wondered, purely the property of Andries Waterboer, who was one of Bloem's major opponents and had gained many advantages from a long and close association with the LMS.[43] On the other hand, not all men can be quite so hypocritical as to subsume all religious feeling to political and social advantages. No doubt many of the conversions that made the Griquas among the favourite, if frequently errant, sons of the mission were genuine and deep felt. The two strands of their inheritance can have been no bar to evangelisation, the Christian self-evidently and the Khoikhoin in consequence of the apparently weak nature of the aboriginal Khoisan beliefs. These did not contain a great pantheon of spirits and cults which had to be absorbed, but, apparently, only concepts of a high god and a devil which were readily assimilable to a Christian cosmology. So later missionaries claimed, at least, and as they did not meet opposition from the remnants of other faiths, their diagnosis would seem to have been correct.[44]

Of course, not all Griquas became believing Christians, and many who considered themselves to be so were not recognised by the church authorities. No missionary, for instance, would have condoned Barend Barend's exhortation to the motley assortment of frontier roughnecks on the commando against

Mzilikazi in 1831 to 'go and murder an innocent [sic] people in the name of God and religion'.[45] There were also those who found the constraints against drink and polygamy intolerable, and so remained clear of the church, although social pressures against such behaviour grew quickly and strongly. Campbell met a village of Bastards lower down the Orange River of whom 'some forsook Griqualand quietly to enjoy a plurality of wives and to live in every other respect without restraint.'[46] Cattle raiding long remained part of the Griqua culture, despite mission pressures, and the scarcity of water always defeated the church's attempts to build a close-knit, agricultural, easily ministered community and to prevent wide-ranging cattle and sheep ranching and long-distance hunting and trading. Yet slowly the mission Christian's ideal began to permeate the society until they became the accepted canons of behaviour.

The combination of these three tendencies — commerce, immigration and Christianity — made the old, clan-based authority structures of Adam Kok II and Barend Barends inherently instable. They remained by far the richest members of the community, and re-emerged as the natural leaders of the Griqua polities in the late 1820s, but by then a new style of organisation had arisen. Alternative sources of wealth had reduced the comparative value of the *Kaptyns'* herds. Firearms could be obtained elsewhere, especially through trading networks which stretched from Griquas to their kin and to frontier Boers in the northern districts of the colony.[47] The influx of population, both from the colony and by the acculturation of !Kora, San and Tswana meant that a powerful group emerged unrelated by descent or marriage to either of the leading families. Christianity, with its stress on education, began to widen the bounds of status, as eminence in the church could be translated into political prestige. Realisation of the advantages of literate government placed a premium on the acquisition of literacy. Thus, while clan affiliation remained important, political alignments began to be based on less personal loyalties, so that the hegemony of the patriarchs broke up.

The first challenge to the rule of the old *Kaptyns* came with the so-called Hartenaar rebellion, when a group of young men defied their authority, withdrew to the Harts River, north of Griquatown, and organised themselves on republican, egalitarian principles. In part the movement represented 'a classic instance of the revolt of frontiersmen against the attempt to impose a system of authority on them'[48] as represented by the mission and the old *Kaptyns*, but the presence of Andries Waterboer among the Hartenaars shows that it was, at least in part, an attempt by those without power in the old system to assert their claim to some share in it. The movement was short-lived, scarcely violent and so successful that within three years both Kok and Barends had to leave Griquatown, abdicating. The vacuum this left was filled by the election of Andries Waterboer as *Kaptyn* at the end of 1819. He was a typical representative of the

19

new style of Griqua, being of San descent (or so it was claimed) and not related to either of the old clans. He did not rely on his own family, and seems almost studiedly to have excluded his relatives from positions of power. An early adherent of the mission, he had been the first 'Hottentot' to preach a sermon, but had had altercations with the church, so that he had been excommunicated for a time in consequence of his adultery. By the time of his election, however, he was reconciled with the mission, and was in fact a schoolmaster in Griquatown, even though his handwriting was anything but a model for pupils to follow. As an upstart, lacking in self-confidence, his actions tended to be impetuous and his government harsh.[49]

Waterboer, however, was not able to gain total ascendancy over the Griqua population. Rather, his election signalled further large-scale revolts, the Bergenaar rebellions. These were complicated, combining political manoeuvres within the Griqua system – by members of the Hendriks and Goeyman families, for example – with seemingly anarchic banditry often connected with the newly-armed !Kora hordes. Such, for instance, was the attack on Kuruman in 1828.[50] The troubles formed part of the great convulsion of the time and were linked to the Mfecane, but they were independent in origin, being the consequence of the absence of any system of authority sufficiently widespread to subsume the tensions caused by the growth of population, the increase in the supply of arms, the decreasing power of many of the southern Tswana chiefs and the general disillusionment felt by many of the exiles from the colony. The Bergenaar revolts, which had their origins in the expanding Cape Colony, not in Zululand, thus added considerably to the general chaos which Transorangia suffered throughout the 1820s.

So far as the Griquas were concerned, the pattern that emerged was that the old Griqua entity was split into four main units. At Griquatown, Waterboer remained in power, strongly backed by the missionaries, the church and the colonial government. Initially he was closely allied with Cornelis Kok II, who had set up in Campbell at the time of the temporary abdication of his eldest brother, and who appears to have retained about him the core of the old Kok clan. There his power decreased, as he lost the friendship of Andries Waterboer, but he remained in the village, with but a few followers, so that he enormously complicated the negotiations half a century later when diamonds were discovered on what was putatively his land. Thirdly Barend Barends, whose following was probably less affected by the Bergenaar revolts than that of Kok, moved north, towards the Harts river valley, brought Wesleyan missionaries to Boetsap in that region and engaged in wide-ranging hunting and trading to the north and north-east. Lastly, Adam Kok II became accepted as the leader of a large number of Bergenaars. These were men who had left Griquatown and its neighbourhood primarily in protest against the election and Government of Andries Waterboer. Although they had found it necessary to live by raiding and hunting, they did not consider this permanent, in sharp opposition to those of their fellows who maintained a warrior's life until they were killed on commando. By 1824, only two years after what had been a rather desultory rebellion, Hendrick Hendricks, the leader of these accommodators, was making overtures to Adam Kok II and Barend Barends.[51] Two years later Adam Kok and this faction of the rebels moved down to Philippolis, for they wished to regain the advantages of respectability and a settled existence. They did so with the approval of Dr Philip, for Philippolis was a station of the London Missionary Society. Thus the Griqua Captaincy of Philippolis, straddling most of the southern Orange Free State, was formed, its Griqua inhabitants consisting of a few mission adherents who had been assistants of the LMS, a rump of the Kok clan, and a large number of unattached ex-Bergenaars who hoped to combine a measure of political independence with the advantages of a settled community.

CHAPTER 3

THE ESTABLISHMENT OF THE PHILIPPOLIS
CAPTAINCY, 1826–37

Implicit in the motives behind the move to Philippolis was the Griqua decision to live in a settled, agricultural, respectable community. The final announcement of this decision was not made until after the Griqua succession crisis of 1835–7, for during the first decade after 1826 there was always the possibility of returning to a wandering, herding, raiding life. Indeed, both tendencies were evident in the Griquas' relationships with the San, long resident near Philippolis, and with their fellow immigrants, the !Kora, the Africans and the trekboers. With these last the Griquas were always correct and commercial, but with the others they tended to maintain the pattern of exploitation and destruction which had been the rule a decade or so earlier. This contradiction was ultimately to be resolved with the Captaincy elections of the mid-thirties.

On the harsh plains of the High Veld, the possible modes of existence were limited by the physical and biological situation, as it had been altered by the impact of man and his flocks over time. Some features have scarcely changed. The Drought Investigation Committee of the Union of South Africa, for instance, claimed that there was no evidence to prove that the average rainfall in South Africa had changed in recent times. Variations from year to year naturally exist. Good and bad years follow each other with no apparent regularity, but no upward or downward tendency in the mean annual rainfall can be traced.[1] Rainfall in the nineteenth century was thus as it has been in the twentieth, averaging between 30 and 45 centimetres a year, but so irregular as to make such figures almost meaningless, and too low and unpredictable to allow agriculture without irrigation.[2] The number of nights of frost a year was high, generally over a hundred, and sufficient to kill off the insect carriers of horse-sickness. In consequence, the southern Free State and Lesotho were the most northerly districts in which horses could be bred, before the introduction of vaccines.[3]

Such constancy was not paralleled by the pasture. At some stage during the nineteenth century, sheep flocks caused sufficient deterioration and erosion to convert the veld from sweet grass plain to bushy false karroo, of considerably lower carrying capacity.[4] This would, no doubt have been aggravated by the pattern of grazing, for in the days before fencing and piped water this was con-

22

centrated in the neighbourhood of the *fonteins*, so that the most valuable areas of land would have been those most quickly eroded. The history of central South Africa must thus be seen against a background of continually deteriorating pasture.

The San, the 'Old Inhabitants' and the establishment of the mission

Since the rainfall was insufficient to permit the development of settlements of an agricultural, Iron Age, Bantu-speaking population in the Philippolis region, it had remained a resort of late Stone Age hunter-gatherers, who had apparently established themselves during the first millennium BC, and who, despite indications of small-scale pastoralist groups on the lower Riet River, had retained possession of the area up to the end of the eighteenth century.[5] The !Kora tribes, who had moved up the Orange River at that time, were, in general, to be found in the north, the valleys of the Vaal, Harts and Vet rivers, and thus it was as a Bushman mission that Philippolis had been founded.

The pastoral settlements of the Riet River had finally been broken up by the Bergenaars around 1823. Their inhabitants had joined two relict settlements of San south of the Orange River, living on abandoned mission stations. These communities had survived for some eight years after the missionaries left them, driven out by the farmers' demands for labour, by the LMS's temporary unpopularity with the Cape Government and by prejudice against the black skin of one of them.[6] Then they had been moved by Andries Stockenström — at that time *landdrost* of Graaff-Reinet — and by the mission-orientated Dutch Reformed Church minister at the same town, to a place which they named Philippolis, in honour of the superintendant of the LMS. It lies in a valley at the point of convergence of the routes through four major drifts in the Orange River and was thought, wrongly, to have sufficient natural water supplies to allow an agricultural village to be set up.[7]

From 1825, the settlement was ministered to by James Clark, a lay missionary of the LMS, and was increased by Dr Philip's sending San kraals scattered across Transorangia to Philippolis.[8] Also a small group of 'Bastard Hottentots' from Bethelsdorp, the oldest LMS station in the eastern province, moved up as a leaven to raise the San up to civilisation and Christianity. Unfortunately, they could not provide the protection needed in those troubled times, so that in 1826 thirty-one San were killed by 'Mantatees' raiding an outpost of the mission.[9]. Arguments against the move of Adam Kok and his followers were thus harder to maintain.

The major initial concern of the Griquas was to impose their control on those who already lived around Philippolis. Although the population was small, it was already exceedingly diverse. In 1827 it was reckoned that the subjects of Adam Kok consisted of 60 families of Griquas and 'Old Inhabitants' (as the Bastards from Bethelsdorp were known), 150 Tswana, 20 !Kora and some 30 families of Sotho,[10] while there were many more who lived within the territorial domain claimed by Kok, which reached 'from the Vaal River as far as the Caledon River', but did not acknowledge his suzerainty.[11] As is apparent from Melvill's categorisation, the old inhabitants merged quickly with the Griquas, for they had to penetrate no cultural barrier before being assimilated. By 1834 they were cheerfully raiding alongside the Griquas and !Kora.[12] Naturally not everything went smoothly. There were clashes over their status, for they had been servants of the mission and were now subjects of an independent chief,[13] but in general they were quickly incorporated, so that they do not form a recognisable party within the later affairs of the Captaincy.

The San, on the other hand, were reduced to labourers or driven out. As the indigenous inhabitants of the area and of the town of Philippolis, they quickly came under Griqua pressure, especially as they were used as cattle and sheep herds, and a ready, if highly surreptitious, market for slave children existed south of the Orange. This occurred with the brutality all too common in dealing with the despised 'Bushmen'. The Griquas behaved in a way that was reminiscent of the Boer reference group, but used even greater brutality. The restraining influence of the colonial officials was not present. The missionaries, indeed, soon found that physical contiguity between Griquas and San was incompatible with the imparting of the Christian message to either, so that they were forced to move about 75 kilometres east to the Caledon River and refound the Bushman station. Those San not under mission protection were then attacked, almost as a pre-emptive measure to ensure that they did not steal stock, although San had taken cattle from Griqua gardens, and a man described as the 'Bushman chief' to whom 'the spring at Philippolis belongs' admitted having stolen from the Griquas.[14] These attacks reached their peak around 1830, when Andries Stockenström, by now Commissioner General, had to cross the Orange to investigate claims that the emigrant farmers had been accessories to the murders. His report is harrowing, for it describes how various Griquas wantonly shot out the San who remained. Boers described how a 'quiet and Peaceable' kraal on the Riet River, for instance, was attacked without provocation by Griquas under Abel Pienaar, and, when asked why, they replied that 'the Bushman steal our cattle, we are determined to exterminate them, so that our cattle may graze unmolested day and night', while they excused themselves for killing women and children on the grounds that 'the children grow up to mischief and the women breed them'.[15] Slave raiding may also have been in their minds. At all events, by 1835, throughout the southern Free State, the San were reduced to the level of labourers or had fled, for instance to the Orange River valley.[16]

The !Kora

With regard to the various groups within southern Transorangia known as !Kora, the Griquas did not so much actively displace them as assist in the creation of conditions which made the mode of existence followed by the !Kora impossible. Although various criteria in terms of physical type, historical grouping and language have been suggested for the !Kora, these do not inspire confidence, and rather it is best to see the !Kora as those who followed a style of life which entailed nomadic cattle herding and raiding in smallish hordes, led by a, theoretically hereditary, *Kaptyn.*[17] It is highly significant that none of the four most important !Kora chiefs in southern Transorangia, Abraham Kruger, Piet Witvoet, Knecht Windvogel and Jan Bloem, had a hereditary claim to pre-eminence. Rather they were frontier opportunists who flourished in the anarchic conditions of the 1820s and maintained a curious alliance with the emigrant trekboers, who saw them as a market for smuggled brandy and firearms. They lived by raiding widely, against Griqua, Tswana, Sotho, Thembu and Ndebele, and many of the groups were broken up following the disastrous defeat of the commando launched by Barend Barends against Mzilikazi in 1831.[18] As conditions became more settled during the course of the 1830s, and the great herds of the Ndebele moved away north, so opportunities for such raiding became scarcer. Some of the !Kora remained in the Caledon River valley, in eastern Transorangia, but this was becoming a battlefield between Moshoeshoe's Sotho and the Rolong of Moroka, in which struggle the !Kora could only act as allies.[19] Others again moved into the debatable land to the west, in the valleys of the Vaal and Harts rivers, where they served to add greatly to the tribulations of the judges and politicians working out who owned the Diamond Fields.

Others again joined Adam Kok. Some quickly became indistinguishable from the Griquas *per se.* Old Philip, for instance was one of those !Kora connected with the Griqua mission from its first establishment. He was considered by the missionaries to be 'a man superior to the generality of his native tribe', and fathered a Griqua *veldkornet.*[20] For many others, incorporation was far less complete. Piet Witvoet, for example, 'avows, when it suits his convenience, allegiance to the chief of Philippolis; but becomes the independent chieftain whenever his interests are to be advanced by such a course'. Such intermittent clientage was apparently quite common. Dr Andrew Smith, the shrewdest observer of the scene in Transorangia during the 1830s, wrote:

It is indeed the custom with marauding parties whenever they see cause for apprehension to attach themselves if they can to some more powerful community, under the idea that it may be surmised they have determined upon changing their way of life; which, they suppose, may perhaps save them from punishment: or because they fancy that such alliances may excite the fears of those who menace them, and in consequence of their newly acquired strength secure immunity. Such a course is even often pursued by the Bushmen who frequently after committing extensive depredations solicit permission to join a neighbouring tribe which is sometimes granted owing to the general desire possessed by all communities of increasing their numbers.[21]

Many of the !Kora of such views joined the mission station set up at Bethany, which lies about 100 kilometres north-east of Philippolis and was officially under its control. The Griqua *raad*, indeed, had doubted the wisdom of setting it up, as they feared it would form a rival focus for political loyalties.[22] The missionaries themselves, who were Germans of the Berlin Society, were remarkably subservient to the Griqua authorities, for, as good Lutherans, they believed that 'the powers that be are ordained of God'. Remarkably, they considered Adam Kok and his council to be such, even allowing the Griqua *raad* to arbitrate in a violent dispute between two cohorts of missionaries.[23] Not surprisingly, the !Kora themselves were less accommodating. Their recognition of Griqua authority produced a peculiar compromise, whereby Klein Piet Witvoet was elected *Kaptyn* by the !Kora, simultaneously with his being appointed *veldkornet* by Adam Kok.[24] This, in fact, did little to stabilise the area, as Witvoet and his close followers were able to expel various clans from Bethany when they opposed his rule, and Adam Kok's nominal suzerainty was unable to prevent them going on commando in company with various other !Kora hordes.[25] Nor did the mission presence do much to stabilise the community. One of the missionaries at Bethany recorded that 'When a heathen chief desires a missionary, then he only means Powder, horses, harness, clothes, gifts of all kinds, not the word of God'.[26] Only as the country became more and more stable did the !Kora with their marauding habits become obsolete, until in modern times an anthropologist could only find 300 pure !Kora throughout South Africa.[27]

The Bantu-speaking people

One of the potential models of existence that the Griqua people attempted to follow consisted of living as aristocrats over the African tribes living north and east of their settlements. In its purest form, such was the policy of Jonker Afrikaner and his followers with regard to the Herero in Namibia, but it also

26

formed the major plank of Waterboer's programme for coping with the decreasing possibility of agriculture in Griqualand West during the 1830s, at a period of long drought,[28] and motivated Barend Barends, if not his followers, during the great raids on Mzilikazi early in that decade.[29] Even in the Kat River settlement, there were many Gona who established patron—client relationships over the Mfengu in the area.[30] For the Griquas of Philippolis similar moves were possible, and were followed, but they did not constitute the gamble that they were for their fellows, either in Griqualand West or in Namibia. When Waterboer was forced to sign a treaty with the Tlhaping chief Mahura, in 1842, which delineated the spheres of influence of the two men, this signalled the end of the northward expansion of the Griquas, and the beginning of the long stagnation and decline of Griquatown. In contrast Adam Kok's failure to absorb Lepui was merely an irritant, with few long-lasting results for Griqua life.

It was necessary to elaborate systems of relationships with the Africans which were different from those used in regard to the !Kora, or, for that matter, the Boers, because the Africans possessed a cultural tradition — language, agricultural techniques, political organisation and so on — far more different from that of the Griquas, than that of any Khoisan or any Christians. Thus gentle osmosis of individuals between the two communities was rare, though not impossible. Moreover, the Griquas had to evolve a variety of stances as against the different African groups, because the maelstrom of the 1820s, generally known as the Mfecane,[31] had reduced the tribes throughout central South Africa to chaos. Following the establishment of the centralised, highly militarised Zulu kingdom, several large war bands had devastated the High Veld, destroying the small-scale Sotho-Tswana chiefdoms that had previously divided the area between them. North of the Vaal, Mzilikazi had set up the Ndebele kingdom around a small core of warriors who had escaped with him across the Drakensberg. The area farther south had been overrun by four or five marauding groups reducing the inhabitants to dire straits that even included cannibalism.[32] From this chaos there emerged several units of far greater political scale than heretofore, notably the Sotho kingdom founded by Moshoeshoe and those groups, above all the Tlokwa under Mma-Ntatisi and her son Sekonyela and the Rolong who settled at Thaba Nchu, who contested with the Sotho for control over the highly fertile valley of the Caledon River.[33] These groups recruited adherents from the mass of totally disorientated individuals who swarmed the High Veld, but many of these also came to live at or near Philippolis, directly under Griqua rule. They appear to have been mainly labourers or squatters, and they never had burgher rights or played any significant role in the political, economic or military life of the Captaincy. Hardly any were sufficiently attached to the Griquas to trek with them into Nomansland. Rather they were the detritus of the Difaqane, families

whose tribal loyalties had been broken, who could but remain, probably dis-
heartened and undoubtedly very poor, in the bottom ranks of whatever society
was imposed upon them. They were sufficiently numerous for services to be
conducted in Tswana as frequently as in Dutch, and in 1852 Walter Inglis was
appointed by the LMS to work exclusively among them, but, in general, all that
can be said of them is that they were there.[34]

To the east, in contrast, the Griquas of Philippolis had to cope with a sizeable
independent tribe, with its own missionary. By 1834 the Bushman mission at the
Caledon River had fallen apart, and the LMS had decided to cede it to the Paris
Evangelical Missionary Society. Jean-Pierre Pelissier had come to the station and
gathered around him some 1,800 Tswana, mainly Tlhaping, under the chief
Lepui.[35] The little community flourished and the name was changed to Bethulie.
In 1835 the boundaries between this settlement and Philippolis were laid down
by Adam Kok II in conjunction with Pelissier,[36] but they were soon challenged,
for after Adam II's death, and perhaps as part of the pay-off that Adam III owed
those who had supported him, the Griquas attempted to gain control over
Bethulie. To the Griqua councillors, Lepui 'is the slave of Adam Kok'.[37] Initially
they employed the classic technique of accusing Pelissier of dastardly crimes —
by analogy with similar cases they should have been adultery — so that he would
be driven from the station. Thus, it was hoped, the Tlhaping would be forced to
submit to Griqua rule for they would be deprived of the diplomatic weight that
a missionary would provide. The attempt failed, because the conference of
missionaries acquitted Pelissier,[38] so that, two years later in 1841, the Griquas
had to use more violent means to achieve their ends. They moved in force to
occupy various farms of what had been the boundary. Naturally Lepui and
Pelissier complained to the colonial Government. The Griquas could not exert
much pressure on the Government, as John Philip and the LMS were not willing
to lend their weight to the Griqua protest.[39] They were thus forced to accept
colonial arbitration and finally agreed to the decision demanding that they leave
Lepui's land.[40] Evidently, the threat of Boer expansion, already very real, had
forced upon them the realisation that further expansion was impossible, for they
needed the colonial Government's support far more than the Bethulie ground.
Apart from occasional trickles, Griqua expansion and incorporation was over,
until they reached Nomansland.

The Boers

Two streams of settlement converged around Philippolis. First were the Griquas
themselves, who had been moving south-east, along the line of the Orange River.
Then, for the trekboers, the *voorlopers* of white expansion, the area provided

28

their first experience of the sweet grass veld of the High Veld. Ever since they had moved out of the south-west Cape, their flocks had been spread over the aridity of the Karroo. Settlement spread fast across the semi-desert, because the land could not support many flocks and because each Boer son looked to an independent life and his own farm. In the course of this expansion, the way of life of the trekboer developed. He was continually on the move, for the same reasons as his Khoikhoin predecessors in the region had been, as winter and summer pasture was to be found in different parts of the interior and he had to beware of exhausting the food and water supply of any one spot. But he was not a true nomad, for the movement was to a regular annual pattern, unless he was diverted by San or Xhosa raids or by drought. Moreover, as the Boers began to recognise each others' rights to particular stretches of country, in both the summer and winter areas, they could begin to build permanent houses, initially rude and sparsely furnished, because a man's status depended on the size of his herds rather than on the quality of his dwelling.[41]

Transhumant pastoralism was not conceived as the only suitable style of life, even if it was the only one to which most Boers could aspire. Where the natural conditions allowed, the Boers would settle permanently, and much more thickly than in the Karroo. By the 1770s a few communities had arisen, notably in the Agter Bruintjes Hoogte, at the head of the Fish River.[42] Nor did the pastoral life lead to total divorce from the society and the concerns of the society as a whole. Even the farthest trekboer needed to maintain commercial relations with Cape Town, to buy the arms, ammunition, wagons, brandy, sugar and coffee that were necessary for existence in the interior, while the south-west and the ships in Table Bay needed the mutton, the draught oxen, the butter, the tallow and the soap produced in the interior.[43] The Boers sold stock on the hoof to travelling butchers and came down to the Cape from time to time to sell such products as they could, to maintain links with their kin in the south-west and to perform the important social rituals of marriage and baptism. Because of these ties, they imbibed the principles of social organisation which developed in the south-west, which were increasingly stressing the coincidence of ethnic and other indices of stratification. Because of their competition with the Xhosa, the San — and in time with the Griquas — for land and because of their need to control Khoisan labour, often with considerable brutality, they reinforced these principles, although the need of a community under intense guerrilla attack from the San for every ally it could get long moderated their exclusiveness.[44]

For long the advance of settlement to the north was held up by the San attacks. Only around 1800 were they finally defeated, so that the Boers moved in large numbers through the Sneeuwbergen, the greatest stock breeding area of the colony, and onto the dry plains between these mountains and the Orange

River.[45] Not until the late 1810s did they move across it, into the country that the Great Trek was to establish as the Afrikaner republics.

Although extensive and thinly populated, this area suffered from crippling droughts and the ravages of locusts and migrating springboks. At irregular but frequent intervals the *fonteins* dried up. As the number of Boers increased, and consequently the pressure of cattle on water and pasture grew, so these became insufficient to supply the community. If they were to preserve their cattle and their livelihood, the Boers of the northern border *veldkornetcies* had to move on. This could only be over the statutory boundary of the colony, over the Orange River and into Griqua territory.[46]

Various Boer hunters had been across the Orange as early as 1819,[47] but these concerted treks to the highland sweet veld did not begin until 1825. Even then they were still occasional. When reports came in that rain had fallen in the colony, all the Boers went back. For a year and a half from the first quarter of 1826 there were no Boers beyond the colony, but 1827 was disastrous. After a trip through the northern districts, Stockenström wrote:

> I am sorry to have to report the distressed state to which the locusts, drought and Trek Bokken have reduced this district. It is impossible to see how every particle of grass has been consumed and not to wonder how the cattle exist. Every attempt at sowing has (with very few exceptions) hitherto proved abortive; no sooner does vegetation appear above the ground than it is devoured. The inner parts have as yet only to contend with drought and Locusts (Phenomena which are known in other parts of the world and therefore credible) but it would be folly to attempt a description of the other scourge: the Trekbokken or migratory Springbucks devastating the border divisions; — as to whose who have not seen the like, it must be difficult to believe.[48]

The Boers had begun to feel that their home was likely to be permanently across the Orange, as they saw little hope of maintaining an existence in the drought-stricken regions of the Cape Colony. By 1829 they were even asking that the colonial Government should confirm land grants in the area north of the River, a request which was emphatically refused.[49]

On the official level the Griquas' reaction to these treks was one of disapproval. Their Government began the oft-repeated, abortive prohibitions on the sale of land to Boers,[50] and they made representations to the colonial Government, both openly, in the form of petitions, which appear to have been drafted by Dr Philip,[51] and snidely, when they attempted to frame Boers with being accessories to the murder of various Bushmen.[52] In the event, however, only the return of rains south of the Orange could bring the Boers back, and they moved south early in 1830, held up — such is the contrariness of African weather — by floods in the Orange, brought about by the rains they had been awaiting.[53]

The return was, albeit, temporary. The Boers of the northern border were becoming accustomed to considering Transorangia as *trekveld*, to which they would move on a transhumant basis. After a brief interlude in the early thirties the droughts returned. From 1834 to 1838 the pasture was continually insufficient, and had probably permanently deteriorated in large areas, while there were many Boer sons, with their own flocks, who could not get farms within the colony.[54] All felt bitter towards the Griquas, who had unrestricted access to the land and grazing which they coveted, and whose cattle — to say nothing of those stolen from the Tswana — could be sold in the colonial markets where, fattened on the northern grasslands, they fetched higher prices than did those of the Boers.[55] Thus the northward exodus was considerable, increasing, unstoppable by the paltry forces of the colonial Government, and, by now, permanent.

The reaction of the Griquas to this settlement was ambivalent. Officially they did not encourage the Boers in their moves to the north. There were rumours that they might trek out again, leaving the Boers in sole possession of the area, perhaps, as Smith was to argue, because 'the almost constant pressure of white men in their country lessens the importance of the aristocratic position of the tribe in the estimation of the lower classes and it offers a party to which the latter may attach themselves and from which they derive confidence and strength in opposing the wishes of their rulers'.[56] Moreover, certain Boer individuals made themselves objectionable to the Griquas. Ockert Schalkwyk and Hendrick Badenhorst, in particular, both of whom set up house near Philippolis, appear to have had quarrels with the Griqua Government that festered on for years. They were, in essence, the type of disputes over land and the rights to it that were all too common in frontier society, but the potential distinction between the parties exacerbated the problem, for there was no recognised arbitrator.[57] As against this, the Griquas were on good terms with many of the Boers. Some Boers occasionally attended church services in Philippolis. During the 1830s Griquas started leasing farms to Boers on an increasingly large scale.[58] They did this because they were poor men, but possessed of considerable assets in land. Only by alienating it in part or by hiring it out to Boer flocks on such terms as 'half the increase' could they hope to realise it. Stockenström's comments, although written long after the event, are highly apposite. On his trip north in 1829,

there were Griquas who were in possession of extensive farms without the means of stocking the same and who were anxious to let their lands to the colonists, many of whom were equally anxious to hire them when driven to

31

extremity by bad seasons. I declared that tho' there was a law to prevent the latter from going over the frontier without authority, there was none to prevent them sending their flocks over and that far from objecting to their hiring lands from the Griquas on the emergencies referred to I should give it every encouragement.[59]

So began the long process of land alienation that was to contribute to the defeat of the Griqua people, but initially the communities were territorially segregated, as the Boers lived in the north, in the valleys of the Riet, Modder and Vet rivers. Thus the initial suspicion that the Griquas had for the Boers wore off and more cordial relations were established. Though antagonistic at the beginning, the Griquas had never been less than correct towards them, as this was defined by colonial norms.

From the point of view of this relationship, the Great Trek was temporarily a clear advantage. It drew off many of the more radical Boers who sought independence for their community to Natal or the Transvaal and left only those whose move to the north had been impelled by economic deprivation. Thus those who remained in contact with the Griquas were conciliatory farmers who retained their links with the colonial economy, went to *Nagmaal* in Colesberg when they could, and maintained a cordial correspondence with the colonial authorities. Their leader, Michiel Oberholster, had been a *veldkornet* on the northern border before he set up permanently on the Riet River, and he stayed in office for some years, even theoretically collecting taxes for the colonial Government.[60] Moreover, the community was stable. Those who wished for land could find better in Natal than in the dusty, parched valleys of the High Veld.

By 1840 the squabbles between Boers and Griquas had settled. They lived so peaceably together that the Government of Philippolis was prepared to make a treaty with the Boer community. In this, they admitted what had by then become a *fait accompli* and allowed their subjects to lease land to the Boers, designating the area in which this might be done. The area which the Griquas had claimed was far greater than they could utilise, and they were prepared to give up part of it. For the rest, the terms were very conciliatory. Although the Griquas promised 'at all times, when required, to render . . . assistance to the emigrant farmers and their directors', and immediately to render justice on any complaints, they did not claim any right 'to call upon these colonists in any case of dispute or war between any of the tribes, but only when we see the necessity of calling in their assistance to conclude a peace between tribe and tribe'. 'Servants' who absconded were to be returned on both sides, and the 'Governing body of the Emigrant farmers', as Oberholster and his close associates were designated, was to be informed of what the Griqua council was discussing. On the other hand, the ultimate authority of the Griquas over land, if not over all persons within it, was recognised, for it was stipulated that 'Although the emigrant farmers acknowledge the Government of Philippolis as proprietors and owners as far as our country extends, also the chiefs of other tribes as chiefs and directors of their rights and laws, yet we declare that the Colonists in the country retain their own colonial laws, according to their customs, and at all times can act without molestation.'[61] By the time this treaty had been signed there had been no serious rifts between Boer and Griqua for six years. The treaty made explicit the *modus vivendi* which had been established and which would last but a year and a half.

The development of internal politics

The tensions and the contradictions that were at work in the interactions of the Griquas with non-Griquas were even stronger with regard to the internal debates within Philippolis. This was the arena in which they had to be resolved. Thus the first decade of the history of Philippolis was one of deep internal conflict, as the final decision as to the direction which the Captaincy was to take had to be made then. There was still debate as to which of the possible models of existence the community should adopt. The controversy came to a head with the succession crisis between 1835 and 1837, for the two candidates represented alternative futures for the Griquas as clearly as if they had been put up by party structures. Therefore, the resolution of the dispute marks the adoption by the Griquas of Philippolis of their future path.

From the foundation of Philippolis it was recognised that Adam Kok II would not rule long. Already he had shown his disinclination to hold the office of *Kaptyn*, when he left Griquatown and surrendered the family staff to his brother Cornelis II at Campbell. He therefore attempted to arrange a suitable succession at Philippolis, so that he could retire. His eldest son, Cornelis,[62] was groomed for the job, in association with Adam's son-in-law, Hendrick Hendricks. During the late 1820s the government was firmly in the hands of these men, who appear to have been seeking a rapprochement with the mission, for as ex-Bergenaars they were out of favour.[63] Adam, indeed, abdicated in favour of his son, but was forced back when Cornelis died, unexpectedly and prematurely, in 1828.[64] From then on there was no heir apparent, and in the dispute which emerged the parties were identified, as usual in South Africa, by racial and genetic labels. On the one hand were the Bastards, who were considered by whites to be partially descended from slave or white ancestors, but who actually seem to have been those who were perhaps newcomers to Griqua society and had accepted more fully the Christian, commercial mode of life. Joseph de Bruin was

33

the prominent representative of this faction. As against these were the 'Griquas', for such was the designation of those within Griqua society who were eager to lead the old way of life.[65] They were far less homogeneous than the so-called Bastards, and represented many positions on the continuum from shiftless stock herders to peasants. Most prominent of these was Hendricks, long secretary of the Griqua Government, but others — Piet Sabba, once a native teacher, Jager Boer, Arnoldus Constabel, the Pienaars, for instance — are occasionally noticeable.

Adam Kok II died on 12 September 1835. The possible candidates for succession were his two legitimate sons, Abraham and Adam.[66] At a high level, Adam was the candidate of the 'Bastard' or 'new Griqua' faction, while Abraham had support from the 'old Griquas' and the ex-Bergenaars. Neither could rely on the Kok clan itself, for most of its members who still felt such ties to be important had not moved to Philippolis from Campbell. Undoubtedly, Adam was the better suited for the job. He alone was literate and had had experience as a member of the *raad* and as *Provisional Kaptyn* in the absence of his father.[67] He was, however, the younger and suffered from the advocacy of the missionary. Moreover, Abraham's illiteracy was only a disadvantage in that it would require the conduct of business to remain with Hendrick Hendricks, as it had done under Adam II. Although deprecated by some, this was to the advantage of others, to Hendricks not least, who hoped to make use of their skill as a resource in the political game.[68] As against this, Abraham lived a rough uncivilised life, showing no sign of wealth or symbols of status.[69] It is thus necessary to analyse the conflict between them in detail, within the context of the political structure of Griqualand.

Although it is difficult to gain definite information on the matter, it would appear, however, that there was a steady breakdown in the efficacy of the kinship ties that had ordered both Khoikhoin and Bastard society. They remained present and could be utilised whenever necessary, so that, in times of communal difficulty, such as the immediate aftermath of the trek to Nomansland, they could be reasserted, but the development of social differentiation between Griquas increasingly rendered them obsolete. Already in the Hartenaar and Bergenaar revolts, there were examples of families completely split. Jan Karse, for instance, protected Moffat against his relative, Jan Bloem,[70] while the Hendricks and Goeyman families were equally divided.[71] Political affiliation was thus becoming far more open than heretofore. In that members of the same family had much the same experiences, they might tend to act similarly, but the implications of an expanding and diversifying society tended to make kinship ties obsolete, for increasing options allowed a wider choice of life, and consequently of politics. Even so, in a small community, many deep personal rivalries would assume considerable importance. The Pienaars, for instance, could not work with Hendricks.

This political activity was expressed within the framework of an elective, limited monarchy, the Captaincy. The *Kaptyn*, Adam Kok II, was by far the richest man in Philippolis, and was the repository of such legitimacy as the Government possessed, but his power was limited by the fact that the majority of decisions were taken within the *raad* (council) over which he possessed far less than complete control.[72] The method of recruitment to the *raad* at this stage is unknown, but even if it was appointed by Kok, it certainly seems to have been effective. Dr Andrew Smith, a sympathetic and competent observer, gave as his impression of the *raad* when he visited it that 'They appeared as a body to be well calculated to manage a small community such as their is, and a very fair proportion of intellect and sagacity was displayed in their various observations.'[73] On the other hand, there were many complaints that the *raad* could not, or would not, impose its rules on those who were related to its members.[74] Its competence was thus only in process of development, especially as, on occasion, mass meetings of the complete burgher body of Philippolis could take decisions and constituted the ultimate repository of authority.

The administration of this nascent polity was largely carried on by the Secretary, who from 1828 to 1850 was the redoubtable Hendrick Hendricks. His power was such that it is impossible to distinguish the office from the man. Born probably in the last decade of the eighteenth century, he died only in 1881,[75] but scarcely impinged on political developments in the last twenty years of his life. Apparently he learned to read and write in Griquatown, and is first in evidence as a trader in ivory around 1816, with close ties to the mission.[76] Later he joined the Bergenaars, among whom he quickly rose to leadership. He became and remained a personal enemy of Andries Waterboer, when his brother was hung on Waterboer's orders during the rebellion,[77] but in fact the two men's careers ran parallel, for they were the two most able Griquas, both men who rose to political ascendancy from relative obscurity. Hendricks's personal qualities were, if anything, greater. He was a consumate pragmatic politician, a fine orator and, when he wished, possessed of winning charms. Certainly his vision was considerable. In 1835, he was arrested during one of his visits to the Cape Colony, because it was remembered that he had prophesied trouble for the colony specifically at the time when the eastern frontier exploded, and was thus thought to be privy to a plot. In fact he had merely expected trouble at the time of the emancipation of slaves, for, as he said, 'I have read many books and I have never seen that freedom has come to a country without fighting.'[78] There are many other indications that his was a literate and trained intelligence. He was always eager to read colonial newspapers[79] and once asked the Cape Government for the 'means of purchasing 12 or 14 Rds. worth of Dutch books on history'.[80] In part his influence over the Philippolis Captaincy stemmed from his literacy, for he was able to conduct the business of government, whereas Kok himself was forced to rely on an intermediary. In part, also, he gained power from his old Bergenaar associates and his marriage to Adam Kok's daughter.

Of the Griquas' external relations, only those with the colonial Government were important within the internal politics of Philippolis. They received their gunpowder from the bonds at Beaufort West, Graaff-Reinet and Grahamstown. They sold their cattle and their ivory in the same markets. They increasingly had to do with colonial subjects across the border and for many Griquas the colony provided the reference group on which they based their aspirations.

The diplomacy of Philippolis was at this time conducted mainly through the medium of Dr John Philip, South African Superintendant of the LMS. Other men might be important. Andries Stockenström, to be sure, was concerned to prevent the migrations of trekboers over the Orange and came closely into contact with the Griquas while he was doing so. Dr Andrew Smith made his great journey of exploration, reconnaisance and treaty-making independent of mission pressure. Nevertheless John Philip's role was paramount, for the missionaries whom he controlled were permanent residents among the Griquas. He was then at the height of his political involvement and was concerned to build up a Christian Khoi elite within the colony to take advantage of the proclamation of colonial equality in Ordinance 50 of 1828. In this he was not alone, for the foundation of the Kat River settlement by Stockenström and others derived, at least in part, from the same impulse and was less wrought with the creeping paternalism which even a good congregationalist like Philip found hard to avoid.[81] But Philip went further. By raising the spectre of Mzilikazi and by pointing to the very real threat to the northern border posed by marauders in the middle Orange valley, who were currently very active,[82] he hoped to persuade the government to extend its boundaries to include the Griquas, who would then form a united block against the northern invaders – and also against the northward spread of Boers. If it were not possible to incorporate the Griquas on the lines of the Kat River settlement, then Philip proposed that the Government should depose Adam Kok II from Philippolis and Cornelis II from Campbell and replace them with more worthy men. Waterboer would then become *kommandant* over the reunited Griquas.[83]

During Dr Philip's northern tour in 1832, he therefore invigorated the political life of Philippolis, which had been quiet if uneasy since the death of Cornelis III, three years earlier. His scheme was not practical. Most of the Griquas of Philippolis and Campbell had moved away from Waterboer, and the colonial forces would have had to enforce the settlement, a step which ran counter to the whole purpose of the scheme and was recognised by the authorities to be militarily impossible, as surprise could not be achieved and the Griquas would merely become marauders again. But its airing caused turmoil, for Waterboer was anathema to a large faction in Philippolis and to Hendricks above all. Moreover, G. A. Kolbe, the minister at Philippolis, was already deeply involved in these matters, for he had denounced the Barends commando of 1831 against Mzilikazi in which many of the ex-Bergenaar faction had taken part, and for which they had been temporarily ousted from the Philippolis council,[84] and had been interfering in various property deals concerning the *Kaptyn*. Even before Philip arrived the tensions were evident, for only the 'Bastard' faction, under Joseph de Bruin was prepared to go out on commando to recover the cattle which a group of !Kora had lifted from the Philippolis Tswana.[85] Certainly immediately after he left, there was a rearrangement of the government of Philippolis. Kolbe, a partisan, described it thus:

> One of the old Griquas[86] had exerted all his influence to eradicate the good counsels of Dr. P. from the minds of his countrymen. He had collected a party of the worst of the people to unite themselves together and then deposed the principal counsellors; subverted the laws and acted as they judged proper — the chief tacitly allowing them to act in this manner — the bastards or new Griquas and all the members of the church expressed their abhorrence of such conducts and steadfastly adhered to the law.[87]

Apparently a general meeting was held at which Cornelis Nels and Lodewyk de Bruin — who both appear to have been 'new' Griquas — were deposed as magistrates, and various laws which had been proposed by Philip were amended.[88] As if to announce the take-over to the world, a party of Griquas proceeded to loot the cattle of the Thembu on the Moravian missionary station at Klipplats (Shiloh).[89]

This *fait accompli* was accepted. By July 1834, Philip admitted that 'the necessity for placing Waterboer over the chief of Philippolis is no longer necessary'[90] and at the end of that year, when Waterboer came to Cape Town to conclude a treaty with Sir Benjamin D'Urban, the Governor, he was treated with considerable pomp, riding in the Governor's carriage and dining at his table, but the treaty he signed only alluded to the territory from Kheis to Ramah, the acknowledged western boundary of Philippolis territory.[91] Adam Kok followed him there in 1835, with the same objective, but the time was inauspicious. The Cape Government was embroiled in the Sixth Frontier War. Despite the highly favourable reception which the treaty between Waterboer and D'Urban received from London,[92] no similar agreement was made with Adam Kok II, nor would it be, for he died at the Kat River on the way home, thus opening the way for the resolution of the struggle for succession.

Politicking was still continuing on 26 January 1836 when the Civil Commissioner of Graaff-Reinet, W. C. van Ryneveld, with five border *veldkornets* and sundry other burghers rode into Philippolis and persuaded the Griquas to elect a *Kaptyn* 'for their own interest'. Evidently the colony, with memories of trouble on the eastern frontier, was not prepared to allow the interregnum to continue.[93] In the resulting election, Abraham received 168 votes to Adam's 68, and van Ryneveld considered it worthwhile demonstrating to his superiors that he had not influenced the election.[94] If he had, he was remarkably inefficient at it, for most colonial officials, like the missionaries, would have supported Adam.

Many of those who supported Abraham did so, it is conjectured, despite a conflict of opinions. On the one hand, they did not wish to see the victory of the 'Bastard' faction, with which Adam was associated, both for reasons of personal animosity and ambition and because this would have installed the church as supreme and would have given much power to G. A. Kolbe, the missionary, who seems to have been particularly insensitive and able to anger all those who were not of his immediate flock. On the other hand, under the pressure of the Boers and with the impulse of increasing trade to the south, they 'acknowledged that their security and existence as an independent people depended entirely on their connection with the Government, and that it was necessary that they should take care to cultivate its favour in order to have its support and countenance'.[95] Thus in the immediate aftermath of the election, the Philippolis government acted in a very circumspect manner. Abraham himself appears to have been merely a figurehead, as Hendricks and the *raad* claimed that they had no intention of attacking Mzilikazi and raised once again the hope that they might enter into a treaty arrangement with the colony similar to that of Waterboer.[96] On being told that this was conditional on an agreement between Philippolis and Griquatown,[97] they assiduously closed the gaps between them and Waterboer, so that a treaty could be signed in February 1837 which provided that war was forbidden without the consent of both parties, that each *Kaptyn* had a duty to come to the assistance of the other in case of rebellion, that the two councils were to meet twice a year to discuss 'matters of state' and that this council alone was empowered to sanction the death penalty.[98] By then, Adam Kok had re-established himself to such an extent that he was one of the main negotiators of the treaty.[99] Not even if he had won the election could a significantly more satisfactory arrangement have been reached.

Simultaneously, a realignment of political forces was occurring in Philippolis. With the arrival of Theophilus Atkinson as a colleague for Kolbe in August 1836, it became possible for the church party to reunite with those who sought similar ends but were restrained from joining the church by dislike of Kolbe, by disbelief or by unwillingness to accept the constraints of sobriety and monogamy. During the last half of 1836, Kolbe was ostracised even by the believers and, classically, accused of adultery with the wife of one of the church members, a Bastard named Andries Wiese who had only moved to Philippolis a few years before.[100] By January 1837, Kolbe had been expelled from Philippolis by the *raad* and ordered to sell the farms that he had bought from Melvill on condition of its being transferred to his successor.[101] As against this, many who were not enamoured of the new direction of Griqua politics began to react during the winter of 1837. It may well be that Abraham Kok was chafing at the developments that could only leave him with the paraphenalia of power and wished to assert his leadership in the only way open to him, as a fighter and cattle-raider. Certainly the temptation presented by the Ndebele herds was magnified by the defeat of Mzilikazi by the Voortrekkers and their allies early in the year. In addition, the treaty with Waterboer aroused suspicion among many Griquas, and by July, Abraham Kok and his party had assembled to go on commando against Mzilikazi.[102] In this he was apparently supported by Kolbe, whose *volte face* was a reaction to the disillusion he must have felt at being rejected as a minister.

The commando was apparently unsuccessful, but it proved to be the end for Abraham. After July, he never returned to Philippolis. By September Barend Lucas had been appointed *Kaptyn* in his absence, and shortly afterwards a large part of the population, going against the wishes of the *raad* and of Atkinson, who both urged delay, but probably with the agreement of Waterboer, who found it politic to be in Philippolis at the time, determined to elect Adam as *Kaptyn*.[103] Abraham did not submit lightly to such deprivation. Gaining an alliance with Cornelis Kok at Campbell, who was at loggerheads with Waterboer, he and his party attempted to retake Philippolis by *coup de main*. Such at any rate was the report, but in fact the 'campaign' seems rather to have been determined by a show of strength, not actual fighting.[104] With what was now a clear majority of the Philippolis burghers and with the support of Andries Waterboer — in defiance of the treaty — Adam Kok was able to establish himself in the position he was to hold for 38 years.[105]

In the early years of Philippolis there had been a close association between recent immigrants, Christianity and a modernising, commercial ideology. The party which these people formed was not sufficient to capture Philippolis, as was shown by the initial decision to elect Abraham Kok. In the subsequent two years, however, the coalition that was arraigned against them fell to pieces, as those who were of long standing in the community, who were not Christian but who saw that a predatory existence was no longer the profitable option, left Abraham when it became clear that they could not ignore him. Had there not been the campaign against Mzilikazi and the expulsion of Kolbe, then the realignment might have been slower and less dramatic. As it was, a large proportion of those who had installed Abraham switched sides with rapid and decisive effect. This marked the final acceptance by the Griquas of the civilised model of existence which they were to follow.

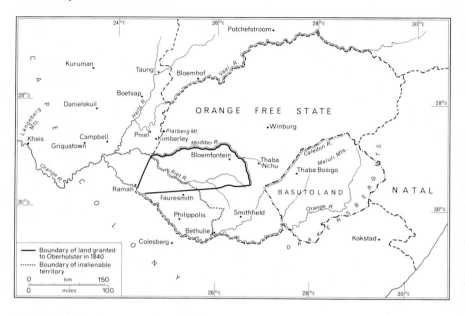

2 Griqualand West and surrounding areas

CHAPTER 4

GRIQUAS, BOERS AND THE BRITISH
IN TRANSORANGIA

During the five years following the election of Adam Kok III in 1837, the Griqua Captaincy of Philippolis was at peace. Internal dissension appears to have ended, as Kok, Hendricks and their allies enjoyed the fruits of their victory. No major quarrels reached the ears of either missionaries or the colonial Government. Conflict between Boer, Briton and Griqua in southern Transorangia had not yet begun. The Griquas were able to accomplish two major realignments of policy, when they finally gave up hope of dominating the Bantu-speakers among whom they lived, and when they made a treaty with the Emigrant Farmers.[1] At this period, therefore, the judicial and administrative structure of Philippolis was fully established. The settlement took on its characteristic shape, both in terms of human geography and social *mores*. The tentative beginnings of later economic growth took place, although the troubles of the late 1840s were to delay them for half a decade.

From the beginnings of Griqua organisation, there had been a council, a *raad*, which aided and advised the *Kaptyn*, and acted as the legislative body for the Captaincy. Precisely how its members were appointed is impossible to say, but its five members were recruited from among the most influential men in the Captaincy. It did its work well.[2] In 1838, the *raad* produced a full code of laws for Philippolis, which showed its maturity. It laid down that the *raad* was to meet every Monday to receive complaints, a frequency that was probably due to the troubles with the Boers, and was not maintained. Its legitimacy was stressed by a provision that the *Kaptyn* and *raad* were to be prayed for every sabbath in church, despite the fact that Kok and many of his councillors were not at this stage members of the church. It made explicit what had been the case for some time, namely that Griqua marriage was to be monogamous, and that those who took a second wife or husband would be considered to have committed adultery and liable both for divorce and punishment, and it served as the court before which all civil cases were to be brought, although provisions were made whereby cases brought against the *Kaptyn* or a member of the *raad* should be tried in their absence.

Simultaneously, the organisation of the local power of the Captaincy, the measures to be taken in criminal cases and the rosta of punishments were formalised. The local officials of the Captaincy were the *veldkornets*, who, so it would appear by analogy with the later situation, were elected by the local population and acted at once as officials of the *raad* and as leaders of the community. The *veldkornet* would be the leader of the burghers of his *wyk*, or district, in battle, but would also be expected to act as police officer, coping with such crimes as robbery in the district over which he held sway. In the case of theft, the *raad* was the court to which recourse was made, and, in the event of a man being found guilty by a majority of the members, with the *Kaptyn* having merely a casting vote, he would be sentenced to a fine of four times the value of the articles he had stolen. In general, however, the laws were not very specific about the punishments to be imposed, being rather concerned to enforce the loyalty of members of the Griqua community to the *veldkornets*, the *kommandant* or general, and to the *Kaptyn*. There were two major exceptions. Because it was a capital crime, and because decisions about it were taken in conjunction with the *raad* of Andries Waterboer in Griquatown, the criteria for conviction in cases of murder were laid down in particular detail. Secondly, a code of laws for the administration of the *dorp* of Philippolis was promulgated. Attention was paid to deciding who had rights to an *erf* in the town and burghers were warned to prevent their stock from straying and damaging other peoples property.[3]

These laws were evidently concerned to prevent tension in the area where it was most likely to arise, namely the town. There was danger here because of the way in which the Griquas were spread over the countryside and the reasons for which they might come to Philippolis. Despite the continual efforts of the missionaries to turn the community into a centralised peasant village which might the more easily receive their pastoral care, there was not enough water in Philippolis to make agriculture feasible. Thus the bulk of the population remained spread over the countryside, living in large extended family groupings on their cattle and sheep farms in the vicinity of the scant *fonteins* which form the water supply throughout the southern Free State. Life here was of an old-established pattern. Many of the Griquas still lived in the traditional 'bee-hive' huts of the Khoisan, made of wickerwork frames covered with reed matting and with skins in the winter. They might keep out the cold, but were highly ineffective against a High Veld thunderstorm. Their major value was their transportability. Those who could afford it, however, were beginning to build more permanent homes, clay on a timber frame, with a thatched roof and a cow-dung floor, and perhaps a coat of whitewash. The difficulty was the supply of timber, for which it was necessary to travel either high up the Orange River or south to the Kat River and the eastern Cape.[4] Clothing, too, was beginning to change. European clothes of cotton and similar stuffs were replacing the buckskin leather, uncomfortably

42

hard when wet, on the backs of most Griquas, and they always covered their heads with bright red, green and black handkerchiefs. For long they retained strings of local beads round their necks, especially the women, and one favourite, an aromatic berry with a sweet smell, was recalled with considerable pleasure by at least one traveller.[5] Colonial-made hats, from the hatteries which seem to have been the first craft shops set up in all the frontier villages,[6] were also worn. Where possible, the *fonteins* were led out to allow cultivation, mainly of wheat, but the great wealth of the people lay in their stock. In 1834, for example, Kolbe estimated that the population of around 700 adults possessed 50,000 sheep, 40,000 goats, 7,000 cattle and 920 horses, but only 22 ploughs.[7] Although Kolbe's estimates are not reliable, never again were there to be any which were as good. Nevertheless, it would appear that there was a steady rise in the numbers of both population and stock, especially horses. Certainly there was immigration from the colony during this period. The Civil Commissioner of Albany complained of the emigration of 'coloured' men from the Kat River to Griqualand at the same time as he worried over the emigration of Boers from his district in the wake of the Great Trek.[8] The devastations of the 1835 frontier war were probably responsible in both cases, to a greater or lesser degree.

The Griquas, moreover, were beginning to become attuned to the commercial market and its fluctuations. A few still maintained links with the trade network in ivory and *karosses* which ran up into Botswana and was speedily re-established in the aftermath of the expulsion of Mzilikazi. In general, however, the men who ran this would seem to have been either independent characters with no firm base anywhere, or else hailing from Griquatown.[9] Also, of course, the farms that had been leased to the Boers provided a ready supply of cash for the Griquas – even if, as the missionaries claimed, a large amount of it was spent on brandy.[10] It is difficult to imagine that even a people as notoriously thirsty as the Griquas could have drunk their way through all the £5010 which they claimed to have received for their farms before 1842, without some proportion being spent on other commodities.[11] Certainly the colonial *smouses* seem to have become more interested in the Griquas at this time, and an English trader set up house in the close neighbourhood of Philippolis – to the considerable annoyance of the missionaries, for he was both 'immoral' and a Deist.[12] Moreover, the Griquas sold cattle and other stock in the colonial markets, often at higher prices than those their Boer neighbours obtained.[13] Schreiner, for instance, attributed the fall in subscriptions to the church which occurred in 1841 to the considerable drop in the price of cattle, which was aggravated by the difficulties which the Griquas experienced in reaching the market at Colesberg. The Orange had as yet neither a bridge nor a regular ferry. It was, probably, not merely wishful thinking on his part to see the major deficiency of the Philippolis area as an environment for a 'respectable' life in this separation from the uncertain commercial situation of the north-east Cape. Despite this, houses were being built, cattle kraals erected, *erven* in Philippolis taken up and a few *fonteins* reclaimed from the Boers to whom they had been let.[14] The evidence on social *mores* is from time to time contradictory — Wright considered Philippolis to be sinking in a sea of alcohol in October, 1842, but commented five months later that the money the Griquas gained from leasing wagons to British troops who had come to protect them went on 'not a drop of brandy'[15] — but it points to an awareness among the Griquas of the potentialities of their country and to a considerable effort to realise them.

Philippolis itself was rather a ghost town. In the early 1840s, it would appear to have had few permanent residents; even the *Kaptyn* built a large house on a farm away from the centre of his government. The missionary, when he was not itinerating, his wife, such traders as had already set up in the town, probably a certain number of riff-raff, trying to live by begging from the traders and their fellow Griquas, and those children who could be spared to attend school (a fluctuating number around 50),[16] formed the core of the town, which had yet to acquire more than a few European-style houses. A British soldier, fatigued after a march from the eastern frontier and resentful at having to fight the Boers, recorded that both the town and its inhabitants stank.[17] Certainly it only came to life intermittently, at times of social crisis as during the election for *Kaptyn* or hostilities with the Boers, or for a church service. As with the Boers, these formed the major social gatherings of the people, so that it was natural for the *raad* to meet the next day. Unlike the Boer churches, services were held every Sabbath, although, no doubt, large attendances were occasional. When the full congregation did gather, however, the church house was too small to hold it. On those occasions, families would move in from the country in their wagons, which were normally rather dilapidated, having been bought second-hand from Boers or in the markets of the Cape Colony, but often drawn by superb teams of matching oxen — Waterboer demonstrated his status by the possession of a team 'of immense height, of a glossy, brindled yellow colour, and striped like tigers'.[18] Increasingly, horses, which allowed their owners to return home the day of the service, were also used.

The missionaries were the only inhabitants who did not enjoy the years of peace. Their role within Griqua society has often been wildly misunderstood. J. S. Galbraith, for instance, claimed that 'Dr John Philip made and unmade chiefs of Griqua tribes'.[19] He was not merely swallowing the claims of Philip himself, but also committing a *post hoc* error, confusing the pleasure which missionaries took from the election of Andries Waterboer and Adam Kok III with evidence for mission involvement.[20] It would be truer to say that Griqua chiefs made and unmade missionaries. In the twenty-five years between the foundation of Philippolis and 1850, there were seven missionaries in the town. Only Peter Wright died there. All the others, James Clarke, John Melvill, G. A. Kolbe, Theophilus Atkinson, Gottlob Schriener and W. Y. Thomson, were forced to leave. The missionaries were actors in the local drama. They did not control it, both because of their own inexperience and of the deepness of their own convictions which precluded compromise.

It was not because their missionaries happened to be particularly incompetent that the Griquas bothered to dispose of them. All of them bar one ministered effectively and quietly after leaving Philippolis. None of them succumbed to the temptations which Bishop Gray described when he wrote that 'Moravians, Independents and Wesleyans all grow rich by dealing in tea, coffee, guns and gunpowder, horses and hides, blankets and ivory.'[21] Rather they were caught in the turmoil of Griqua indecision. They were symbols of the modernisers, and saw themselves as the head of a party in that cause. They were concerned with more than religious conversion. John Philip himself claimed:

> In a country like this the mechanic may do as much for the Kingdom of God as the missionary, and the man who subscribes money to purchase a pump to raise the water of a river at a missionary station does a service as truly acceptable to God as the man who lays out his money sending missionaries and Bibles to the heathen; for what can a missionary do for the salvation of such people if he has no means of bringing them together to receive the first elements of Christian instruction or of keeping them together till those instructions give rise to the formation of a society which will give a permanent footing for the Gospel, with all the apparatus of printing and schools that must follow in the train of the missionary before he can have any security for the effects of his labours.[22]

Missionaries saw themselves as total social revolutionaries. In a society which was only slowly accepting the line they propounded, and was politically skilful enough to remove a man whenever he failed to walk the narrow path between not preaching (which was inconceivable) and offending important Griquas, they were obviously highly vulnerable.

The missionaries were not merely agents of western Christian culture. They were also representatives of the power of the Cape Colony. The colonial officials recognised and encouraged this. Andries Stockenström said:

> I do not think the missionaries have done so much in the way of Christianising as I think they have been useful in a political point of view . . . because these natives looked upon them as a sort of medium of communication between them and the government . . . I think they can be principally beneficial . . . in

making representations on behalf of those natives and warning the government of the state of things, as also their advice restraining the depredations of the natives.[23]

Such influence as John Philip possessed over colonial policy towards the north depended primarily upon the superior net of information provided by his missionaries. The Griquas were conscious of this facet of missionary work. John Melvill found that his pastoral work was greatly hampered by his previous role as Government agent,[24] but Peter Wright, who by 1834 was fully trusted by the Griquas, was appointed the confidential agent of the Governor with Waterboer.[25] Nine years later he was transferred to Philippolis, which Philip correctly predicted would be the ground over which the claims of Boer and Imperial power would be fought.[26]

The British had become involved in events north of the Orange mainly in reaction to the Boer advance, but nevertheless their actions there were in general accord with the processes of Imperial activity in southern Africa. There was continual vacillation in the attitudes towards South Africa of the British Government, whether the Colonial Office and its successive parliamentary masters in London or the Governors and their staff at the Cape, who, because of the time needed for messages to pass between South Africa and Britain were always forced to act independently, except for the threat of veto for their decisions and the sack for themselves. The Griquas knew this well, for they were left in the lurch three times by changes in British policy, which sacrificed them while seeking other objectives.[27] It has generally been argued that the pressures on the British Government were threefold. There was the military and strategic view of the situation. Even the most fervent anti-expansionists recognised the importance of the twin harbours of the Cape peninsular, which were considered vital for the defence of British interests throughout, commanding as they did the sea-route from the Atlantic to the Indian Ocean. However, few could see much potential beyond them. The third Earl Grey summed up the feeling well when he wrote:

> Few persons would probably dissent from the opinion that it would be better for this country if the British territory in South Africa were confined to Cape Town and to Simon's Bay. But however burdensome the Nation may find the possession of its African dominions, it does not follow that it can now cast them off, consistently with its honour and duty.[28]

On the other hand, the clashes with African tribes, which had been in progress intermittently since the first settlement at the Cape by the Dutch, continually sucked the military further and further into the country. This was probably exacerbated by the fact that from the annexation of the Cape in 1806 until

1854, virtually all British Governors at the Cape were military men, with a consequent tendency to view the scene as a strategist, not as a politician.[29]

This was expensive, and the second main determinant of British policy towards southern Africa was the need for economy. The British Parliament did not relish disbursing cash on colonial matters, and least of all on South Africa, which seemed to have no economic potential and yet, in consequence of repeated frontier wars, was remarkably expensive to maintain. A 'Kaffir War' was the worst misfortune that could be inflicted upon an unfortunate Colonial Secretary or Cape Governor, so that all their actions were performed in the knowledge that above all they had to keep the peace, both on the eastern frontier and to the north. Money was too tight to do otherwise. In contrast, there were few who had a vested interest in South African commerce, for it was as yet dependent on Cape wine, which was notoriously execrable, and wool. This latter trade was admittedly growing, but less fast than elsewhere in the world, and the South African contribution formed too small a proportion of British imports to make Yorkshire concerned with events on the karroo.

Thirdly, in forming their policies towards South Africa, the British Government had to take cognisance of the views of the humanitarians and missionary societies. The great May meetings in Exeter Hall could whip up considerable support for a cause. The 'Saints' in Parliament were a force to be reckoned with, and officials at the Colonial Office might be sympathetic to them, but, at the final count, they could only sway what had been agreed upon already. Certainly, after the death of Wilberforce and the emancipation of the slaves, the humanitarian influence of colonial policy never seems to have been decisive, at least with regard to southern Africa.[30]

It must also be remembered that South African issues were frequently forgotten in the general melée of politics in England. For instance, the decade between 1837 and 1846 seems a momentous one in South Africa. It saw the consolidation of the Voortrekker position, the British annexation of Natal and the beginnings of British involvement north of the Orange, with the threat of war in 1842–3, the battle of Zwartkoppies in 1845 and the establishment of a British resident in the next year. Yet not once did the British Parliament call for information on any of these issues. Only with the breakdown on the eastern frontier in the War of the Axe, and the consequent expense, did they again become interested. Otherwise decisions remained with the Colonial Office, and in South Africa.[31]

Nevertheless, behind the apparent uncertainty of British policy, there lay a regularity of action which had profound effects on South African history. Particularly with regard to the eastern frontier of the Cape Colony, the advent of the British changed the power relationships within southern Africa. In the first forty years of conflict, the Boers and the Xhosa had been at least balanced, militarily. If anything Xhosa might was generally greater than that of the Boers.[32] However, the advent of the British meant that the balance shifted decisively in favour of the whites. Clearly, no other force in southern Africa was sufficiently formidable to take on the British Empire, if it was disposed to exercise its full power.[33] From 1806 on, the security of frontier life was always underwritten by the British army, especially after the establishment of British settlements in the eastern province. The only time thereafter when whites were evicted from an area that they had colonised was in the northern Transvaal in the 1860s, far beyond the aegis of the British.[34] However much they might prevaricate, the British were ultimately not prepared to allow the destruction of their 'ideal prefabricated collaborators', on whom alone could be based any hope of turning what was essentially a military base into a profitable colony.[35] Occasionally British spokesmen might toy with the idea of leaving the Boers, particularly those of the interior, to their fate. The third Earl Grey once wrote, in private, that Britain 'must cease to act with such quixotic philanthropy as to insist on preventing the savages and semi-savages (the Boers) of Southern Africa from cutting each other's throats and thus bringing them all as enemies against ourselves.'[36] However, this was an aberration. Consistently the British supported the colonists in their disputes with Africans and 'coloureds' for land. The process of law and the more naked exercise of force were used, perhaps unwittingly, to establish *baaskap* throughout southern Africa. In the ordering of social stratification along the lines determined by pigmentation, the role of the British was immensely important, mainly because the British in South Africa itself were naturally aligned closely with colonial society, and were thus receptive to its wishes. The level of policy as determined by long-term objectives and that ordered by the pressures and visions of the local social situation both tended towards the same end, that of the establishment of social and political hegemony for the group which defined itself as white.

This is not to say that there was a uniform coincidence between the actions of the British and the desires of all members of the white community. On the contrary, they were frequently in conflict, particularly after the Great Trek, which spread Boer settlement far beyond the bounds of the Cape Colony. The possibility that another European power might control the harbour of Port Natal (Durban) forced the British to become embroiled in the conflict. Thus in 1842 the British annexed Natal. After a short struggle, the Trekker Government that had operated there for the previous four years was extinguished, but the underlying conflict with the Imperial Government did not end there. Rather it was transferred back across the Drakensberg on to the High Veld, embroiling those who had had no part in the original quarrel and breaking the peace and stability

of Philippolis. During the next twelve years, the chances of politics would establish the republics of the Orange Free State and the Transvaal, and in so doing
considerably reduce the possibility for an effective Griqua organisation.

The British presence on the northern border of the Cape Colony began with
the Civil Commissioner of Colesberg. For twenty-one years from the establishment of the magistracy this office was held by Fleetwood Rawstorne, a highly
competent, well-liked, rather anonymous man, with experience on the eastern
frontier. He was served in his role as intelligence officer and mediator by various
of the leading Boers of the northern border, who had maintained contact with
their fellows over the Orange. Most notable among these were *Veldkommandant*
N. J. van der Walt and *Veldkornet* Gideon Joubert. Rawstorne was subordinate
to the Lieutenant Governor of the eastern Province, a position which was held
through the crucial years of the 1840s by Lieutenant Colonel Hare. From him
the chain of command ran to the Governor, a post held during this period by Sir
Benjamin D'Urban, who was highly competent but unfortunate, being caught
between a frontier war and a London administration dominated by the pressures
of philanthropy; Sir George Napier, a military man from the normal school of
Cape Governors, the Peninsular War; and Sir Peregrine Maitland, from the same
source, but basically too old, who left most of the actual work to his nephew.

To continue the *dramatis personae*, the Voortrekker community was split, as
might be expected of a body spread from the Mzimkulu to the Limpopo. The
maatschappies of Potchefstroom and Winburg had been formally part of the
Natal Republic, and Hendrick Potgieter in the Transvaal was still the hero of the
more republican Boers and might hope to gain support further south. In
Transorangia itself, Oberholster on the Riet River was concerned to maintain his
allegiance to the Cape Colony and his friendship to Adam Kok for as long as
possible. He had even written to the Commissioner, who was concerned to
establish British presence in Natal, asking specifically not to be included, as he
hoped to maintain contact and eventually be re-incorporated into the Cape
Colony. In major opposition to him were Jan Mocke, Jan Kock, and their
following, most of whom lived around the Modder River or in the region of
Winburg. They were fervent republicans and had formed a very sizeable proportion of the Boer forces which resisted the British take-over of Natal during
the winter of 1842. On returning across the Drakensberg, disillusioned, no doubt,
with the way in which the Natalians were prepared to deal with the British, they
proceeded to carry on the fight.[37]

The immediate reaction of the British Government to the widespread emigration of Boers to the north had been to pass an act, for which there were
various precedents elsewhere in the Empire, by which all crimes committed south
of latitude 25° south might be tried in the Cape courts, irrespective of the

49

boundaries of the colony. No means of enforcement was provided, however, and up to 1842 it had never been invoked, at least in Transorangia.[38] After the return of Jan Mocke, Jan Kock and the Modder River Boers from their winter's excursion to Natal, where they had been concerned to make life difficult for the new British Government, Sir George Napier chose to remind them of that Government's powers and issued a proclamation in which he made known to the emigrants, and most particularly to those who resided in the neighbourhood of the native tribes north of the Orange that 'Her Majesty will regard with the liveliest indignation any attempt upon the part of any of her subjects to molest, invade, or injure any of the native tribes, or to take or maintain unlawful possession of any of the land to those tribes belonging.'[39] Moreover, those who did so were to lose any right to the protection of the British Crown and render themselves liable to be punished in its courts. The arguments of the missionaries on behalf of the various tribes, which may have been given independently but were certainly not disavowed by the chiefs of those tribes, were being heard.

Partly in reaction to this, and in part as a move in internal Boer politics by which he hoped to rally the non-committed and loyalist factions within Transorangia to the support of the Natal *volksraad*, Mocke proceeded to take action. The Boers had, moreover, been stimulated by the arrest of two of their number on the suspicion of murder. Thus, during October, rumours began to fly that the Boers were assembling to proclaim the independence of the country north of the Orange, and the information leaked out that on 24 October Mocke was to raise the standard of the Natal republic at a ford in the Orange River known as Allemans Drift. Kok and his council went to Colesberg a few days before this to confer with Rawstorne. They claimed that

> our purpose in coming to Colesberg at this time is to seek the aid of the British Government, in accordance with the proclamation, to protect us and to prevent bloodshed. For should we do anything to oppose the Boers outside the intervention of the British Government, there will surely be bloodshed which we should very much like to avoid.[40]

To Mocke they protested in much stronger terms:

> We hereby protest most strongly against your fearless and unlawful action, namely that you are entering *our borders* by force with a few hundred armed men with the professed intention, be it said, to erect a beacon *within our borders*. We have already called upon the justice, power and intervention of our ally and friend the British Government to come to the help and protection of ourselves and the other surrounding peoples against your inhuman force. Should Captain Adam Kok be at Alleman's Drift on the 24th, then it shall be

neither at your calling nor with any intention to make any arrangements with you over this action.[41]

By chance, there was in Colesberg at the time one Judge Menzies, in the course of his circuit. He became embroiled in the matter and took it upon himself to take possession for the British Government of the land north of the Orange River as far as latitude 25° S and longitude 22° E. Both Adam Kok and Peter Wright were consulted about this. Both agreed and both were present at the ceremony at which it was done on 22 October. Two days later the Boers arrived. Menzies, Rawstorne and various of the colonial *veldkornets* went out to meet them, but it had been decided that, to avoid provocation, no Griqua would be present. The meeting was argumentative, fiery, inconclusive, and in many ways irrelevant, for as soon as he heard of Menzies' actions, Sir George Napier disavowed them. It was, he claimed, against general British policy, and could not be maintained without considerable force, which was not available.[42]

On the other hand, the episode had the effect of increasing, albeit temporarily, the unity of the Afrikaner population, which had been one of Mocke's objects in staging the occasion. Various of Oberholster's followers began to secede to the republicans. Rawstorne became worried that he would have to resist the Boers, which he could not do, as the only forces at his disposal were the colonial burghers, many of whom were sympathetic to the emigrants.[43] Throughout the rest of the year armed parties of Boers roamed the area, and there was one major incident of provocation, in which the Boers visited an outlying Griqua farm, took the seven guns there, held the owner captive for several days and drove off all his stock.[44] During December, however, the British took the chance of stripping the eastern frontier of troops, moved up to Colesberg and beyond and were thus able to induce the Boers to disperse. Lieutenant Governor Hare's prestige, and the redcoats at his back, were sufficient.

The Griquas maintained their policy of complete loyalty to the British Government throughout this period. At any rate, such was the impression they were concerned to project, and there is no reason to suppose that it was a false one. Thus they released to the *South African Commercial Advertiser* a description of a meeting which occurred between Mocke and Hendricks in the immediate aftermath of the Allemans Drift affair. Mocke was attempting to secure a rapprochement with the Griquas, claiming that Boers wished to check the English Government, to form alliances with the black nations, and by including them in the Boer Republic, to strengthen its opposition to the British subjugation of the country, for the 'real design' of the beacon that Menzies had erected 'was to reduce the country under the tyrannical yoke of the British Government, and the Griquas and other nations would not be able to bear the oppression of that

Government, for they [the Boers] powerful burghers had not been able to bear them and how could the black nations bear them'. Hendricks's reply stressed that the Griquas were the allies of the British Government and had received much benefit in return. They had only allowed the Boers into Griqua country for as long as they remained faithful subjects of the British Government, but the Boers had behaved most treacherously, so that it was only the advice of Judge Menzies that prevented the Griquas from rising up to destroy Mocke.[45] In this last he was certainly exaggerating. In less rhetorical moments, the Griquas knew that they were short of ammunition, short of guns, short of experience and short of numbers with which to take on the Boers, and frequently called on Rawstorne to rectify such of these difficulties as were within his power.[46]

The views of the Griquas were most forcibly reiterated at a conference which was held at Colesberg on the last day of the year, and continued two days later. Most of the main protagonists — Hare, Rawstorne, Oberholster, Adam Kok, Gideon Joubert — were there, but once again it was Hendricks who stole the show. Wright claimed of the latter occasion that 'Hendricks made the best speech I ever heard from a native, it touched the feelings and called forth the praise of His Honour and Rawstorne'.[47] His two outbursts deserve to be quoted at some length. First, he was concerned to refute the uncomfortable fact that the Griquas were but newcomers to the land. The experience of the Griquas' ancestors, who had been driven from the colony as coloured men, was in his mind. He said:

> The farmers say 'the Griquas now occupy the Bushman's land'. Who was it that drove us there? — let the names 'Kapstadt', 'Stellenbosch', 'Tulbagh' give the answer — it was the Dutch people who sent us forward — it was not until later years until the English name 'Colesbergh' [sic] was heard in the land, that the Griquas had rest. It was the English who made the Hottentot free. It was not until England put her hand on the land, was there any resting place for the Griquas — and never, never will there be security for the Griquas, and the Black nations of Africa until England continues to hold her hand over the whole country.[48]

Two days later he dilated further on the same theme:

> The whole of our confidence is in the British Government. It is through the Government that the slaves are free — that we possess a country and are a people this day and we feel ourselves under deep obligation to the Govt. for its support — all this is contrary to the wishes of the Boers. We are a Christian nation — we thank God that we stand on such relation with a Christian nation which has acted consistently with us and all others — which is the cause that Waterboer and Le Puy[49] and Moshesh are still in existence, contrary to the

intentions of the Boers. We have no other refuge than the protection of Government — we cannot be separated from that Government — it is our life — our support — We are viewed by the Govt. as an independent nation and yet are protected and assisted as if their own subjects — nothing can repay our obligation — were we to renounce the Govt. we should be annihilated — this is the wish of the Boers — they would fain have that Govt. should reject us — they would hide their true feelings until they have an opportunity of crushing us.

The arrival of Your Honr. at such a moment when our very existence was endangered, when we see all the preparations made for our assistance, calculated all the expense, see all the waggons — how shall we be able to repay all the obligations?

Many a time have we come to Colesberg for help and assistance and have found the Civil Commissioner struggling under the same difficulties as ourselves.

For my part, regards me, on account of my strenuous opposition to the Natal Republic, I am obnoxious to the Boers, who have even proposed to carry me off to Natal and punish me.

We are thankful to your Honor — the whole Griqua Nation thanks your Honor for what has been done for them.[50]

Obviously Hendricks, a canny politician, knew how to mould his subject to suit his audience, and his rhetoric was high flown — and was no doubt more so in the original, before Rawstorne's translation and precis. But the Griquas' actions are consistent with his rhetoric.

During these troubles, the Griquas (because they had to go into *laager* in Philippolis) could not gather what promised to be the best harvest that the community had yet seen. Moreover, their flocks and herds, which had to be gathered together to avoid capture, suffered badly from overcrowding and the consequent shortage of water and grazing.[51] On the other hand, they made a considerable killing out of supplying the British troops who had come to protect them. For the supply of wagons they received £578, so that some 25 houses were in process of erection in March of 1843.[52]

The Griquas were also able to turn the event to political advantage by securing a satisfactory relationship with the colony, as had been denied them earlier by the death of Adam Kok II and by the difficulties consequent upon that. The achievement of this was hindered by the death from typhus of the Rev. Peter Wright, on 15 April, 1843.[53] Wright was one of the very few missionaries trusted by the Griquas, because he had been frequently partisan on their side in various disputes, notably that with Robert Moffat in the late 1830s, and because he was known to be a highly competent diplomat in his dealings with the colony. The Griquas then asked James Read the elder to become their minister. Read was notorious as a protagonist of 'hottentot' rights, with a reputation stretching back thirty years to the Black Circuit. What the Griquas wanted from their missionaries seems evident, although in this case they did not get it, as Read declined to move from the Kat River.[54] So they had to continue their negotiations with colonial powers without such help, a situation which they distrusted, for even Hendricks, who had much to gain from his position as Secretary, admitted that 'With no one to assist us, in a written agreement between two nations, one of which is highly civilised, and the other not so civilised or enlightened, it never goes well.'[55] John Philip was, however, as ready as ever to profer his advice. Thus by November 1843, and despite objections that Adam Kok was not as powerful a chief as Waterboer, and therefore did not deserve as large a salary — a belief that by this stage was erroneous — a treaty was signed between him and the Governor, Sir George Napier. It resembled that concluded with Waterboer eight years earlier. In return for £100 per annum, £50 per annum to the LMS for education, and 100 stand of arms, Kok was to take all measures necessary to keep the peace, guard the colonial border, gather intelligence for the colony and 'cooperate . . . with the colonial government in preserving peace and extending civilisation to the native tribes'. Significantly, no mention was made of the Boers, who had precipitated the move.[56]

No one, except perhaps Napier himself, expected the treaty to bring permanent peace to Transorangia, for that evidently required the pacification of the Boers, and the way to that end was certainly not through the Griquas. As an example of frontier opinion, the 'Northern Correspondent' of the *Grahamstown Journal*, who was probably an English merchant in Colesberg, wrote of the Griquas:

> The tribe of which [Kok] claims the chieftainship does not possess one redeeming quality to rescue them from the odium resting upon them as arrant imposters and petty depredators. Besides they are as destitute of the power as of the disposition to fulfill any treaty — except be it one which shall give them authority to plunder a poor 'smous' [hawker, or travelling trader], commit some acts of petty tyranny towards some destitute and unprotected emigrant farmer — or cut the throats of some wandering bushmen.[57]

The sort of animosity that this entailed could not be a basis for a lasting peace. It marked the beginning of serious pressure on the Griquas' lands and independence, in the face of which the Griquas closed ranks. Men who had been excommunicate since before the Bergenaar revolt, above all the *Kaptyn*, his half-brother Gert Kok and Hendrick Hendricks, were once again received into the church.[58] Waterboer and fifty of his men spent some two months in Philippolis as a precaution against Boer aggression.[59] But at the same time they attempted to take the maximum benefit from the Napier treaty.

Between the signing of the Napier treaty late in 1843 and the next major breakdown in relations during early 1845, there were a succession of annoying incidents, all of which threatened to spill over into war. In March of 1844, for example, Adam Kok had arrested a Boer called Van Staden who had killed an Englishman, George Mills, and sent him to Colesberg to stand trial. In this he was within his rights as he saw them to be defined by Napier and by the Cape of Good Hope Punishment Act, but the move was, wittingly or otherwise, calculated to annoy those Boers who were attempting to build a *maatschappy* of their own, and to enrage all those revolted by the suggestion that they were under the jurisdiction of a black man.[60] This incident was exacerbated by a law which Kok had recently passed and promulgated, forbidding the sale of liquor within his territory and regulating the amount of their beloved 'Cape Smoke' that the Boers were allowed to take through Philippolis.[61] War was evidently a definite possibility.

That these difficulties did not produce an open breach was due primarily to the other concerns which the Boers had at this time. With the routes to the sea through Natal finally cut off, two readjustments had to be made. First, there was the need to establish a more effective political order, for the Natal *volksraad* was evidently impotent and in the pocket of the British. In April 1844 the men of Winburg and Potchefstroom produced their own system of legislation, and placed Hendrick Potgieter, the old Voortrekker leader, at the head of a theoretically united community which stretched from the Orange to the Limpopo and was to be based, so Potgieter hoped, on the village of Andries-Ohrigstad, in the far north.[62] Secondly, this new polity had to establish relationships with its neighbours. Thus Potgieter himself successively made an expedition to Delagoa Bay and an arrangement with the Pedi of the northern Transvaal for a considerable cession of land. He was followed north by Jan Mocke, who failed to find a way through the tsetse-fly belts, but had long and fruitful talks with Potgieter.[63]

While Mocke was away in the north there was a short conference in Philippolis, at which Adam Kok, Oberholster, and the colonial leaders, Joubert and van der Walt, agreed that those who had been hostile to the British Government should lose the land they had hired from Griquas. This was evidently to the advantage both of Oberholster, who could hope thereby to strengthen his position in the emigrant community, and to the Griquas, who might thereby regain much of the land they had hired; but equally the 'disaffected' Boers, led by Jan Kock, who was also present at the meeting, could not stomach such proposals.[64] Nor did the Governor, who saw the conference as one more attempt by Kok to follow up 'the views he has for a long time been aiming to accomplish, namely the establishment of a military post at his headquarters, Philippolis, to support his measures and his laws'.[65] If he could manage otherwise, Maitland hoped to avoid this eventuality.

Throughout the rest of 1844, southern Transorangia gently smouldered as Boers and Griquas eyed each other warily. Oberholster was finding it difficult to maintain control over his followers.[66]

Finally at the end of November a Boer commando once more assembled under Jan Kock, and was countered by the gathering of the Griqua forces in Philippolis.[67] The Boers then surprisingly dispersed and Potgieter, through Jan Kock, attempted to arrange a meeting with Adam Kok III. Kok's initial reaction was to tell Potgieter that 'he does not feel himself at liberty to meet officially or to make a treaty with anyone who assumes to himself a supremacy over Her Majesty's subjects'.[68] However, he did agree to allow twelve men into Philippolis, whereupon Potgieter put in a document which read in part:

> We [the Boers] are emigrants together with you [the Griquas] and are regarded as such and regard ourselves as emigrants who together with you dwell in the same strange land and we desire to be regarded as neither more nor less than your fellow-emigrants, inhabitants of the country, enjoying the same privileges with you.
>
> It is by no means the intention of the Head Commandant [Potgieter] and his council to bring any native chief under their laws and authority, but to leave each one to exercise his own authority. But in the case of any crime committed by a white against a native, the native shall complain to the leader of the whites and when a crime is committed by a native against a white, the white shall complain to a ruler of the natives. In case of hired servants of either party absconding they shall be mutually delivered up by both parties.[69]

The Griquas' reaction was as ever a re-avowal of their trust in the British Government as the final arbiters of this dispute. Such at any rate was the version that they allowed to reach W. Y. Thomson, who had succeeded Peter Wright as missionary in Philippolis, and hence Dr Philip and the colonial Government.[70] There is, however, no reason to believe that they told Potgieter anything else. The Griquas had staked heavily on being able to maintain themselves through the British, for their distrust of frontier Boers was of long standing, running back to the experiences of their Bastard and Khoisan ancestors on the farms of the interior in the previous century. The British were powerful, they were apparently occasionally well-intentioned, various Britons were among the Griquas' closest friends and allies, and they were seen as extraneous to the situation of frontier South Africa. Thus they were thought to provide the best hope of reaching a satisfactory conclusion, if they could be manoeuvred into a situation where they had to act. In the long run, however, this hope would necessarily prove vain, as ultimately the British would never sacrifice their collaborators.

In the event, it was the Griquas who precipitated the crisis. After their troubles of two years previously they waited until the harvest was in, but early in March 1845 Adam Kok once more invoked the powers he claimed to hold under the Cape of Good Hope Punishment Act by sending a party of Griquas, 100 strong, to arrest a Boer named Jan Krynauw, who was resident in the Griqua *gebied*, and who, so it was claimed, had seized two Tswana subjects of Adam Kok. In fact they missed Krynauw and conducted a long and acrimonious conversation with his wife, but the move had the effect of driving both Boers and Griquas into *laager*.[71] Even Oberholster and his followers joined the republican Boers, while Waterboer brought a contingent over from Griquatown to join his fellow *Kaptyn*. The British, too, viewed the situation with alarm and began to take measures to move troops up to the Orange River.[72]

The breakdown finally came on 6 April, when shots were exchanged between the Boer *laager* and a small group of Griquas under Adam Kok, who had gone out to parley with them. What precisely happened is very unclear, as both sides naturally claimed that the other had fired first. For the next fortnight or so there was desultory fighting. In the many skirmishes, and in two engagements of major importance by local standards, there were only ten Boers killed, even by the calculations of their adversaries, and only one Griqua.[73] The correspondent of the *Grahamstown Journal* was no doubt accurate when he claimed that 'the Griquas are found to be quite a match for the Boers, number to number — but both parties are alike in not venturing, if they can help it, within shot of each other.'[74] The much-famed Boer marksmanship only arose with the breech-loading rifle, while in the days of the *voorlaier* it was necessary to get close to an adversary, or more frequently to game, in order to deliver a telling shot. Against an enemy as well armed this was foolish, and the Boers contented themselves with driving off large numbers of Griqua cattle.

After some three weeks, there was a concerted effort to achieve peace. Various of the colonial burghers, who could act as intermediaries, brought word that the Boers were willing to treat with Adam Kok and with Rawstorne, provided the latter was admitted to be a representative of Kok, not of the British Government. This was allowed and a meeting took place on Allewyn's Kop, the Boer headquarters a few kilometres from Philippolis, at which Rawstorne demanded the return of the 3,600 cattle and the 260 horses that the Griquas claimed had been taken from them. He also demanded that Krynauw and any others who had committed crimes be given up to British justice, reminded them of their own allegiance to Britain, ordered them to disperse and stressed that the

Griqua claims would be enforced by the British troops then on the way north.[75] The Boers refused these terms, because their *raad* had not sanctioned them, but agreed to retreat from their position. They were also amenable to returning the Griqua cattle, provided those of their own which were in Griqua kraals were also returned. Because of their fear of the Griquas, which resulted from many of them living interspersed with Griquas in Griqualand, they hoped for a definite line of demarcation between the two communities.[76] They then retired from Allewyn's Kop, but did not disperse. Rather they reformed at Zwartkoppies, 40 kilometres north-north-east of Philippolis. Nor were the requisite number of cattle immediately forthcoming. Therefore when contingents of the 7th Dragoon Guards and the Cape Mounted Rifles had reached Philippolis, they found it necessary to go into action against the Boer encampment. They achieved the desired result with remarkable ease. This was because they did not fight fair, but appeared to be prepared to accept casualties in the expectation of inflicting them. After the Boers had been lured out of their camp by a Griqua division, a British charge put the Boers to flight.[77] Only one Griqua and two Boers were killed in the fight, but in consequence the armed parties of Boers moved as quickly as possible north to the Modder River, while Oberholster and his followers made peace so quickly that by 8 May, nine days after the battle, 280 of the emigrants had taken the oath of allegiance and about 2,000 cattle had been returned to the Griquas.[78] Many other Boers, even of the republican faction led by Jan Kock, hoped to exculpate themselves by returning Griqua cattle.[79] All parties then awaited the arrival of the Governor, Sir Peregrine Maitland, for he was to arrange what was hoped to be a durable solution to the problem.

Maitland arrived with his staff about the middle of June. His object in making such a trip was 'to secure their land and freedoms to the numerous native tribes inhabiting the country for many hundreds of miles beyond the colony to the North-East against the encroachment and aggressions of self-expatriated British subjects, superior in combination and arms and too often ready as well as able to dispute successfully with the rightful owners for the simple necessaries of a half-civilised life'.[80] Essentially, to do this he followed suggestions put to him six months earlier by Thomson and Philip.[81] He proposed to locate the British subjects on the land of the native chiefs which they had already occupied, but to stipulate conditions for such locations by treaty with the chief concerned. Arrangements for leasing would have to be agreed and a British Resident, with a force preferably made up of local native levies, established at some central point.[82] Maitland therefore called a meeting of all the chiefs of Transorangia at which to explain his plan. In the event it only applied to Moshoeshoe, who was agreeable, and to Adam Kok, for all the others either controlled too little land for leasing to be possible, or were engaged in border disputes with Moshoeshoe, so that a settlement was impossible. It was therefore with Adam Kok that Maitland had most difficulty, for the peculiar situation in Griqualand, where farms had been leased to the Boers by individual Griquas or by the *raad*, led to considerable complications. The Boers could not be expelled without 'unmerited hardship' — or considerable expense — while to do so would have been to 'precipitate them . . . on still more defenceless tribes in the interior, to work havoc and massacre beyond our reach.'[83] The negotiations were actually mainly carried out between Maitland's nephew, who combined the offices of chaplain and secretary, and W. Y. Thomson, so that detailed drafts survive only in the LMS files, where Thomson sent them. Thomson, however, must have had Kok's agreement for everything he wrote to Maitland.

The argument between Maitland and the Griquas centred on the question as to which Boers should be expelled from Griqualand for their part in the recent troubles. To both sides this was evidently the key issue. If the Griquas could make the definition wide enough, then they could regain almost all the land they had previously leased away. To Maitland, however, widespread expulsions would be both expensive and dangerous. He therefore proposed that all those British subjects who had not forfeited their rights 'by some act of conspicuous criminality' against either the Griquas or Her Majesty's Government should be allowed to retain the farms which they had hired.[84] Thomson asked for amplification of this formula.[85] The reply was based on the fact that Adam Kok could not maintain order within his own territory. Moreover, so it was claimed, he had provoked the emigrant Boers by the attempted arrest of Krynauw, and therefore they could claim that they had gathered together in self-defence. Thus because the Griqua laws with regard to land, and the maintenance of title after the committing of treasonable acts, did not coincide with the British, 'the simple fact of having been recently in arms against Captain Adam Kok does not of itself require that every person proved to have been in arms should be expelled by British troops'. On the other hand, various definite criteria were laid down. The ringleaders at Allewyn's Kop when Rawstorne's conditions were refused, those who fought against the British at Zwartkoppies and those who offered violence to Griqua lives and property before the late troubles were to suffer 'absolute and unconditional expulsion'.[86] Thomson and Kok, in their reply, stressed the corporate nature of the Boer opposition. They noticed that at least one Boer had remained quiet and unhindered on his farm throughout the troubles. They pressed for the expulsion of all who had taken up arms, both against the Griquas and the British. Even by the narrower criteria which Maitland offered, so they claimed, few Boers would have remained in possession of their farms, had the provisions been vigorously enforced.[87] As it was, not even the most notorious of the Transorangian Boers was expelled. Some moved north, disgruntled with the imposition of British authority, but none was forced out.

By concentrating on the problem of expulsions, the Griquas and their advisers conceded the rest of the proposals put forward by Maitland, albeit reluctantly. In this they made a tactical error of considerable magnitude, as the future would show. The Griquas may have seen the British Resident as the forerunner of a British take-over, but if so their fears were shown only in a single, snide query as to 'how the fact of [Adam Kok's] sovereignty over the whole of his country should be made a reason for the extension over his people of the powers of a British Magistrate'.[88] Basically, they accepted the necessity of a Resident to perform the variety of administrative and judicial tasks which were required under the settlement. Above all he was to collect quitrent on Boer farms, half of which would accrue to the Griquas. Rather more questionable was their acceptance of the suggestion that Griqualand was to be divided into two parts:

> One division to consist of land in regard to any part of which it shall not hereafter be competent for Captain Adam Kok, or any of his people, to grant leases, or make sales, or give any right of occupation to any British subject, or generally, to any person of European birth or extraction; and the other division to consist of land which may be let to British subjects and all others indifferently.[89]

This was, of course, not new. Kok had made a very similar arrangement with Oberholster five years before. Moreover, 'That the Griqua people committed a great political fault in admitting into their territory a large number of British subjects Adam Kok is willing to acknowledge; and he had consented to atone for that fault as far as possible by allowing the permanent settlement of part of his territory by British subjects.'[90] He might complain about the continued presence of those who had attacked him, but he was prepared to let the alienable territory go. What is rather remarkable is that no complaint was made against the boundaries of the two divisions. It might have been assumed that the line should follow that of the Oberholster treaty, which was hard to define on the ground, but fitted the realities of settlement. Maitland's division, which was present from the first draft, however, ran quite across this previous demarcation, so that the major Boer settlement of the lower Riet River was partially included in the inalienable territory, while many Griqua farms in the better watered area to the north-east of Philippolis were excluded. To be precise, some 59 per cent (85 out of 143) of those farms which had been leased were within the inalienable territory, while only 40 per cent (58 out of 146) of the farms in the alienable territory had been leased.[91] Perhaps the members of the Griqua *raad* themselves

60

mainly possessed farms near Philippolis and so were not affected, so that they did not notice. At all events, the pattern was a considerable disadvantage to the Griquas in the succeeding decade.

In the end, the Griquas agreed to the plan put forward by Maitland, and hoped that it might be carried out. After the various technicalities of the drafting had been ironed out in Cape Town, the treaty was signed in February 1846.[92]

The Maitland settlement was ultimately unsatisfactory to almost everyone concerned, but initially there was no particular problem, as it did not impinge greatly on the lives of the inhabitants of Transorangia. The hostilities of the previous years had caused very considerable disruption and were followed by a bad drought during the summer 1845—6, but nevertheless several Griquas began to build houses and repair the damage of the war. Church attendance began to increase, as did the number of Griquas at school. At the end of 1845 there were some 150 pupils in the mission school at Philippolis and another 80 at outstations. Despite the destitution of crops and stock, some £90 was subscribed for the repair and enlargement of the church. This money had probably accrued from the various side benefits of the war, primarily the supplying of the British troops with transport and, perhaps, fodder.[93] The indices of economic advancement are thus somewhat contradictory, but they show that the Griqua community was at the least prepared to utilise the possibilities which might occur in the future.

Politically, however, the situation was highly precarious. The British Resident had to hold the ring between many conflicting forces without the power to accomplish anything. In real terms, his appointment changed little, except that there was now an authority who might mediate in the various differences over land and wages which had built up between the loyalist Boers and the Griquas. In the two months of his tenure Captain Sutton, the first resident, appears to have done little else but settle disputes of this type. A few examples may perhaps illustrate the nature of the relationships which had been built up in the area. For instance, Johannes Coetzee admitted lashing a 'hottentot' subject of Adam Kok's. His defence was that he considered Stuurman to be 'myn hottentot', but all the same he was fined 14 rix dollars, and bound over to keep the peace for £24.[94] Two 'Bushmen' brought a complaint against a Boer, that he had shot another when out on a shooting expedition, but the claim was dismissed for lack of evidence.[95] There were several complaints that Boers were trespassing on Griqua land in the inalienable territory, and even more problems as to the exact status of land which Boers held from Griquas. These were usually settled after the pattern of a case between Gert Oerson and Adriaan van Wyk. Van Wyk had paid in all some £154 15s. 0d. worth of goods to Oerson for the hire of the two farms Touw Fontain and Doorn Kraal, so it was adjudged that he could hold them until this money and what he had paid for improvements had been paid off, at a rate of £11 5s. a year.[96] In the south there was thus an atmosphere of relative calm, but to the north, in the area of Winburg and Potchefstroom there was little sign of peace. Major Warden, who was Sutton's successor and a man who does not seem to have been capable of adjusting from a military to a civilian ethos, had to lead an expedition against Winburg in May 1846, in consequence of rumours that Jan Kock was calling his followers out to drive out the Resident. It would appear from his rather incoherent report that shots were exchanged,[97] but despite the presence at his back of a contingent of the Cape Mounted Rifles and one of Griquas, it is clear that the British Resident's power extended only to where he was a useful mediator in local disputes. In Winburg and across the Vaal he was irrelevant, especially after the return of Andries Pretorius from Natal, disgruntled at the way in which the Governor refused to listen to his complaints about the amount of land which the Boers were allocated. In Basutoland and the Caledon River valley, the squabbles went on without Warden being drawn in, as yet. Warden's most decisive action was to attack a group of Thembu who had moved up from the Transkei across the Orange River. He did this without provocation, in consequence of a bad attack of the jitters — excusable in a military man surrounded by hordes of potential enemies, with a mediocre force at his back and left on his own with no advisors or superiors within call — brought on by the progress of the War of the Axe of 1846–7 on the eastern frontier. Pottinger, then Governor, would have sacked Warden for it, but decided to leave the matter to his successor, who had just been appointed.[98]

Over the course of the previous decade, the British had been more and more embroiled in the affairs of Transorangia, basically against their will. Always they had tried to limit their commitment to the minimum compatible with the maintenance of their prestige and the prevention of a war which might spill over into the colony. To Maitland, head of a cautious administration, annexation, though perhaps desirable, was impossible on account of expense.[99] His next successor but one, Sir Harry Smith, was a man of another stamp. Almost a caricature of an early Victorian expansionist, he was colourful, attractive, flamboyant, given to temperamental extremes, but a superb battle general with a considerable and deserved reputation from his Indian exploits. His major political faults were an egotism that believed that the sheer force of his personality would steamroll any problem, and a consequent tendency for dramatisation. Above all he was a simplifier. When faced with the problem that beset all colonial governors in the era before the carve-up of the world among European powers, of how to cope with disorder beyond the borders, in the frontier zone of debatable authority, his response was to generalise:

My position has been analogous to that of every Governor General who has proceeded to India. All have been fully impressed with the weakness of that policy which extended the Company's possessions, and yet few, if any, especially the men of more gifted talents [sic], has ever resigned their Governorship without having done that, which however greatly to be condemned by the Theory of Policy, circumstances demanded and imperatively imposed upon them. Such has been my case.

The security of all Countries *within* depends not only upon their sound internal condition but upon their security from without; and the existence of a relationship on the borders calculated to inspire confidence.[100]

Thus in the first two months of his governorship at the Cape, where he had served as head of armed forces some 13 years previously, he almost doubled the size of British Dominion, annexing the districts of Namaqualand and Bushmanland, south of the Orange, extending British power on the eastern frontier to the Kei, acceding to requests to take in the area east of Colesberg and then proclaiming the Orange River sovereignty over all the area south of the Vaal River.[101] He did this last after a progress through the area in which he claimed to have ascertained that the opinion of the Boers was favourable to the step. Given the contact he had with them, this would have required telepathy. As he was a keen advocate of economies, he hoped to run the sovereignty at a profit, and therefore was concerned above all to establish suitable relations with the local population, to prevent conflagrations. With Moshoeshoe this was easy. Smith merely reiterated what Maitland had arranged, and probably never noticed that this left room for great trouble on the border of Lesotho.[102] With the Boers and Griquas there was much greater difficulty.

Smith considered that the major threat to the order which he hoped to establish in Transorangia came from the disaffected Boers. Thus he was concerned above all to woo them. The Griquas had to be sacrificed to placate the Boers. On 23 January 1848 Smith called Kok, Hendricks and the *raad* of Philippolis to Bloemfontein, the military camp which Warden had set up as his headquarters. The meeting that followed was extraordinary, although in character for Smith. The account of it that Kok authorised is the best, for it both expressed its flavour and describes the concerns of the Griqua Government. He wrote:

His Excellency commenced by saying to the chief, Adam Kok you have done exceedingly wrong in permitting the Boers to settle in your country – hired your lands to the Boers for their money – the Boers have now a right to the lands they hired – you must not hinder them – they must hire them for ever whether in the reserved or that part of the territory which may be let to

British subjects — I shall make you rich — Why will you not be rich? I shall give you personally £200 a year and to your people £100. What must I give you? The Chief replied it is not in my power to give away my people's lands — I am satisfied with even the £60 a year (the sum to which the quitrents had hitherto amounted). We were satisfied to let it remain as it were according to the treaty of Sir Peregrine Maitland. Will you then, replied His Excellency, kick my children out at the expiration of the 40 years? (Getting up and suiting the action to the word). No. NO. I am their old Pap — The chief upon this replied according to the treaty between Sir Peregrine Maitland and myself when the time of hire of the places in the reserved territory is expired the Boers are to leave, and go over into the leasable territory and there they may hire — His Excellency upon this replied you will not give the land I will take the lands for ever for the Boers. You may now go and consult with your council — The Chief and his council then adjourned to their wagons and having consulted together, resolved that they could not without the consent of the people, give away their lands and private property.

  His Excellency then sent for the Chief and his Council — they went and on being seated His Excellency asked what have you resolved upon? The Chief then replied that they have resolved that it was not in their power to give away the private property of the people without their consent. You have replied His Excellency taken in lands which did not belong to your father. I will prove to your Excellency that my father did possess those lands which I now claim even before Morocco [sic] was in that country. Why then is it not inhabited? said His Excellency. It is because of the constant disturbances of the Boers — I am satisfied with the treaty of Sir Peregrine Maitland which has been approved by Her Majesty the Queen. Upon this His Excellency exclaimed in a passion, Treaty is nonsense — Damn the treaty. And taking off his glasses he dashed them on the table — Southey His Excellency cried tell him I am Governor General. I shall hang the black fellow on this beam — tell him, Southey, to leave the room immediately.[103]

Not unnaturally, Kok complained about such cavalier treatment until the year he died,[104] but his protests did have some immediate effect. Next morning an agreement was drawn up whereby the Griquas were to retain the farms in the inalienable territory after the leases had expired, on payment for such improvements as the Boers might have carried out. The value of these was to be assessed by a three man commission consisting of Warden, Hendricks and a representative of the emigrant farmers. More important 'the . . . sum of Three Hundred Pounds a year shall be payable in perpetuity for the farms leased now only for forty years in the alienable territory; and which leases shall be in perpetuity for the consideration aforesaid'.[105] So began the long wrangle over the 'Forty Years Money' that was to continue until the end of the century.

Smith's roughshod charges over Griqua rights coincided, more or less fortunately so far as he was concerned, with a real possibility of peaceful Imperial advance. Of all the groups in South Africa with which the British had to deal, the Griquas were the least likely to cause trouble by rebelling. A few years later, one of the leaders of the Kat River Rebellion wrote to Kok trying to persuade him to join the revolt, in aid of Hottentot unity. Kok's reply was symptomatic: 'I cannot but consider you as the enemies of all the coloured people of South Africa, for by your rebellion you will impress a strong prejudice on the minds of all thinking people against the character, the rights and the claims of the coloured races.'[106] The Griquas were collaborators of the British, not because the British provided some advantage in recompense, but because there was no other way in which the Griquas could hope to fulfil the aspirations which they held as a community. After the British found, as they did by the time of the Maitland treaty and the battle of Zwartkoppies, that the Griquas could not perform the functions of collaborators in maintaining the peace beyond the Orange, and consequently began to scout out the High Veld for other, more effective ones, even then the Griquas remained loyal to the British. The colonial Government had noticed that the disturbances north of the Orange were caused by dissident Boers, and therefore took steps to humour them. It considered initially that it had succeeded,[107] but the basic aim was what it had been a decade previously, namely to maintain order as cheaply and as efficiently as possible north of the Orange. In attempting this the British had been pulled in, from time to time consciously by the Griquas, but when they arrived they took a line which was to cause great hardship to the Griquas themselves.

CHAPTER 5

THE YEARS OF THE SHEEP

The fundamental changes in the South African economy after the mineral dis-
coveries of the last third of the nineteenth century have threatened to blind
historians to the less spectacular developments of the previous two-thirds.
Although the alluvial deposits of the Harts and Vaal rivers and the 'blue ground'
of Kimberley and Jagersfontein were discovered to be diamondiferous during a
decade of slump in the agricultural economy of southern Africa, both the
potential and the achievement of that economy in the earlier period were considerable.[1] Throughout the middle of the century there was a long trend of
readjustment, which produced a definite shift in the balance away from the old
agricultural heartland of the south-west Cape towards the east and the north.
Small *dorps* were founded and thrived, after their fashion, throughout the
eastern division of the old Cape Colony and north across the River into what was
to become the Orange Free State. This restructuring was founded mainly on
merino wool, and the Griquas, or at any rate some of them, joined in it successfully, building on their experience in long distance trading to the north and
transport riding to the south, and on their traditions as a pastoral people. They
took, perhaps, a small part in the subcontinental play, but viewed from
Philippolis the development was highly significant.

Before about 1836, the economic life of the colony had been dominated from
the south-west, by the agriculturalists of the winter rain belt, in the mountain
valleys behind Cape Town. Many observers felt that the future of the colony lay
in the production of wool, in the pastoral, frontier mode of existence that this
implied,[2] but the most profitable farms in the colony were still those that grew
wines or wheat. Barrow calculated, around the turn of the century, that the net
income of the average corn or wine farmer was rather over 2000 Rix dollars,
£400 at the rate of exchange then current. This was about five times that of a
frontier grazier.[3] This dependence on the agricultural sector of the South African
economy increased during the early part of the nineteenth century, as the
country was becoming far more of a commercial entrepot, which could be
financed only by the profits on wine. To exemplify, in 1827, 56.5 per cent
(£123,000 out of £218,000) of South Africa's exports consisted of wine, while

during the first five years of that decade 37.5 per cent of the twelve and a quarter million gallons of wine which had been produced were exported. Insofar as the South African economy was linked to that of the rest of the world, it was linked through wine.[4]

Much of the reason for this monocultural tendency can be seen in the transportation system of South Africa. Cape Town, which was the only port in the colony, is tucked away in the far south-west, protected by the folded mountains of the Boland from the interior of the country. In the early part of the nineteenth century the roads over the passes were execrable. Even the much-vaunted ox-wagons tended to break up if frequently subjected to the rigours of the Roode-zand or the Hottentots Holland Kloofs, and ox-wagons were the only means of bulk transportation available to the colonists at the time.[5] South Africa has no navigable waterways, coasting traffic was scarce and undeveloped and the ports from which it might start were hidden behind the same mountain ranges as was Cape Town.[6] In consequence, the only products of the interior which could be sold in any sizeable market were those which could be driven on the hoof from the interior, namely cattle, sheep and horses. This might be sufficient to tie the frontier Boers to the Cape. It was not sufficient for any talk about the economic development of the east to be meaningful.

The change of emphasis away from the south-west towards the pastoral sector as represented by the eastern division began around 1830 and continued until the discovery of diamonds firmly settled the economic future of South Africa in the interior. It was based primarily on two developments. First, a new harbour was developed in the east, at Port Elizabeth, to which access was much easier than to Cape Town. In the old anchorage of Algoa Bay the port remained open to south-easterly gales, and as it long possessed no jetty, had to be worked by lighterage. For long, 'the back of a Fingo native allows the only means of locating dry shod'.[7] Labour, however, was cheap, and the port provided a ready outlet for the goods of the eastern Cape, especially after the contingents of British settlers, more happy as traders than as farmers, began to lubricate the commercial intercourse of the interior. Port Elizabeth was first allowed to export directly in 1825,[8] when a customs post was set up there, and it continued to grow until, by around 1850, the value of its exports equalled those which flowed through Cape Town.[9] The expensive, difficult and drawn-out trek across the karroo and over the mountain passes was thus obviated and the east and the north-east of the colony could grow unimpeded.

The growth that did occur was based almost exclusively on wool. Sheep, of course, had long been the basis of the frontier economy of the trekboers, supplying them with meat, tallow, and fat, and providing their main source of cash to buy those necessities — gunpowder, iron, wagons, tea, coffee, sugar and brandy —

without which the primarily subsistence life of the frontier would have been impossible.[10] But these sheep were of the old Cape breed, with fat tails, small, stocky frames and hairy coats. Their value lay in their carcasses, not in their wool. The transformation of the sheep farmer from the poor relation *ober die berg* into the motor of the new economic development came with the introduction of merino sheep into the colony on a large scale. Merinos first entered the colony about the turn of the century, and indeed the flock that began the Australian sheep industry had remained for a time in the Cape. Throughout the first third of the century there was a steady stream of propaganda to encourage the switch from hairy sheep to merinos, but the unsettled conditions on the eastern frontier, where many of the prime sheep lands were, cannot have enhanced the willingness of farmers to invest in an expensive flock of imported sheep. Slowly, however, the change was made, often by hybridisation with the existing herds of hairy sheep and then 'breeding up'.[11] Some indication of the extent and speed of this transfer can be seen from the figures for the export of wool and for the trade of Cape Town, which sent some wool to Europe, as against Port Elizabeth, which was very largely a wool-exporting port, in appendix 3. From these the changing structure of the colonial economy of South Africa can be clearly seen.

Although much of the growth of wool farming was in the hands of large-scale farmers in the Albany and Somerset East districts, often financed by the capitalists of Cape Town, or even Yorkshire, the Boers on the northern frontier of the old colony began to respond in like fashion at about the same time. Fleetwood Rawstorne reminisced of the twenty years he had spent as Civil Commissioner at Colesberg as follows:

> The Division has not deteriorated, but owing to the fortunate adoption by the major part of the farmers of the wooled sheep has become more flourishing than ever. In 1837 farm profits were derived from the several sources of the breeding of horse, cattle and Cape sheep. Wooled sheep were then scarcely introduced, and the farmers were dependent for a market on the uncertain and precarious purchases made by the butchers 'knegts'. At present the attention is nearly concentrated on wool, which, besides that it is equally remunerative, has the advantage of always commanding a market at any of the district towns.
>
> The number of wooled sheep in 1838 (derived from the 'opgaaf returns', and which were not likely to diminish the number as wooled sheep were exempt from duty which Cape sheep were not) was less than 20,000, or about one fortieth part of the total number of sheep in the Division.
>
> By the returns of 1855, the wooled sheep were 555,000, whilst the Cape sheep were but 387,000.[12]

The extent of this switch to a cash-orientated existence shows the truth of the dictum that 'the economic impact of international markets was carried into the interior not in the wagons of the Voortrekkers but upon the backs of merino sheep.'[13]

At the same time as this development, and consequent upon it, the mercantile system of the northern districts began to change. The *smous* was going out of business, or rather was being driven north. In his place, small *dorps* were being established throughout the Cape Colony, except in such backward areas as Namaqualand. Their resident store-keepers came from the commercially-orientated English-speaking community of the eastern Province. The Boers themselves do not seem to have gone into this line of business. Either they could not raise the capital necessary to finance the opening of a store or the provisioning of a wagon with the necessary trade goods, which the English could get on credit, or they were too successful as farmers to branch out into new and hazardous enterprises. Banking was as yet rudimentary, confined to the main towns and dominated by the same class of people as controlled the rest of the credit in the colony. The Boers — and Griquas — in general remained beyond the pale, as farmers rather than in commerce. Nevertheless, during the second quarter of the century several dorps were established. Graaff-Reinet grew in size from a messy collection of huts centred around the church and magistracy into a flourishing small town. Cradock arose to serve the Tarka area, Somerset East was the metropolis for the fine sheep lands of the Bruintjes Hoogte, Colesberg dominated the northern frontier and Middelburg, established a little later in time, catered for the pastures north of the Sneeuwberg.[14] The *smous* followed the trekboers north into the Free State and the Transvaal. Even there permanent stores were founded. On the establishment of the Orange River sovereignty, Bloemfontein gathered to itself a large coterie of shop-keepers and businessmen, financed by eastern Cape money. Within two years it had a newspaper, significantly owned by the *Grahamstown Journal*, the spokesman of frontier opinion and wealth. Fauresmith, Smithfield and even Winburg and Harrismith began to flourish, while across the Vaal Potchefstroom benefited greatly from the new route to the ivory of the interior, which ran through Natal and the southern Transvaal. Philippolis was but one of many similar settlements which began to attract shopkeepers and southern money at this time, so that in the course of time six shops were operating in the *dorp*.[15] It was in the main line of South African development of the time.

During the period of the Orange River sovereignty, Transorangia became fully integrated into the colonial economy. By 1853, there were estimated to be 139 traders, speculators and the like in Bloemfontein itself, and approximately forty more on their farms.[16] Certainly the period was marked by a boom in land prices, consequent upon considerable speculation but also on the realisation that the land could be put to commercial use. The exports of the territory soared, as wooled sheep were increasingly introduced. As ever, such trends are difficult to quantify, so that it is necessary to rely on the testimony of William Collins, who was long a member of official society in Bloemfontein. He claimed that

> Already early in 1856, that staple article of commerce, 'Merino Wool', was beginning to make a good show in the State, the quantity delivered in Bloem-fontein in one season, being estimated to number at least 1,200 bales, and throughout the entire state at least 5,000 bales; this valued at £10 per bale, totals £50,000. This marked a great contrast with the year 1850, when one of the most active 'wool dealers' who, in fact, had the monopoly of nearly the entire wool trade, secured what was then considered an exceptionally large clip of wool, i.e. 'fifty bales'.[17]

His impressions are confirmed by the census which the Free State Government took of its burghers' holdings in 1856, when it was discovered that over 85 per cent of the flock was at least partially of wooled race.[18] To cope with this new product the wool-exporting firms of Port Elizabeth began moving agents up to Bloemfontein, and there are many examples of advertisements for transport riders to take bales south to be found in the *Friend of the Sovereignty*, the paper which was established in Bloemfontein during 1850. Some farmers began to take pride in the quality of their stock and agricultural produce. The first show in Bloemfontein occurred in April 1853, and horses, cattle, butter, cheese, tobacco, potatoes and hay were exhibited as well as sheep.[19] A market was beginning to develop, particularly for horses, which were always in demand either for the British troops or for the northern Boers, whose strings were frequently ravaged by horse-sickness, and for cattle which were sold to the butchers in the Cape Colony. Sheep and their wool, however, were established on the commanding heights of the economy of what duly became the Orange Free State.

The Griquas shared with their neighbours in the production and the benefits of this economic growth, so that the Griqua community of Philippolis had a short but conspicuous flowering during the 1850s. This is not surprising. The Griquas had always been a commercially orientated people. In the early days of the community, when they still lived in the region of Griquatown and the middle Orange valley, its extent can best be defined by the measure of integration into the cash economy which stemmed from Cape Town. Those who were not so integrated were 'Koranas' or 'Bushmen', still beyond the fold. This trade was based on the sale of cattle in the Cape Colony and on the products of the hunt, above all ivory and the luxurious jackal and civet skin *karosses* of the Tswana.[20] It continued throughout the century in varying forms. In the last years before the

70

Difaqane, various important Griqua leaders, above all Barend Barends and his entourage, were deeply involved in the politics of the central Tswana chiefdoms, which provided them with large quantities of ivory and *karosses* in return for beads and such commodities as coffee and tea. This relationship was broken by the advent of Mzilikazi, who was particularly anxious to keep all the relations between his subjects and outsiders in his own hands.[21] Thus the attacks that the Ndebele suffered from the Griquas under Barend Barends and Jan Bloem were, in part at least, because these men had been deprived of a very valuable source of income and went to war to regain it. On the other hand, after Mzilikazi had been expelled, the pattern of trading took on a different shape. No longer were the 'big men' of Griqua life involved. Rather the network was re-established by men who had little or no attachment to the old polities, but who were full-time traders, with close attachments to the Tswana chiefdoms in which they worked. In time they might retire and become leading citizens of the Captaincies, above all Griquatown. Adam Januarie, for instance, was one of the most important traders and later became a member of the *raad* of Griquatown.[22] Initially, however, they were more likely to have come directly from the colony, or even to have been Tswana who saw the advantages of this style of life, attached themselves to Griqua traders and later set up independently.[23]

In addition to the professionals, there were those who from time to time went on an 'annual hunt'. These were men who moved north, again mainly from Griquatown, for a few months and then returned with the profit.

The heyday of this system came during the late forties and early fifties. Until then the traders had been working mainly among the Tswana tribes of eastern Botswana. After 1849 the routes that ran north and west from the Ngwato capital, Shoshong, towards Lake Ngami, Barotseland and the Ndebele kingdom were opened. Solomon described the effect this had on the way of life in Griquatown:

> The hunting expeditions of our people are in many respects injurious to themselves — involving as they do their absence from the means of grace for five or six months — living at that time a rude and certainly not the most civilising kind of life — besides losing the *best time of the year* for agricultural labors, but I suppose they *will* pursue them as long as they *fancy* them profitable in a temporal point of view. For the past few years the yearly hunts had lost much of their attraction — but the discovery of the Interior lakes last year and the large quantity of ivory brought by a few of the Griquas who went into that neighbourhood, very naturally revived their love for the hunt, and excited their desire for gain; so that this year more than average number of people have gone to the interior to hunt elephants. However, as in all probability

these hunts will become year by year less profitable, the evil is likely to work its own cure.[24]

Tales of elephant tusks being left to rot on the ground worked their magic quickly,[25] and for a while profits were considerable. One of the earliest white traders, for instance, made £1,700 for the outlay of but £150 worth of trade goods, which was not surprising when 'one elephant tusk, if large is worth £12 or £15, and it can be purchased for a handful of beads worth 2s. 6d. I have seen a musket worth £1 sold for three tusks worth between £30 and £40.'[26] More generally it was claimed that the traders in the first few years 'carried on a very lucrative traffic with the natives, some of them bringing home ivory to the value of £1,000 for goods which had cost £200'.[27] For a time large convoys of Griquas moved into the interior to overawe the reluctance of the Tswana chiefs, who disliked allowing large numbers of muskets through to their enemies. After a visit to Shoshong in 1853, James Chapman wrote:

> During our stay at Sekomi's about a hundred Griqua and Bechuana wagons from Kuruman and from Griqua Town and Philippolis arrived here on their way towards Moselekatse's country. The wagons, which were very showy and too good for this rough work were ostentatiously drawn up in two long lines facing the town, to display them to the best advantage, so that the people remarked that the Griquas must be a powerful and rich nation. From the conversation of these Griquas we learnt that their object in bringing such a force was to deter Sekomi from opposing them in their intended visit to Moselekatse, he (Sekomi) having on a former occasion nearly cut off the whole of their party by a strategem during a like expedition.[28]

The majority of the men who went on these expeditions probably came from the west, from the region around Griquatown. There were several, however, who hailed from Philippolis, although these seem to have been rather more ephemeral figures in the interior, and are in consequence less well known. It is certain, for instance, that a man named Jan Pienaar, son of 'Rooi' Jan, was on the borders of the Ndebele kingdom in 1853, for he died there.[29] Equally, David Livingstone met a party returning from the north directly to Philippolis, and sent letters back to the colony with them.[30] The Griquas of Philippolis were quick to respond to these possibilities, but interior trading was never the regular means of making a living for many of them.

In the more immediate neighbourhood of Philippolis, there were opportunities for earning cash other than the sale of stock to colonial butchers which was the most important source before the advent of wooled sheep. For instance, one man realised that he could profit from the steady traffic on the road from Colesberg

72

to Philippolis. He therefore built a cottage about an hour and a half by horse-wagon from the Orange River 'expressly for the accommodation of travellers and strangers'.[31] Others bred horses, exploiting the advantage of living on the northern edge of the area in which horses could be bred. One of Adam Kok's brothers, probably Gert, owned a stud of 400, for which he no doubt found a ready market.[32] Missionaries who worked in areas susceptible to horse-sickness kept their spare horses in Philippolis, under the care of the *Kaptyn*.[33] The Griquas were by no means well supplied with cash in the 1840s,[34] but there was a ready realisation of the value of commercial achievement and a desire to partake in it.

After about 1850 the Griquas joined their neighbours in the Orange Free State in exploiting merino-sheep farming on a moderately large scale. To exemplify this is difficult. Although Kok once claimed that the Griquas possessed 200,000 sheep,[35] there is no reason to think that this was anything but an unsubstantiated guess, but there is no better estimate of the movable wealth of the community. It is thus necessary to fall back on the testimony of the various missionaries who ministered at Philippolis. Fortunately Edward Solomon was sympathetic towards the Griquas, well liked by them and a good correspondent, so that for the period from 1851 to 1857 an impression of social progress can be presented through the experience of the man most likely to form a correct one. Thereafter he was replaced by W. Buxton Philip, who was accepted by the Griquas as the son of his father. Unfortunately he seldom described the town to the LMS in London. Perhaps this is not surprising. Because the Philippolis congregation became independent of the mission connection in 1855, he was not responsible to the secretaries of the society. Luckily, however, his later reminiscences are most useful.

Even by the end of the 1840s Philippolis was decidedly prosperous, in comparison with its position at the beginning of the decade. During 1847 it was possible to collect enough money to build a new stone church, capable of holding 600 people, which admittedly did not yet contain any furniture, windows or doors.[36] James Read Snr., who visited the country in 1849 after seven years absence, considered that there had been considerable improvement since his last visit. Not only had a new church and a new school been built, but the circumstances of the population had evidently improved. 'Scarce a man but has a wagon, and a team of oxen, and upwards of twenty horses. Wagons with 8 horses attached to them [are common]. They had sown much wheat this year and were likely to get the most of it harvested before the locust could engross it.'[37] This praise was not universal, however. After a short visit, Freeman claimed that they 'are not quite so far advanced as those living in the colony; I mean those of coloured race living within the colony'. He did allow, however, that 'some of them individually are far advanced; there are men who have got good houses and

73

dress in European clothing very comfortably; a few of them unite to pay for a schoolmaster at their own farms for the education of their children; they possess immense flocks of cattle and their houses are furnished in capital style'.[38] Nevertheless, Solomon, who had ministered for ten years at Griquatown and had had the experience of Cape Town upbringing under the aegis of Dr Philip, was probably right when he wrote that 'The country round Philippolis is very fair and fertile, abounding with springs of water, and is very favourable for raising corn and cattle of every description. However [sic] the people here are the wealthiest natives with whom our Society has to do in South Africa, several of them possessing property to the amount of several thousand pounds.'[39] Evidently the disagreement between the two men was concerned with the extent to which the wealth which was being generated was spread throughout the community, a point which will be elaborated below.

During the early fifties a succession of good rains replenished the *fonteins*, allowing the Griquas to grow the largest crops of wheat they ever produced. Solomon wrote in 1852:

> This year more grain has, I believe, been sown than in any previous year since the establishment of the Griqua mission. At some of our Griqua farms, where fountains were sufficiently strong, above twenty muids of grain were sown, and altogether considerably more than 200 muids of grain have been sown this year by our people, — a pretty large quantity when it is remembered that in this country all our crops must be raised by means of irrigation.[40]

At the same time, the pastoral side of the Griqua economy, which must always have been the dominant sector, was being developed:

> Another system of progress is the greater attention they have paid to the improvement of their flocks. They have begun to appreciate the value of the merino sheep — many are now doing their utmost to get a flock of these and some of our people have already flocks, varying from 300 to 1,500 in number. This year they have sent to market about 20,000 lb of wool, the produce of their own flocks, a quantity in itself but small, yet sufficient to induce the hope that a good beginning has been made. It is unnecessary to point out the many advantages, social as well as economical, to be hoped for, from the Griquas devoting themselves to this branch of enterprise, for which their country is admirably adapted.[41]

Various Griquas were spending up to £400 to reclaim some of the farms leased to the Boers, and paying much attention to the spring in Philippolis. Up to £140 was spent in trying to lead the water down into the town more satisfactorily.[42] The euphoria of this early period did not last long. Locusts almost obliterated the crops of the succeeding years.[43] However, the foundations of the later prosperity were laid during the first years of the Orange River sovereignty.

This development raises certain problems. The switch from the Cape sheep which formed the basis of the Griqua flocks to merino could not be effected immediately. Rather it was necessary to build up a flock of wool-bearing animals by cross-breeding between merino rams and hairy -- or in time half-caste -- ewes. That this could be done moderately quickly is illustrated by the speed of the change which the Boers effected in Colesberg, and in the Free State itself. The sheep were not used by their owners for meat. They could still live off the considerable herds of game which roamed the plains of the High Veld, and could supply all the protein needed by the mounted huntsmen of Griqualand. Moreover, although pure-bred merino flocks evidently produced wool of a higher quality, there were farmers who considered that a strict pedigree was too much trouble, that in strict economic terms hybrids paid better.[44] On the other hand, a certain leavening of high-quality animals was necessary, and these were expensive. By 1855, first-class Saxon rams were selling in Bloemfontein for between £40 and £50.[45] How the Griquas raised the cash to buy their animals is uncertain. It could be argued that various individuals disposed of some of their land to Boers, in order to raise the cash to utilise effectively the land which remained to them. If this was the case, then the practice contributed directly to the difficulties in which the Griquas found themselves *vis-à-vis* their Boer neighbours.[46] Others again may well have raised the necessary money on credit from the local shopkeepers, who were thereby able to exert pressure on their creditors, causing greater difficulty than they alleviated. These arguments are necessarily highly speculative, but they may nevertheless contain a reasonable explanation of the events which occurred. Particularly they may go some way towards explaining the troubles into which the Captaincy fell, for it would be the poorer members of the polity who felt most need to behave in this fashion. However, other sources of cash were available to the Griquas during the early fifties. Perhaps some of them made money from the boom in northern trading at this time. Others again may have been able to sell stock to the butchers, or corn from the good harvests that blessed these years. Specifically, the conflicts between the British and the Sotho under Moshoeshoe during the early fifties must have provided opportunities both for running guns and horses, the prime war materials, into the Lesotho, and for acting as transport riders for the ponderous British columns. Although the evidence does not allow more than tentative suggestions, the opportunities must have been there for some Griquas, at any rate, to raise the sums they needed without dangerously depleting their political capital. Certainly they raised them in some way or other. During the last half of the decade, the Griqua Captaincy of Philippolis flourished as never before or after.

The flowering, short as it was, came after about 1855, just as the Free State itself was beginning to enjoy similar expansion.[47] Solomon commented then that 'the Griquas' clip of wool is better than they have ever had before. One of our members has realised £180 for his clip this year and several individuals will realise from £50 to above £100 each for their clip — and this tho' wool is selling at a lower rate than usual.'[48] Over the next years he dilated further on the same theme. Late in 1856, after the annual sheep-shearing, he wrote that

> several good homes have been built this year in the village, considerable attention has been paid to the raising of wool — at least 200 bales of wool have been produced this year from the flocks of our people and have realised to them in the market about £2,000 sterling. This year we anticipate a much bitter clip. This is one of the best proofs of progress in temporal matters and affords one of the best guarantees for the formation of habits conducive of peace and prosperity. Should our relationship with our European neighbours remain satisfactory, we have every reason to hope for external prosperity and this we [trust], will be accompanied with those spiritual results which are the grand objects at which we aim.[49]

The prosperity gained from this bonanza of merino sheep was turned into material advantage. Solomon wrote further:

> Our village is improving in appearances. 15 new houses have been erected during the past year — all of them built of stone and burnt brick and some of them very excellent [sic] houses — one in particular is an excellent comfortable dwelling containing parlour, dining room, 3 bedrooms, kitchen, pantry and store room — all the timber used in the house is good English deal and the house has cost the proprietor about £300. This is the best and largest house but two others almost compete with it, and it is a cheering proof of the progress of civilisation when individuals are willing at such an expense to raise comfortable houses.

This was achieved despite the loss of almost £10,000 worth of cattle through the spread of lungsickness which was devastating the South African agricultural and transportation system at the time.[50]

There is confirmation for Solomon's descriptions. A photograph taken about 1860 from the hills overlooking Philippolis and giving a panoramic view of the town allows over 35 houses to be identified, some of which are evidently of high quality and workmanship.[51] Those Griqua houses that have remained in

Philippolis certainly increase the impression of moderate opulence, even if their proportions do much to increase the quaintness of the town. Traders came into Philippolis in some numbers at this time, where they were put under the control of a town board to which they had to pay tax. They had a fair amount of freedom, however, and entered various contracts with Griquas for the erection and later hiring of trading stores. John Barker, who traded with the Griquas for so long, both before and after the trek to Nomansland, that he claimed to have made and drunk three fortunes off them, agreed to build a house for Gert Kok, which he would then hire for three years. Kok was to provide the building materials, and Barker was to pay the labour charges in cash, which there was every expectation he would be able to do.[52] By the final years of the Griquas sojourn in Philippolis there were six shops in the town (more than in 1972), and these were doing profitable business mainly by relying on the Griqua trade.[53]

The Griquas seem to have maintained this wealth to the end of their stay in Philippolis. W. B. Philip, reminisced a decade later of the town named after his father. He wrote of them when they had to trek:

> The people were in a prosperous state; they had their titles to their farms, on which they had built substantial cottages and out-buildings; orchards, stocked with good fruit trees, garden grounds and lands for cultivation, were in many cases enclosed with stone walls; good stone kraals and one or two dams were to be found on most farms; troops of from twenty to one hundred horses, about the same number of cattle and hundreds of well-bred wooled sheep, were running on these farms and many a man brought his ten, fifteen, twenty, and twenty five bales of wool at once for sale; while the shopkeepers found them as good customers for clothing, groceries, guns, saddlery, carts, and furniture as any of the Boers. Of course there were many poor people, whose poverty was brought on by their own laziness, pride and drunkenness.[54]

It was a description that could have been applied to many communities, both black and white, during the late 1850s. The Griquas were in the mainstream of the country's economic development.

The growth of prosperity had important results for the ecclesiastical situation in Philippolis, for the old paternalism that pervaded mission churches was broken, in this particular case, by the achievement of 'independence'. This meant that the LMS no longer financed the minister, but rather that he was paid by the congregation to which he was called. The LMS had long wanted this.[55] As an offshoot of the Congregational Church in England, the Society obviously had leanings in the direction of local autonomy. Autocrats did exist within the movement, Robert Moffat being the prime example, but in general there was a far higher regard for the capabilities of their congregations allowing them a

77

greater place within the government of the church than, for instance, within the centralised, authoritarian Wesleyan establishment. Also the LMS was short of money and felt guilty about expending its meagre resources on communities which had long had the benefit of missionaries when it could be used to spread the gospel further to the lands of the heathen. Self-support would therefore relieve these interlocking tensions.

There had been moves in this direction from the end of the 1840s onwards. John Philip in his last years as superintendant mooted the idea, but the reaction of W. Y. Thomson, then minister at Philippolis, was that the Griquas were not as then ready for it, especially as the political tensions of the time made it imperative to have a missionary in Philippolis to cope with the necessary diplomatic correspondence.[56] More determined efforts were made by the LMS in the succeeding years. Joseph Freeman, the secretary of the Society, made a visit to South Africa in 1849, primarily to discover whether any stations were ready to become self-supporting, but the reaction of the man who was then in Philippolis, C. J. van der Schalk, was not favourable, for he had been brought up in the colony, had hoped to find the Griquas, among whom he laboured for an unhappy two years, as docile as the emancipated slaves of the colony and considered the moves towards self-support as a Griqua trick to gain more control over their missionaries.[57] Independence for the community was therefore not achieved until another five years passed, by which time Edward Solomon, well liked, well trusted and a congregationalist bred if not born − the family from which he came were originally St Helena Jews[58] − was ensconced in the *dorp*.

In 1855, the parlous state of the LMS's finances required a further move on the part of the secretaries to decrease the cost of the South African missions, and once again the remedy of self-support was adopted. For a time Solomon doubted the Griquas' capacity to pay him adequately, as they had just recruited a schoolmaster to teach in the *dorp*.[59] The Griquas themselves did not. The church leaders and deacons wrote that 'We feel that it would not be right any longer to enjoy our privileges at the expense of you our fathers (Directors) and of our brothers and sisters the churches in England, many of whom, we hear, are poor as regards the things of this world.'[60] Having plagued successive missionaries with their difficult political demands, they no doubt realised that he would be more than ever under their control. Previously they had formulated definite criteria as to the style of minister they desired. His qualities should be

> strict piety, an impressive preacher and one who can go about the whole neighbourhood to preach, who would take similar interest in promoting education to what is done in Kat River, and one who would assist in improving the internal constitutions into the English and Christian model as the

South Sea missionaries do, and also who would help us in our co-operations with the Colonial Government.[61]

Whatever the actualities of the situation, when Philippolis joined the three other stations of the LMS which were completely self-supporting, the enthusiasm of the congregation for the church grew mightily. In every succeeding year the income of the Philippolis mission more than covered its expenditure. The actual figures for subscription run as follows: 1856, £381; 1857, £457; 1858, £511; 1859, £584; 1860, £612, despite setbacks in the Griqua economy in 1858 due to a poor harvest and the financial crisis in England which lowered the price of wool. At times the Griquas were even able to subscribe to the furtherance of the mission which had worked among them, even sending £12 to the Indian Relief fund in the year after the mutiny — although it is not clear which side they wished to relieve.[62] At about this time it was even considered possible to found a newspaper in Philippolis. It was very amateurish. W. B. Philip, who seems to have been largely responsible for its production, wrote that 'We have been compelled to commence with type nearly worn down, and a small rough home-made printing press; our first productions must therefore be very imperfect.' He hoped that money would be found from the grant for the improvement of natives which Sir George Grey had allocated from the colonial expenses, for he considered that its largest sale would be in the colony. The editorial policy was clear. Its object was 'the increase of morality, religion and knowledge' among the natives.[63] Despite these protestations it did not last long, and no copy seems to have survived, at least in any obvious depository. Thus for a brief Indian summer the Griquas of Philippolis achieved their ambition to be a wealthy, Christian, respectable people.

Nevertheless, the foundations of Griqua wealth were not solid. The increase of wealth had multiplied the economic differentials always present within the Griqua community. While those who still possessed farms were enjoying the fruits of the new prosperity, those who did not were perpetuating the image of the Griquas as a poverty-stricken, drunken rural proletariat, who lived by sponging off their richer fellows or off the tradesmen in the town. All observers noticed this incipient stratification. The oft-made distinction between the 'Griqua' section, who reinforced the stereotype, and the 'Bastards' who showed progress and drive remarkable to the eyes of an outsider, probably stemmed from this awareness, although, in the way that South African minds would tend to, it was translated into racial terms. Moreover the relative importance accorded to the various sections of the population varied almost exactly with the political stance which the particular writer held towards the Philippolis Captaincy. To the missionaries, for whom the increase of material prosperity was an index of the moral uplift they were striving to achieve, the continued existence of the 'poor Griquas' was an embarrassment, a reminder that their work as social and religious revolutionaries was not yet complete. W. B. Philip acknowledged their presence only in a throwaway remark.[64] Edward Solomon, in his time, was even more cagey about admitting their presence, particularly in his more public pronouncements.[65] The attitude of the Free State Boers, who coveted the land which the Griqua sheep farmers still possessed, was diametrically opposite. They made much play of the idleness and destitution of the many Griquas, and treated the 'Bastards', the rich ones, as sports. At the distance of a century the historian cannot make a judgement between the claims of the two sets of witnesses who knew the Griquas best. He can only point out the existence of the two parts within the community, both of whom were integral parts within a single whole. Neither could escape the pressures which the other imposed on them, and together this relationship provided the lever by which the aspirations of the wealthier section of the Philippolis Captaincy were brought down.

CHAPTER 6

LAND AND AUTHORITY

At the time of the great increase in Griqua wealth, their political position was becoming more and more parlous. The establishment of the Orange River sovereignty did little to settle Transorangia. It merely provided another forum in which the debates between Boers and Griquas on the control of land and the authority over persons could be played out. The scuttle by the British six years after they had penetrated north of the river marked the Boers' victory over the Griquas, just as much as it derived from Moshoeshoe's successes at the battles of Viervoet and the Berea. There was now little possibility that the Griqua Captaincy at Philippolis could maintain itself as an independent entity.

The problems began immediately upon the establishment of the sovereignty. Sir Harry Smith had extorted from Adam Kok and his council the concession that any farms in the alienable territory of Griqualand which had been leased for forty years or more were to be considered as permanently alienated. Some 42 farms passed out of the Griquas' hands by this arrangement, but their owners can scarcely have expected ever to possess them again. Only ten of the 42 owners were alive in 1888, when the leases would have fallen in.[1] The £300 *per annum* that the Griquas received was thus not too bad a bargain. When it came to the administration of this settlement, however, the Griquas were astounded to discover that the British administration of the sovereignty were treating all the farms within the alienable territory as though they had been leased for the full forty years.[2] Major Henry Warden, the British Resident in Transorangia, who was now the sole administrative officer in the sovereignty, began issuing Boers with land certificates throughout the area.[3] In February 1848, two months after the original agreement, Kok complained about the way in which it was being put into practice. He asked that the Griquas might be allowed to distribute the land north of the Riet River which was as yet unclaimed. In fact the Griquas had lost both the empty land and all those farms which they had leased. In the wake of this agreement, officialdom took from the Griquas another 88 farms which they had never let.[4]

Not unnaturally, the Griquas used all the diplomatic leverage they could exert in an attempt to change the situation. Sir Harry Smith was no use. In his bullying paternalist self-confidence, he considered that he had done the best for the Griquas.[5] Moreover, his conduct can scarcely be considered a political error. It was motivated not by a concern for justice, but by the necessity of placating the Boers. Therefore, Kok and Hendricks turned elsewhere. In December 1848, Hendricks visited Sir Andries Stockenström, who had by now become one of the leading figures in the amorphous political scene of the Cape Colony. For many reasons, Sir Andries was prepared to blacken Smith's conduct, and sent a complaining letter to the Secretary of State in London. He also attempted to create a furore in the Cape press.[6] Kok and Hendricks also wrote to John Philip and to John Fairbairn, editor of the *South African Commercial Advertiser* and leader of the liberal press in the colony.[7] But these efforts came to nought as did those made by the Rev. Joseph Freeman, one of the directors of the LMS, who made a long tour in South Africa in 1850. By then the Griquas had many complaints, and Freeman's letters received wide publicity, but Smith remained adamant.[8] In any case, by 1851, the land in the disputed territory had largely been distributed. The Boers who had received it were more likely to prove a nuisance to the British than the Griquas who had lost it.

There was, perhaps, more than the altruism of *Realpolitik* behind the actions of the British at this time. The sovereignty administration, small as it was, was in a very favourable position to indulge in land speculation. By 1853, 'the Civil officers of the Orange River Territory are generally occupied with their land speculation to a degree which of course occasions some neglect of real public business'.[9] It may be that the immense acreages that officials managed to acquire were bought before they entered office, but they still point to a very definite interest among those who ran the sovereignty in bringing as much of Griqualand as possible on to the market. A small clique of businessmen and officials formed almost the total British society in Bloemfontein. The Griquas' case conflicted with their advantage, weighting the balance of the argument severely against Adam Kok and his subjects.[10]

Simultaneously, the Griquas were engaged in a test case over land. The Dutch community settled in the general neighbourhood of the Riet River wanted to found a church for itself. They lived half-way between the centres of Bloemfontein and Colesberg. They were relatively stable and settled and were prosperous enough to support such a venture. There would have been no trouble but for the confusion over the status of the land on which they wished to build. They hoped to erect a church at Sannah's Poort — alternatively known as Zuurfontein and later the town of Fauresmith — which lay within the inalienable territory of Griqualand. They had persuaded its owner, a Griqua named Petrus Hendricks, to sell them the land for 10,000 Rix dollars (£750).[11] Kok, however, would not agree. He knew that the church would form the focus of a *dorp*, with

82

stores, permanent residents and farmers' town houses. He knew that once such a settlement was established, it would be impossible to evict the occupiers when the lease expired. His response was vehement:

> The Boers hold farms in my country on lease and the longest one expires in about 37 years, why then are persons having land on such tenure so anxious to purchase Zuurfontein, for which I hear they offer 10,000 Rds. [rix dollars] and then express the like sum in the building of a church? Because they want to gain a firmer footing in my country! I and my *Raad* well know that if land were sold to the Boers they would not only build a church but a town, then apply to Government for a magistrate and their wants would not cease until the Griquas were in some way or other deprived of the best part of their country.[12]

His protests and prophecies were accurate, but in vain. By the end of 1849, the Boers of the Sannah's Poort consistory had obtained Warden's consent to the sale.[13] A further part of the Griquas' patrimony had disappeared.

By 1850, the affairs of the sovereignty were such that Major Warden could attempt to carry out one of the provisions of the agreement which Sir Harry Smith had made with Kok two years before. He began to assess the value of the improvements which the Boers had made on their farms, so that the amount the Griquas would have to pay to redeem them would be known. This caused a major political crisis in Philippolis. Hendrick Hendricks, the only figure whose stature could rival that of the *Kaptyn*, had been nominated two years before as the Griqua representative on this Appraisement Commission. During the early part of 1850, however, he fell from his position as Secretary because of his conduct on the commission and because he advocated sanctioning land sales to the Boers. Although he lived another 31 years, he never regained any influence.

The main charge against Hendricks was that he sold himself to the Boers for brandy. Therefore, so it was claimed, he put too high a value on the improvements that he was judging, so that the Griquas could never hope to regain them after the leases expired. In the first bout of valuations, twenty-three farms were reckoned to have had £5,820 worth of building and other works done to them. Adam Kok considered that this was too high and that much of the work had been done after 1848, which according to the agreement should have been discounted. 'Hendricks could not resist the glass of brandy offered by the Boers, and the Captain thinks they took advantage of that.'[14] Once he realised that he was on the way out, Hendricks seems to have tried to curry favour with the Boers, even advocating land sales in the *raad* at Philippolis. He even attempted, so it was alleged, to raise the Griquas in revolt against the Government of Adam Kok, but had no support, at any rate from the propertied Griquas who formed

83

the paramount political class in the Captaincy. In consequence he was dismissed from his post as Secretary, and for a time was kept as a state prisoner in Philippolis.[15] Finally, the *Friend of the Sovereignty* of 16 September 1850 carried the announcement that all documents drawn up and signed by Hendricks were fraudulent and 'of no value whatever'. Hendricks's 24-year tenure of the office of Secretary had ended.

This account of the affair is coloured by being based almost exclusively on the reports of C. J. van der Schalk, who hated Hendricks. For most of the time Hendricks had been in power, the missionaries would have been glad to see him go and now van der Schalk was jubilant. Counterbalancing evidence is difficult to discover, but British officials considered that the appraisals would be such that the Griquas would never regain their land.[16] Hendricks was but one of three members on the Commission, and could be outvoted by a combination of the others, who were Warden himself and an Englishman called Allison, who was appointed because Hendricks claimed that the Griquas would trust no Boer to be fair.[17] On the other hand, Warden wrote, defending his actions, that 'with regard to the property appraised in Griqualand, I am prepared to prove that with the exception of the two Englishmen, Norval and Roberts, the farmers are highly satisfied with the amount of appraisement done at each place, the amount being in most instances higher than the farmer expected.'[18] There is thus no doubt that the Griquas lost out in these transactions. There is also no doubt that Hendricks enjoyed his brandy and may have been susceptible to inducement offered in this form, or alternatively may have been so fuddled that he was unable to mediate the doings of Warden and Allison. If he had not been prepared to acquiesce in the actions of his fellow Commissioners, he could in all probability have disowned them before the results were made public. His dismissal by the *Kaptyn* seems fair, if rather disappointing for the historian, for Hendricks was an engaging figure of high intelligence, who occasionally pointed out the way in which Griqua society thought and acted more acutely than any other witness.

Conceivably, however, there was a deeper side to the episode than Hendricks's drunken incompetence. Perhaps he was consciously attempting to define a new path for Griqua policy based on an alliance with the Boers among whom the Griquas lived rather than on reliance on the Imperial power which was showing itself to be a worthless ally. Hendricks's political acumen was considerable, and he could well have read the portents which showed that the Boer community was going to become increasingly dominant in Transorangia. If that was the case, as it was, then the only hope for the Griquas was to achieve a rapprochement with the Boers, and hope that henceforth the region would be dominated by a colour-blind class of landholders, both Griqua and white. If he hoped this, even so he was probably unduly optimistic. Physically there might be little difference

84

between the two groups. Waterboer addressed the Free Staters as 'my fellow whites.'[19] Twenty years later, Sir Charles Warren wrote that although the Griqua 'is just as white in many cases as the darker Boer and quite as much civilised, yet he must be classed among the blacks and have no right to land' in the eyes of the colonists.[20] Certain individuals could escape from the status of 'coloured'. In particular cases the Boers might even promote this. The *veldkornet* of the Marico district in the Transvaal, Jan Viljoen, once described Adam Januarie, who was later to become one of Nicholas Waterboer's *raadsmen*, as 'a burgher of the Transvaal community', because he hoped that Januarie might safeguard the Transvaal's — and, specifically, Viljoen's — interests in the interior.[21] But in the more settled districts to the south it was too late. Even if the matter had not been settled before the forebears of the Griquas left the Cape Colony during the eighteenth century, a decade of conflict north of the Orange had defined the groups concerned too tightly. Notoriously the *volksraad* of Potchefstroom laid down that 'no bastard shall be allowed to sit in our sessions as member or as official up to the tenth generation', and there were many examples of similar attitudes.[22] Men thought not of 'land-owners' and 'labourers', but of 'Boers' and 'Griquas', increasingly of 'white' and 'black'. Their actions had driven them apart, and there was no threat to bring them back together. The colour line had hardened, and Hendricks's brandy could not wash it out.[23]

Throughout the troubled years of the Orange River sovereignty, the Griquas maintained their old and well-established policy of unmitigated alliance with the colonial authorities. Perhaps their last chance for a change of line came with the rebellion of Andries Pretorius in July 1848. The Boers from the Transvaal and the north of the sovereignty were successful for a time in ousting the unwanted overlordship of the British. Warden was confined to Bloemfontein. Pretorius was able to establish himself as master of Transorangia. Throughout these proceedings the Griquas temporised, awaiting results. When Warden appealed to him in desperation to send troops to his aid, Adam Kok received ammunition from the Civil Commissioner at Colesberg, but did not move north, surmising, probably correctly, that the help he could give would be too little and too late to re-establish British power.[24] When Pretorius moved south in an attempt to gather to himself all possible allies in face of the threat of Sir Harry Smith and the British troops which he was known to be moving up from the eastern frontier, the Griquas reaction was equally equivocal. Tactfully, Adam himself was away from Philippolis, consulting with Waterboer. Hendricks and Piet Draai, now emerging as one of the leading councillors of the Captaincy, were prepared to enter into an arrangement of neutrality, which would need to be ratified by the *Kaptyn*.[25] The Griquas no doubt realised that a showdown between the Boers and the British could have only one result, and when Sir Harry arrived, 250 men, the followers

85

of both Waterboer and Adam Kok, joined his train. In the sharp engagement at Boomplaats which followed, the Griquas appear to have kept themselves out of the way of the main fighting, but busied themselves with such tasks as guarding the baggage and mopping up the last Boer resistance after Pretorius had been defeated. In consequence, there were insinuations as to their courage, but they received the praise of officialdom for their 'most exemplary fidelity to their engagements of alliance with Her Majesty notwithstanding the attempts of the rebels to undermine their loyalty'.[26] In fact they had no choice. It was not with the republican Voortrekkers of the north that they could have reached a rapprochement but with the generally loyal farmers of the southern districts. Moreover, open rebellion against the British must have been disastrous to their survival. The incident only served to increase the antagonisms between Griqua and Boer.

The Griquas behaved similarly when Major Warden's crass government had managed to involve the British in conflict with Moshoeshoe, who was at that time a match for any force in southern Africa, barring the full might of the British Empire in the sort of campaign they were unlikely ever to have been prepared to mount. Warden was inveigled into partisanship in the deep quarrels between the southern Sotho chiefs about control of the Caledon River valley. As the British were aligned in opposition to the Moshoeshoe, so the Griquas were forced to follow suit, although they cannot have relished it. Moshoeshoe was an ally of long standing and one of the participants in the highly informal and tacit arrangement for carving up Transorangia of a decade or so earlier.[27] Thus, at the meeting of chiefs that led up to the battle of Viervoet in June 1851, Kok was forced by the decisions of the other chiefs present to agree to war, although his own instincts were all for 'making up matters', particularly as 'there are cattle in Basutoland belonging to my people, and as soon as they learn that I am engaged in the war we shall never get them back'.[28] Warden was always anxious to involve the Griquas as deeply as possible in his struggles, for he feared for their loyalty.[29] A year later, however, when the major expedition of the High Commissioner, by now Sir George Cathcart, moved against Moshoeshoe in the campaign that led to the near fiasco at the Berea, the Griquas were not called upon to supply auxiliaries. For once their conflicts of loyalties were not exposed.

These two defeats were the final spurs for the colonial Government in London to take the decision which had long been germinating and abandon the Orange River sovereignty. Mainly in consequence of the frontier war of 1851 and in line with a general retrenchment in British colonial policy, the Colonial Office was concerned to reduce British responsibilities in South Africa.[30] The sovereignty was obviously the prime candidate for the assegai. Recently and haphazardly acquired, it contained a very small white population which was primarily Dutch and of suspect loyalty. Its black population was large, quarrelsome and formidable. If its commerce expanded significantly, which seemed unlikely, it would be controlled by the British ports on the coast. By October 1851, Lord John Russell, then Prime Minister, was prepared to state, if not publicly, that 'the ultimate abandonment of the Orange River Sovereignty should be a settled point in British policy'.[31] This announcement did not close the matter, nor bring it to immediate fruition, but such was the British intention.

Realisation of this policy was difficult. As Lord Grey, Lord John Russell's Colonial Secretary, began to lose confidence in Sir Harry Smith he sent out to South Africa two men as Assistant Commissioners, Major Hogge and C. Mostyn Owen, to work under Smith to clear up the troubles of the administration. In fact, as Sir Harry was primarily occupied on the eastern frontier, Hogge and Owen became virtually free agents, especially when they became concerned with the affairs of the interior. Until his death, moreover, Hogge was the close confidante of Grey, and his letters became one of the main bases on which British policy was based.[32] This pair was able to negotiate the Sand River Convention with Andries Pretorius, and thus allow for the recognition of the Transvaal as an independent republic. The repercussions south of the Vaal were obviously enormous, for no longer were all British subjects (i.e. all white men) under the legal authority of Britain. With the Transvaal independent, it was far more difficult to maintain either the dependence or the loyalty of the inhabitants of the Orange River sovereignty.[33]

Thereafter, two steps were necessary before the Orange River sovereignty could emerge from its cocoon as the Orange Free State. First, Sir Harry Smith had to be dismissed, for far too much of his personal reputation was bound up in the sovereignty for him ever to acquiesce in its abandonment. This was duly done with a stinging despatch early in 1852.[34] Secondly, a suitable Government had to be manufactured for the new country. Here there was more difficulty. The enthusiasm of the white population of farmers and traders who would have to form the basis of Government was small. The dubious advantages of independence were more than countered by the insecurity of the Sotho frontier. Psychological self-sufficiency could not compensate for the withdrawal of British troops on which white society had relied for the last forty years. Thus it was necessary not only to encourage the republican aspirations of many of the farmers, so that those who a few years before had been 'rebels' were now 'collaborators' and the erstwhile 'loyalists' became 'obstructionists',[35] but also to provide considerable concessions to the farmers. In the circumstances, the best counter the British could play was to guarantee security of tenure to those Boers who had hired land

from the Griquas. It was with this in mind that Sir George Clerk, formerly
Governor of Bombay, who had been sent out from Britain to make suitable
arrangements for the territory, came to Philippolis.[36]

Clerk was a forthright man who realised how deeply the Boers felt on the
question of the Griqua land and how necessary it was to find some solution to it.
He was aided by Henry Green, who had taken over from Warden as British
Resident and had the prejudices of officialdom against the Griquas. Whether
from the source, from personal experience, or out of a realisation of what was
politically the most advantageous attitude, Clerk had these prejudices too. When
he and Green met Kok and his *raad* early in February 1854, the Griquas were
presented with a draft of a settlement to modify their current agreement with
Britain. According to this, 'the Griqua people, subjects of Adam Kok shall have
the right (hitherto denied them) of selling their farms, whenever they are disposed to do so'. This was the crucial point, but others were as controversial.
'Every person of European extraction purchasing a farm in the Inalienable
Territory shall be subject to the laws of the Independent Government, now
established in the Sovereignty.' An agent was to be appointed to act as intermediary between the dealers in land, a magistrate was to look after the interests
of the farmers within the inalienable territory, and the annual payment of £300
which the Griqua chief and council then received in lieu of nutrients from the
farms in the alienable territory was to continue 'to be paid to the Griqua Chief
Adam Kok personally, during his life time'. Finally, 'Payments ranging from Rds.
500 [£37 10s.] to Rds. 1500 shall be made to such Griqua proprietors who have
lost farms in the alienable territory by the above mentioned agreement . . . Such
payments to be made in proportion to the relative value of the farms at the time
the arrangement was made.'[37] The reply of Kok and his *raad* was that the proposal that Europeans could buy farms within the inalienable territory would have
the effect of 'entirely annulling the Maitland Treaty — filling our country with
aliens — destroying our nationality — and ultimately compelling us either to
leave the country or to subject ourselves to the new Government, a Government
of which we have no knowledge, and consequently in which we can have no
confidence. We are therefore constrained to say that we cannot consent to such
a proposal.' The Griquas had broken no treaty with the colonial Government.
Moreover, Kok was most annoyed that compensation for farms which had been
taken from them by Harry Smith should be made conditional on their agreement
to Clerk's current proposal, for the Griquas considered that settlement to be
both unjust and a violation of the Maitland treaty, which they considered still to
be in force.[38]

Although Clerk had already managed to extract from the whites of the
sovereignty a Convention (the Bloemfontein Convention) by which the Orange

Free State was set up, Griqua intransigence was probably based on the hope that the difficulties of making suitable settlements might even yet force the British to remain in the sovereignty. Certainly such ideas were current in Philippolis at the time.[39] Ironically, there were difficulties, avoided by sheer chance, which would have caused such embarassment to the colonial administration in London that they might have been forced to remain in control,[40] but the complications at Philippolis were not of that order. When they felt it necessary the British officials could impose their will on the Griquas without compunction, for there was no political danger in doing so and the gains were considerable. Thus when the Griquas met Clerk and Green, they were reduced to scoring debating points off the commissioners,[41] who themselves could lambast the Griquas. Green's speech was reported as follows:

> I have on the part of the British Government made you the most liberal offers, merely for the preservation of the future peace of this territory. Your case simply stands thus: the farmers on the other side of the Riet River are in occupation of certain lands on which the Griquas have a claim; while on this side of the Riet River many Griquas occupy farms which they have sold to Europeans or colonists, but which they will not surrender to the purchaser because they say the sale of land is opposed to Griqua law. On behalf of the British Government I have come between you and offered to satisfy your claims on the farms beyond the Riet River provided you will give possession to the purchasers of the ground you have sold them on this side and abrogate a law which leads to so much dishonest and underhand dealing. You decline this liberal offer, you are willing to take all the money the British Government will give, you will keep the money you have received for your lands and you will keep the land as well! Can such dishonesty prosper? I think not; and I perceive a day of reckoning approaching. The British Government and Captain Kok are both willing to allow the Griquas to sell, but the people themselves, many of whom have already sold, and been paid for their property, refuse through their council to remove the last and only impediment.

Thus he had no qualms in stating that 'The offer of payment which I made for land beyond the Riet River is withdrawn as the object in offering it, the preservation of peace, will probably be frustrated through the unsettled state in which the land tenures must be left in consequence of your resolution.'[42] When, some months later, the Griqua *raad* realised that it had lost the chance of compensation for farms in the inalienable territory and therefore wrote to Clerk asking that they might now take it up, this was refused, as Clerk no longer felt it in his power to maintain it.[43] The Griquas attempted to call the British bluff, only to realise that it was no bluff. By Solomon's calculation they lost £15,000.[44]

This bout of negotiations signaled the end of the traditional Griqua policy of relying on the British against the Boers. The myth that had been fostered that the British were somehow just and would set all to right had finally been exploded. There was only one more flicker of such arguments before the Griquas trekked over the mountains. In general, however, they were bitter, a bitterness echoed by at least one Englishman:

> I must say the Griquas have been shamefully treated; they have been offered as a peace offering to Standers and his party.[45] Since Adam Kok has been in treaty with the English he has been twice called upon to fight against the Boers, twice against Moshesh, once against the Tambookies,[46] and now the upshot is, the Boers, against whom Kok fought, become the friends of the English, are supplied with ammunition, and Kok is deserted and left to the tender mercies of these ragamuffins, without even being allowed to get ammunition to defend himself. However, this is quite in keeping with the policy pursued by the Government towards the natives during the last few years.[47]

In the arguments between the Boers and the Griquas which accompanied the scuttle from the sovereignty, the battlefield, as well as the prize, was land. Sir George Clerk could claim that he was justified in dealing as he did with the Griquas because they had broken the Maitland Treaty by allowing land to be sold to the Boers within the inalienable territory. With even greater fervour, the Griquas protested against the way in which they had been deprived of many valuable farms. It is therefore necessary to examine the question in rather greater detail. Evidence comes in two forms. First there were the propaganda statements which both sides produced to show how they had been dealt with, and how the other had broken some agreement. These are not necessarily false, for it would have been stupid to base a case on allegations which could have been disproved, but they are evidently the spectacular instances, atypical within the process. To balance these, then, it becomes necessary to look at the Orange Free State land registers, which are certainly chaotic and incomplete, but nevertheless yield valuable information on the way in which land was transferred from Griqua to Boer.

But the exceptions were important, both because they could be used to demonstrate particular points and because they did much to decide how land matters were viewed by the various actors. The Boers' case for the abandonment of the Maitland treaty was primarily based on the fact that the Griquas had been selling land. To prove this they put forward the following document:

15 April 1853

I, Adam Kok, Captain, Griqua Chief — of the district of Philippolis — acknowledge herewith, that Jan Isaak, one of my subjects, is the lawful owner of the
farm Dassies Poort, conformably with the ground certificate subscribed and
given to him by the Griqua Government, bearing date the 29th May, 1849,
and I further declare that I have not the least objection in case the said Jan
Isaak with Kootje du Tooit, a British subject now living on the said farm
Dassies Poort, shall make such agreement to sell or to dispose of the said farm
as his property.

(signed) Adam Kok.[48]

Adam Kok would later deny any knowledge of the deal, but Jan Isaak was quite
prepared, apparently, to let his farm go.

On the other hand, to give but one example, there was the trouble that ensued
over the farm of Matjes Fontein. This farm, which was situated in the alienable
territory, was leased by a Griqua, Stoffel Vesasie, to a certain Petrus Pienaar.
This was done in 1840, and the lease was to last 10 years. Pienaar then died, and
his widow married a man called van Colder (?Coller). After the Maitland treaty,
Vesasie leased the farm to Gideon Joubert, who was to obtain possession in 1850
and was to pay Rds. 3000, 1200 of them in advance. Then, at the time of the
battle of Boomplaats, van Colder fought against the British, and had his land
confiscated, along with remarkably few of his companions. The farm was put up
for sale, and was bought by Joubert for Rds. 1550. He also paid Vesasie another
Rds. 250, so that in all he laid out Rds. 3,000 for the farm, but over half of this
was lost to Vesasie, although he had fought with the British at Boomplaats. Not
unnaturally the loss annoyed him, and he complained to the British Government
for the next ten years, hoping to get compensation, but apparently without
result.[49]

This sort of story was not unusual, although the details were obviously idiosyncratic. Piet Draai, for instance, had a similar tale to tell over the farm at
Boomplaats.[50] It is necessary, however, to aggregate the dealings, to produce an
overall pattern. In so far as it is possible to discover, the Griquas let a total of
136 farms in the years before 1848. Of these, only 58 were in the alienable territory, north of the line from the Riet River to the Krom Elleboog Spruit. By the
agreement which the Griquas made with Sir Harry Smith all these were lost,
although only 42 of them had been leased for 40 years or more. Moreover,
another 88 farms which had not been leased, but which were in the alienable
territory, moved out of the control of the Griquas when Major Warden began
distributing them among the Boers and the English land speculators.[51] There was

obviously a certain amount of complaint about this but surprisingly little, so that it would appear that the Griquas were either resigned to the loss or, alternatively, that they had never really been in effective occupation far from Philippolis. There remain 74 farms which were leased at some stage. A few others may have been hired out and then returned to the Griquas, but although various missionaries enthused about this possibility, there seems to be no record recoverable of such a transaction. It would not appear in the Orange Free State records, on which perforce these figures must be based. The freehold of the others was at some time or another sold to a Boer, most often the one to whom the farm had been let. A further 163 farms had never been let, or had been regained, and were sold to the Boers direct. The timing of these sales is important. They appear in appendix 2 which refers to the date entered on the bill of sale between a Griqua and a burgher of the Orange Free State, as recorded in the Registry of Acts in Bloemfontein. From this table it is evident that the boom year for sales of both hired and unhired farms was 1854, which was only outstripped by the last year of the Griquas' occupancy of Philippolis, when the last holdings had to be disposed of, and a number of small parcels of land, which had never been allotted to any Griqua, were given out to prominent members of the community, who made quick money by immediately selling them to Boers.[52] But the transfer of farms that occurred in 1854 was something different, especially as virtually all were sold in the five months between June and October.[53] In part, perhaps, it may not have been the consequence of any real change, but merely dependent on the establishment of a registry in Bloemfontein. Boers who had previously occupied Griqua farms by virtue of verbal agreements may now have decided to regularise the situation and place their ownership on record. As there was often a considerable time between the drawing up of the deed of sale and its registration, however, there may be a deeper explanation. At least in part, it must represent a definite shift in Griqua consciousness. Many Griquas must have sold land in defiance of their own laws because they considered that they could not hope to maintain them against the pressure of the new Orange Free State community. The Griqua officials railed against this, but could do nothing. Kok complained bitterly to the new Government about a notice in the *Government Gazette* that all land within the inalienable territory that had been sold should be registered with the *landrost* of Fauresmith.[54] At the same time he was becoming depressed and lethargic. Solomon wrote of him:

> Kok is shrewd enough to see his own difficulties but has no resources to meet them, he sees himself surrounded by enemies and betrayed by a portion of his own people, hence he has become perplexed and depressed, unwilling to make any move, preferring to let things take their course. In fact I think he is so

tired, annoyed and at his wits end that he would be glad to get out of his
position altogether by sacrificing everything and leaving his country. Vigour
and sound judgement at the head of affairs here might at least have delayed
for a time the catastrophe, but *now* I have no hopes. It is difficult to save
people in spite of themselves.[55]

In the early years of its existence, the Griquas cooperated reasonably well
with the Free State Government. The various officials generally acted in concert,
when it was appropriate to do so.[56] If anything, the major political contact of
the Griquas was with the Cape rather than with Bloemfontein. They hoped to
gain some redress for the wrongs which they claimed had been done to them, to
buy gunpowder and to have the pension which had been promised paid.[57] But
the relationship between the Boers and the Griquas was as suspicious and wary at
this period as at any other. Boshof, the second President of the Free State, complained vehemently about the granting of ammunition to the Griquas.[58] Rumours
flew that the Griquas were going to lead a coalition to stab the Free State in the
belly when the burghers were away on commando against one of the minor
Sotho chiefs at the north of the Drakensberg.[59] In the atmosphere of mistrust
the Griquas made a self-fulfilling prophecy, selling land on the assumption that
they could no longer maintain a position in the new order of the Free State.
Only the wealth that they accumulated over this period stopped it from being
fulfilled earlier.

CHAPTER 7

THE GRIQUA TREK

By the end of the 1850s, the ambiguities inherent in the Griqua position were becoming more blatant. The individualism of particular Griquas in the situation of small capitalist agriculture was becoming less compatible with the strong community which was necessary if the Griquas were to survive, even as individuals. In the face of Boer pressure, the alienation of Griqua land and the absence of succour from the British, the Griquas could either cease as a community or they could trek. They chose to trek. In many ways this was not surprising. Mass migrations of people have been one of the characteristics of South African history, at least since the early nineteenth century. The *Völkerwanderung* of the Mfecane and the incessant trekking of the Afrikaners, of which the Great Trek was only the most spectacular, are the most notable, but there are others. In this century, there has been the gradual move into towns by both rural Afrikaners and Africans. In the last, there were such movements as the trek of the Bastards from de Tuin to Rehoboth. But of these migrations, the Griqua trek of 1861−2 is among the most spectacular. It was not of great size. Perhaps 2,000 people left Philippolis to establish themselves in Nomansland, over the Drakensberg.[1] But the great caravan of ox-wagons and donkey carts, 300 in number, journeyed over a road which the Griquas cut themselves across the high ridge of the mountains, in one of the most remarkable engineering feats of South African history. The pass over Ongeluks Nek, recently reopened as a jeep track, is a remarkable testimony to Griqua endurance and expertise.

It would seem that the Griquas trekked for two main reasons. First, and possibly most important, there was a country for them to go to. In consequence of the chance of the Mfecane and the sourness of the grazing in Nomansland, modern East Griqualand, it was one of the few tracts of empty country remaining within South Africa. Others coveted it. The Mpondo, under their chief Faku, claimed that it was within the area of their jurisdiction.[2] Theophilus Shepstone, the Native Secretary of Natal, had hoped to form a settlement there to rid Natal of its large African population. This would have appeased the settler population who considered that Africans had a place only as labourers, not occupying land and growing their own food and thus obviating the necessity of working for the

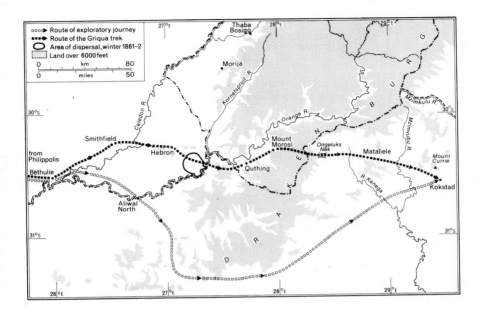

3   The route of the Griqua trek

whites. The small, faction-ridden community was perhaps the most insecure of the white settlements in South Africa, for it had to live in the shadow of the formidable Zulu kingdom and seems to have compensated for this with a particularly vehement rejection of the possibility of African equality and a strong assertion of their communal and nascent class solidarity. However, Shepstone's scheme was thwarted, mainly by Sir George Grey,[3] who in fact gave the Griquas permission to move there. He based his decision on an opinion of the Griquas higher than that of any other British official and on his hopes to annexe the whole of the country between the Cape and Natal.[4]

Secondly, the Griquas trekked because they could no longer abide their position within the Orange Free State, for it was becoming more and more parlous in consequence of a variety of specific political events. Unfortunately it is impossible to know precisely how this discontent was expressed. The *raad* minute books do not exist for this period. The last missionary in the town, W. B. Philip, was a bad correspondent. It is therefore necessary to rely on inference and on the testimony given in various forms much later. For all that his first-hand experience of the Griquas was limited to a short visit in 1861, the Rev. John Mackenzie was surely right when he wrote:

95

In the case of the Griquas there was added the strong caste feeling, or prejudice, on account of their colour. They might be good, intelligent and wealthy; they were only 'bastaards and Hottentots' after all. This had not been so manifest in the early years of their contact with the Dutch in the district of Philippolis . . . but as the colonists increased in numbers their clannish feelings returned . . . The . . . feeling has modified the use of certain Dutch words; for instance 'menschen' is used by Dutch colonists of themselves, to the exclusion not only of black people but of Europeans also; 'volk' is used by them of all coloured people, and never of white persons, although, of course, no such usage obtains in Holland or in the Dutch Bible.

Therefore the Griquas

sought a place where they might again become 'menschen', and cease to be 'volk' and 'schepsels' (creatures). They were selling, it was true, some of the finest sheep runs in South Africa; but they were getting hard cash in return; and there was no sentiment binding them to the country, which was not 'the land of their sires', except to such of them as happened to be Bushmen.[5]

But such feelings had been growing slowly over a long period of time. To explain the timing of the trek, it is necessary to look to particular events during the late 1850s.

On 31 January 1857, the *Friend* carried a notice from the Orange Free State Government which announced the creation of *veldkornetcies* within Griqualand. Until then the Fauresmith district had had few local officials, but now it needed five *veldkornets* spread through what had been the inalienable territory. Once more the jurisdiction of Kok and his *raad* was seriously challenged. The local officers of the Griqua *raad* were no longer the only accredited officials within their *wyk*, although, to be fair, it seems unlikely that they had been able to control the Boers even before this move.[6]

At about the same time, the Free State published various articles of agreement which it claimed the delegates of the Orange River sovereignty had reached with Sir George Clerk in 1853. The most important of these read: 'That whenever any Griqua lands shall be sold to any person of European descent, such lands shall fall at once under the Orange River Government.' A further article stated: 'That when Adam Kok departs from his territory, the treaty between Her Majesty's Government and him lapses.' Clerk acceded to them both with the proviso, in the latter case, that the knowledge of such a clause might tend to delay any Griqua migration.[7] There was some controversy as to whether or not these articles were genuine, or forged additions on behalf of the Orange Free State. Clerk himself wrote that he 'do[es] not recollect such stipulations', but that he 'may, nevertheless, have assented generally to those remarks'.[8] Certainly, however, they did not improve relations between the Griquas and the Boers. By such measures 'Griqua subjects were seized on Griqua farms by Free State subjects, and by them confined in Free State prisons, instead of being reported and handed over to the Griqua Government.'[9] It was said later that there had been rumours of war between the Griquas and the Boers.[10] In fact the Griquas seem to have remained remarkably quiet during 1858, when war between the Orange Free State and the Sotho broke out. They did attempt to revenge themselves on the burghers who they considered had usurped their lands. They co-operated with the Boer *veldkornets* in apprehending roving cattle thieves.[11] Kok ordered his subjects to remain quiet, and they obeyed him.[12] The whole episode seems to show that the Griquas were as yet unsure of what their policy ought to be and where the community was going, although in later years they were most adamant that this had been the time when they were finally swindled by British and Boer connivance.[13]

It was at about this time that the first moves towards the exodus to Nomansland were taken. Apparently, in August when Sir George Grey was in the north attempting to settle the Free State—Sotho dispute, the question was broached as to the possibility of moving, unless some other way could be found to modify this anomalous state of affairs:

> War was out of the question, and the British Government wanted no such complication with its ally, and if the Griquas could remain in quiet [sic], their children could not purchase farms for themselves at the rate offered by the Boers or Englishmen.
>
> The best solution of the problem seemed to be that those Griquas who still held farms should sell them, and all should move to some other part. A few suggested Namaqualand, a few more the Campbell Grounds, others suggested the eastern side of the Drakensberg, Nomansland. Sir George Grey warmly supported this proposal.[14]

The Griquas had apparently heard of the area from a man called Smith Pommer, who had been one of the rebels at the Kat River in 1851 and had then become the leader of a band of marauders who established themselves in the debated land beneath the mountains during the 1850s. They were hard pressed because they had aroused the enmity of the Bhaca, one of the largest Bantu groups in the area. Pommer would certainly have welcomed the arrival of a large contingent of Griquas, and is known to have been in contact with Philippolis at about this time.[15] At any rate, the Griquas would go and see.

At some stage during 1859, a party of more than a hundred men, with wagons, oxen, horses and guns left Philippolis for Nomansland. The exact date of their departure is of some importance, but it is impossible to determine. They had gone by early July, but the tone of the report suggests that they had left but recently.[16] They went south-east, through modern Dordrecht and around the northern borders of the Transkei, through Maclear and Mount Fletcher and then down into the plains between the Mzimkulu and Mzimvubu rivers. To a people brought up in the dry plains of the High Veld, with its turgid *fonteins* and recurrent drought, the green hills, flowing waters and bracing air of the Drakensberg hills must have seemed a Promised Land. Its disadvantages were only apparent afterwards. Most of the party remained in the area, where they found few inhabitants, but some visited Faku of the Mpondo and others visited towns and sugar or coffee plantations in Natal. 'Pleased with the capabilities of this Nomansland and promising themselves unlimited supplies of coffee, sugar, and rice, which they were to raise for themselves', they determined to return by a direct route over the Drakensberg, for by now the winter must have been over. They drove a route across the Kenega River and up the scarp of the mountains at Ongeluks Nek, which they named because a man accidentally shot himself while unloading his gun from a wagon. From then on they went down the steep slope behind the ridge, across the spurs of the higher Orange valley, past the mountain fortress of Morosi and through Hanglip and Smithfield back to Philippolis.[17] They arrived, at the latest, by December 1859.[18]

By the time of their return, the last incentive which might have kept the Griquas in Philippolis had disappeared. The British Government had squashed the scheme for a South African Federation which had been put forward by Sir George Grey, and had recalled Grey to London.[19] President Boshof, whose policy had been concerned to a large degree to increase the union between the Free State and the Cape, had resigned, and Marthinus Wessel Pretorius had been elected in his place, presaging a reorientation northwards.[20] This meant that there would be no alleviation of the pressures which the Boer community exerted on the Griquas. If federation had been achieved, then the *status quo* could have been maintained. At any rate Grey believed that it could. In January 1859 he wrote to London relating Kok's problems and claiming that the British should 'maintain the treaties at all hazard', for despite possible trouble with the Orange Free State, 'this is the course justice required us to take'. On the other hand:

> in the event of . . . federation, Adam Kok, who is a man of very considerable private wealth, and who is tired of the cares of his position, has expressed to me his desire to resign his sovereignty and to allow his possession to be incorporated in those of one of the Federated States, if due provision is made for the interests of his subjects, which I would take care was done.[21]

Perhaps Grey was speaking above his brief, a habit of his. But he may have accurately reflected the feelings of at any rate some Griquas, and the coincidence of timing between the readjustment of South African politics consequent on Bulwer Lytton's June dispatch and the Griqua trek may be more than pure coincidence.

In January 1860 there was a meeting in Philippolis to decide whether or not to transplant the community to Nomansland. The decision was not unanimous but 'by far the majority agreed to move thither'.[22] Some few who had mainly lived around Rhama in the west of the Captaincy decided to stay and were received without too much hostility by the Free State.[23] At least one retained his farm and fought alongside the Boers in the war with Moshoeshoe in 1865.[24] Others again went west to Namaqualand, where the Oorlam leader, Jan Jonker Afrikaner, had newly-arrived Griqua councillors in about 1863.[25] Many others remained in Griqualand West, living on the lands of those Griquas who in the 35 years since the establishment of the Captaincy of Philippolis had never left the area.[26] But most of those who could afford the transport went east over the Drakensberg. It may be surmised that the poor acquiesced in the move because they hoped to recoup their fortunes on the farms which would be given out in this land of green hills and running streams. The rich also had to move, for while South Africans viewed men as members of distinct groups, almost of separated nations, they could not hope to maintain themselves in the manner to which they had become accustomed other than as Griquas. They were Griquas before they were individuals, or members of a society, or of a class of landowners. They would seem to have presumed that if the community of Griquas was broken, as it was being broken by the various actions by which the Orange Free State demonstrated its control over what was officially part of its territory, then they would not long be able to run sheep on the farms they owned. In this they were probably correct. At any rate they sold out at the top of a boom, if not for such prices as were obtained shortly afterwards by those to whom they had sold.[27]

Obviously such calculations cannot have been the only ones in the minds of those who left Philippolis from 1860 onwards. The sentiment of friendship and long association would have made many men unwilling to be parted from their kin and their fellow Griquas. Again, all agricultural communities in South Africa depended on continual territorial expansion, or on the continual subdivision of land. A 3,000-acre farm was looked on as the birthright of a Griqua as much as it was of a Boer, and property was divided, by Roman Dutch law, equally among the children. This could no longer be provided in the area of Philippolis. In Nomansland, they may have thought, there was the possibility of living again as they hoped and had been taught to live.

During the next year the Griquas tried to smooth the way for their trek into Nomansland. This consisted primarily of settling affairs with the Orange Free

State and the British, selling up the land and making a road over the mountains. Remarkably little contact was made with the Africans who would become their neighbours. Only the briefest discussion seems to have taken place with Faku of the Mpondo. Adam Kok did not meet Moshoeshoe until early 1862, after all the preparations had been made, despite the fact that the route would be skirting the southern edge of his kingdom and that his son, Nehemiah, was attempting to establish himself as a semi-independent prince at Matatiele, near where the Griquas hoped to settle.[28] With the Free State it was different. Following a visit to Philippolis in March 1860 by Marthinus Wessel Pretorius, it was agreed that a Land Commission should be set up by the Griquas to mark out the boundaries of the various farms before they were sold, thus minimising the difficulties which the purchaser should have in the future, and, incidentally, probably allowing the Griquas to charge higher prices for their land.[29] This commission, which consisted of Kok himself and two leading raadsmen, Isaac Read, later *veldkommandant*, and Hendrik Swarts, later chairman of the *raad*, met throughout the year, and those people with whom they were dealing seem to have been well satisfied with the results.[30] At the same period, Kok appointed an agent in Philippolis to look after his business after he had gone. Initially this function was given to David Arnot, a coloured lawyer with a chip on his shoulder and a shrewd eye for an opportunity, who had practised in Colesberg for at least ten years.[31] Later a local trader and farmer named Henry Harvey took over. He was to prove disastrous, for during the 1860s he went bankrupt, so that much of the money still owing to the Griquas, particularly for the sale of Government land, was lost.[32] Kok's attempt to arrange an agent in Cape Town, however, was considerably more successful, for he persuaded Saul Solomon, one of the most powerful political figures in South Africa — he was Member of the Assembly for Cape Town and edited its leading newspaper, the *Cape Argus* — to act for him.[33] Solomon was no doubt persuaded above all by the fact that his brother had long been the missionary at Philippolis, and had remained on good terms with the Griquas, even going up to Philippolis shortly before they left to say good-bye.[34] In Cape Town, at least, they had an energetic and powerful advocate.

Land sales in Philippolis went on briskly throughout 1860 and 1861. The Griquas were fortunate that the depression that hit the wool farmers later in the 1860s had not yet struck,[35] so that they enjoyed good prices for the farms and had no difficulty finding buyers. In general the first payment of the sale was made in kind, in oxen, sheep and wagons. Apart from this, only a very few held security for later instalments. The purchasers were often indignant at the want of trust which was implied in the Griquas' requests for a mortgage bond, and many declined to purchase if one was required. 'Still very few of those who sold without a bond received the price agreed upon.'[36] Nevertheless, as W. B. Philip commented, for those who had been used only to handling small sums, the hundreds of pounds[37] which they received seemed inexhaustible, and the stores of Philippolis did good business.[38]

Before the trek could take place, an agreement had to be reached with the British Government as to the exact boundaries of the land to which they were going and the status of the Griquas when they got there. The negotiations were conducted by Kok during a visit to Cape Town during 1860 and by a series of letters over the next two years. The main reason why they were complicated was that in 1850 Faku had ceded to Natal the land between the Mtamvuna and the Mzimkulu rivers.[39] This included the main part of the area to which the Griquas wished to trek. It had never been taken up. Nevertheless, the Natal colonists, working through the Lieutenant Governor, were anxious to prevent it being settled by Griquas, as this would mean a large tract of land into which the country hoped to expand passing out of the hands of the whites. They therefore used the fact of the cession of 1850 to try and take full possession of Nomansland, although white settlement in the Colony had scarcely spread so far south.[40] On the other hand, Sir George Grey was trying to use the Griquas as counters in his scheme to gain control over the whole of the Transkei.[41] He wrote:

> They muster at least 2,000 fighting men, mounted and well armed [a considerable exaggeration] . . . During the many years they have been on the borders of the colony, they have not only abstained from thieving but it has never been alleged that thieves have escaped through their territories, and they have, on different occasions acted with us against both European and native races as our allies. They would thus form for Natal an important bulwark on one point of danger and, lying as they would do in the rear of the Kafir tribes, might, in as far as this colony is concerned, prove most important auxiliaries in the event of another Kafir war.

Moreover, he stressed that they farmed on European principles, and would clear the land, so that in time Europeans might buy up the land and the Griquas move on again. For the time being, they would be *bona fide* occupiers of land, not speculators.[42] Above all, Grey insisted that the Griquas should go into the new land as British subjects, and should come in some way or another under the control of the British.[43] For their part, the Griquas no doubt found the negotiations which were continuing about and around them rather irrelevant, if they knew of them at all.[44] Once, at the beginning of 1860, the Philippolis Captaincy had decided to trek, nothing would have prevented it, short of armed force. Too much had been thrown into the gamble for it to be abandoned. They proceeded to get ready to leave in their own good time.

Nevertheless, although the diplomacy had but little impact on the years

between 1860 and 1863, it was to leave marks which bore important consequences for the later history of Nomansland. The details are not of value for the
present purpose, but the results are. Essentially, the Griquas received all they
hoped for, except — and this must have been a wild dream — a port.[45] The highland area between the Mzimkulu and Mzimvubu rivers passed into their hands, at
any rate that part of it north of the Ingeli mountains. But in the course of these
negotiations, the Griquas created a powerful enmity with the Natal Government
and many of the colonists, which was to last throughout the period in East
Griqualand.[46] The correspondence between the Cape and Natal over the next
twelve years is full of accusations and anecdotes as to the way in which the
Griquas were running their country, all aimed by Natal to blacken the name of
the Griquas in the eyes of successive Cape Governors. They are a useful, if one-
sided, source for the historian, but, cumulatively, they must have created an
impression which led finally to the annexation of the Griquas. The negotiations
of the trek also left a dangerous ambiguity as to the status of the Griquas. Were
they or were they not British subjects? The legal situation seems to have been
highly confused, for they were trekking to a country which had been ceded to
the British crown, but which had never been administered in any way whatsoever
by the British. Still, this was to be a powerful weapon in the hands of the
expansionists a decade later.[47]

These problems lay some way in the future. Kok came back from Cape Town
with six two-pounder cannons and much ammunition,[48] with which to blast
through any opposition in the mountains. From the beginning of 1860 onwards,
the Griquas began to sell up such farms as remained in their possession. They
used the proceeds to buy wagons and stock and to move out towards the new
land. Some left after the winter of 1860, moving on to Hanglip near the Orange
River (in the region of the modern Zastron) which was then still Sotho territory:

> On the road . . . might be met a single bullock wagon with its span of oxen,
> while before and behind small numbers of different kinds of stock were driven
> on; further on you would meet one household encamped, with tents, a large
> tent wagon, a good horse wagon, a buck wagon, a tent cart, and large
> quantities of stock, quite a patriarch moving with his children, at a greater
> distance you would meet two or three families moving onward together with
> their wagons and stock; vehicles of every description, shape, and age were
> pressed into service, some forming a ludicrous contrast to the new brightly
> painted wagons.[49]

Over the course of the next year, the rest of the people began to move. The
government sold its highly profitable salt pan to the Orange Free State for
£3,000,[50] and such ground in Griqualand as had not been given out fetched

£4,000 as a lump sum.[51] The church and parsonage were sold to the successor church, the Nederduitsche Gereformeerde Kerk, for £900, although £218 was still outstanding two years later.[52] After the winter of 1861, the rest of the community moved off to Hanglip, where they had decided to see out one more winter before making an assault on the mountains themselves. There they spread themselves over a radius of about 15 miles and erected an iron church to serve them through the winter. W. B. Philip spent the winter staying with the French missionary at Hebron. But the year was one of very heavy drought which crippled the Griquas. Draught oxen were recorded as fetching £12 to £14, where the price the year before had been £9.[53] Even by May Philip considered that 'the approaching winter will be a time of suffering for many; they have had no crops the last year; they have no prospect of crops next year if they lose this sowing time, and starvation must come to many, almost as bad as in Namaqualand.'[54] By the end of the winter his fears were fulfilled:

> Hundreds of cattle and horses, and thousands of sheep and goats, died in every direction; the air seemed tainted, and the vultures, numerous as they were, could not devour the carrion. The losses were especially great where a good many were encamped together, and not a blade of grass could be seen for miles round their camp. Many a man lost five hundred sheep, and was left with two or three score; many of them lost 900 out of 1,000, others 1,300 and 1,500 sheep out of their flocks; the poor as well as the rich lost most or all of their milch cows, on which they had depended so largely, and numbers of horses died.[55]

To make matters worse, the mountain chieftains of southern Lesotho, above all Poshuli, began to harry the Griquas, taking all the cattle and horses they could,[56] while the mountain San, who were at least in part the clients of these chieftains, took their toll.[57] The cannon obviously helped the Griquas to drive their way through, but at least one group, that led by 'Gamga' Jan Pienaar — always the most independent of the 'big men' — decided to travel round by the north, through Witsie's Hoek and Natal, to Nomansland, and thereby deprived the main body of a useful contingent of fighting men.[58] But the others remained. 'Every morning scores of men set to work with pick and crowbar, hammer and drills, powder and fuse to dig out a passable track on the mountainside.'[59] In the course of the summer of 1862–3 they dragged their wagons over the mountains and down the precipitous pass of Ongeluks Nek. So many wagons were destroyed on the way that it was said that they supplied the local Sotho with iron for many years to come.[60] The Griquas came down through Matatiele, where Nehemiah Moshoeshoe had set up his kraal, and on to Mount Currie where they set up a *laager* from which to settle and farm the country. In the travails of the two-year trek they had become an impoverished and demoralised people.

CHAPTER 8

NOMANSLAND

The history of the Griquas in Nomansland, after the trek, has the quality of an unreal afterthought. Its pattern parallels that of the era in Philippolis, as the attempts of the Griquas to build themselves into a self-sufficient community were baulked, this time finally, by the activities and concerns of the white colonists. But the circumstances within which the pattern was played out were different. The Griquas did not have to contend with the expansion of the trekboers and the political systems they created. Rather they had two main tasks. They had to tame the land and begin the agricultural development on which they based their hopes of prosperity, and they had to establish some form of political order over the country into which they had migrated. Only when these tasks had been accomplished could they hope to become an aristocracy, as they envisaged themselves, living in part on the fruits of the land and in part as overlords of the African population which surrounded them.

Of the two problems, the first was more difficult. Nomansland is fine farming country, similar in all respects of Alan Paton's Beloved Country, across the River Umzimkulu where:

> About you there is grass and bracken and you may hear the forlorn crying of the titihoya, one of the birds of the veld. Below you is the valley of the Umzimkulu, on its journey from the Drakensberg to the sea; and beyond and behind the river, great hill after great hill; and beyond and behind them, the mountains of Ingeli and East Griqualand.
>
> The grass is rich and matted, you cannot see the soil. It holds the rain and the mist, and they seep into the ground, feeding the streams in every kloof.[1]

However, various problems made acclimatisation difficult for the Griquas. The region is almost all over 4,000 feet above sea level and in consequence the winters are cold. There is no shortage of water, but the wet valley bottoms harbour liver fluke. Used as they were to the droughts of the High Veld, the Griquas would instinctively have sent their sheep into the neighbourhood of water, and so lost many of them. The veld around is primarily sour, so that the very high carrying capacity it enjoys in summer, when the rain allows the grass to grow, disappears in the winter, for the grass does not turn to hay and is unpalatable. Because of these difficulties, the Griqua flocks that had crossed the mountains were further reduced, until the wealth that they retained was but a small fraction of that which they had previously possessed.[2]

In the immediate aftermath of the trek, the Griquas set up a *laager* on the slopes of Mount Currie, five kilometres north of the modern town of Kokstad. Initially, the settlement was built of wagons, but increasingly these were replaced by semi-permanent shacks, of stone, wood, or, most usually, turf. It was meant to be a temporary residence, but they actually stayed there for nine years. It did not impress visitors. A typical reaction was that of a prospector:

> To our disgust and disappointment, found it a very dirty place, consisting of about 200 mudhuts, a few old waggons and a lot of dirty Griquas, sitting or lying outside their dens. A small church and a fort stand in the middle of the village and Adam Kok's palace at one end . . . Adding to the miserable appearance of the laager, a number of houses are only half built and allowed to remain with their four walls standing. It is, indeed, as one of our party called it, a village in ruins before it was built.[3]

It certainly was a squalid shanty town, perhaps, as was claimed, because those who had survived the trek with any wealth at all moved out into the countryside to begin farming, while those who remained in the town were the destitute.[4] At the same time, a general air of despondency and defeat spread through the community. Read and Solomon noted that many who had previously been strictly sober had turned to drink, a sure sign of social and individual collapse.[5] Adam Kok himself was particularly badly affected, by the failure of his hopes if not by drink, and he left government almost entirely in the hands of his cousin, Adam 'Eta' Kok, and of the *veldkommandant*, Isaac Read, both of whom appear to have been men of considerable competence and energy.[6] The old clan loyalties that were present in Griqua society may well have reasserted themselves much more fully at this point. One observer wrote at the time that 'national laws are proposed and considered by general gatherings of the heads of the recognised families' and that 'the Kaptyn can veto the attendance of any family representative; and need not give any reason for the act'.[7] Such a view does not accord with the descriptions of other writers or the records — maybe only five years later — of the Griqua *raad*, and its timing is significant. Simultaneously, other manifestations of familial ties were manifest. The families, in particular, tended to settle together — for instance, the Draais at Riet Vlei, the Marais clan on the Mvenyana River or the followers of 'Gamga' Jan Pienaar in the Witteberg, north of Matatiele and this last clan, which had trekked by a different route, returned en bloc to Griqualand West early in the 1870s, where they were to become

105

prominent in the rebellion of 1878.[8] The information is certainly sketchy, and, as that from Philippolis is even more so, it is impossible to be definite on the matter, but the impression is certainly one of increased atomisation of society.

But not everything disintegrated. A few traders began to move into the region, from around 1865–6, and began supplying the Griquas with many of the goods which marked the status of civilised men. Of these men, the most important were the partners of Donald Strachan and G. C. Brisley. Strachan had been living on the Mzimkulu River since before the Griqua advent, and he was a man with deep roots in the country. More than anyone, perhaps, he embodies the ambiguity of status which surrounds racial distinction in South Africa. Grandson of an immigrant from Scotland, he was genetically 'white' and was accepted as such, serving, in the fullness of time, as member of the Cape House of Assembly for East Griqualand.[9] On the other hand, during the late 1860s and early 1870s he became one of the most important figures within Griqua politics, and was appointed both magistrate and *veldkornet* for the Umzimkulu district, the sensitive area where Griqualand bordered on Natal. To add to the difficulty of classifying him, he was a superb linguist, spoke all the Bantu dialects of the area flawlessly, and was accepted as the leader of a 'regiment' of African tribesmen.[10] He was a successful and well-liked trader, who worked on what was then the frontier of the Natal economy among the Griquas, those Africans who were moving towards peasant agriculture and the few whites who had settled so far from their fellows. His partner, Brisley, traded at the *laager*, where he managed to gain much influence over Adam Kok, so that he became Secretary and was able to advance to a considerable extent the interests of the firm, and of himself.[11] But other firms operated in East Griqualand. Balance and Goodliffe, who appear to have been a fairly substantial Natal-based operation, maintained a store at the *laager*, as well as on the fringes of Pondoland.[12] Various other men – Hall, Stafford, Scott – worked for longer or shorter periods on the borderland between the Griquas and the African tribes to the south, and not infrequently ran foul of the Griqua Government.[13] At least one man, John Barker, crossed the Drakensberg with the Griquas, because his experience in Philippolis had convinced him that Griquas meant good business.[14] His decision was echoed by others. Scott wrote that 'whatever faults the Griquas had, they had one good quality for traders; they would buy anything'. He never hoped, however, to persuade them to work for him.[15] Dower, too, commented that the traders did well, although he noted that there were many risks associated with a traffic which had to be conducted almost totally in barter for stock and other agricultural products.[16] The beginnings of the infrastructure of trading activities was not totally beneficial. Prices were ruinously high, even for bread and other foodstuffs, and many Griquas drank considerably from the *canteens* which the traders provided.[17] At times no food was obtainable in the *laager* apart from meat. The luxuries of coffee, tea and sugar, which the Griquas had come to expect as the leavenings of an otherwise monotonous diet, were only obtainable from Natal traders, who made extortionate profits on the bartered deals,[18] but did provide the incentive to drive the Griquas to begin commercial activities which would take the community out of the slough of poverty into which it had descended.

On another level of achievement, the church functioned effectively right through the period of the trek, even though there was no minister from the time, around 1862, when W. B. Philip left them until 1867. The church indeed may well have been one of the major centripetal forces that kept the community together during the troubled era immediately after the trek, as the church deacons maintained regular worship in the *laager*.[19] When visiting clergy arrived, they were surprised and gratified by the size of the congregations, if not at the quality of the accommodation. Edward Twells, first bishop of the Orange Free State, preached to several hundred squatting on their heels in a mud hovel.[20] Solomon, a year later in 1866, considered that the congregations were around 600.[21] A Griqua marriage officer was appointed from among the deacons, although at least some of the young couples preferred to be married by an ordained minister and went to the Wesleyan station at Emfundisweni for the purpose.[22] The Griquas even asked Thomas Jenkins, the missionary there, to come and be their minister, but he refused as such a move would have disastrously complicated the political balance of the region.[23] Insofar as it could without buildings and without a minister, the church organisation flourished, as was to be expected from a strongly congregational community.

An attempt was made to solve the problems consequent upon the lack of an ordained minister by seeing if any of the Griquas was of sufficient standing to be himself the clergyman they desired. Thus in 1867 James Read Jnr. and R. B. Taylor, Congregational ministers from the eastern Cape, came to Nomansland and proceeded to ordain Johannes Bezuidenhout, an old man who had been a deacon of the church since 1845. He was described as 'a man of high character, and very gentle manners, but withal energetic and firm when required'.[24] He was moreover promised support to the extent of £150 a year, but this was never forthcoming, an index of the Griquas' poverty.[25] Bezuidenhout was thus placed in a very difficult situation, and had to spend much of the time on his farms, to the detriment of his pastoral activities. The experiment was therefore not a success, and although Bezuidenhout remained active in the church and was performing marriages for the Griquas many years later,[26] the position in which he was placed made him rather unpopular, for he had to live at a level he could not afford, if he was to fulfil the accepted position of a Griqua minister. The community was therefore happy when in 1869 William Dower, moved up to Nomansland as a stipendiary missionary of the LMS.

The third major achievement of the early period in Nomansland was the expulsion of Nehemiah Moshoeshoe from Matatiele. As the Sotho kingdom expanded and came into conflict with the Boers of the Orange Free State, it had been necessary to discover some further outlet for the growing population. In addition, Nehemiah was one of the ablest of Moshoeshoe's sons, but was debarred from high position because he had been born to one of the lesser wives. He was driven by ambition to attempt to set up a principality of his own. In 1859 he had moved down into Nomansland, where, in much the same way as the Griquas, he hoped to establish hegemony over the primarily Nguni-speaking peoples of the northern and eastern Transkei, bringing them loosely under the aegis of Moshoeshoe, but more directly under his own power.[27] He did not have much physical force directly at his disposal — Sir Walter Currie in 1861 considered he had only 50 fighting men at his back[28] — but he could call on the strength of the mountain chieftains of southern Lesotho, above all Poshuli, which had already been used in raids on the Mpondomise.[29] Although initially they had been friendly,[30] and had various interests in common — Nehemiah later claimed that he had been responsible for clearing the raiding San from the highlands of Nomansland[31] — the Griquas were evidently competing with him for a single niche within the political system of the area. It is thus not surprising that they came into conflict. Grudges between the two parties began during the trek, when Sotho stole much Griqua stock, and flared to life in the early 1860s. 'A regular system of stealing' developed.[32] The Griquas heard rumours that Nehemiah was intriguing with other African chiefs to drive them out.[33] Finally, when war between the Sotho and the Orange Free State broke out in 1865, Nehemiah lost the main bulwark of his position, for the unspoken threat of backing from Lesotho proper was no longer available. Only a very weak push, not even directly aimed at the kraal at Matatiele, was then sufficient to send Nehemiah scuttling back over the mountains.[34]

During this time of disintegration the first moves were made towards the resuscitation of the Griqua community. It had held together through the period of trouble because of the need to preserve unity in face of a large, potentially hostile surrounding population, because of the maintenance of the institutions of Griqua solidarity, of which the church was the most important, because of the brotherhood in arms on the commandos, which might be up to a hundred strong and which were led by an extremely able man, Isaac Read,[35] and because there was no prospect of future wealth elsewhere. Naturally some men dropped out. There was an influx of Griquas into the Herschel district in the north-east Cape, comprising men who had dropped out on the trek.[36] But the solidarity that was maintained was substantial.

Moreover, in the early years in Nomansland the Griqua community became a focus for immigration as it had not been to any degree since about 1840. The source was the same as it had always been, namely the Khoisan (or by now 'coloured') population of the eastern Cape, but the route taken was different. When, during the early 1850s, the Kat River settlement, the largest 'coloured' rural area in the Cape Province, broke up, after an abortive rebellion, many other 'coloured' peasants in the area were also displaced.[37] Numbers of these people moved across the Kei and various communities were established. Smith Pommer's banditti were the most notable of these, but there were others.[38] In the Gatberg (modern Maclear) a group which constituted the *raad* of Freemansland, led by a man named Esau du Plooy, was the most organised. By the mid-1870s they were a community of 354 persons, generally prosperous and well thought of by Europeans.[39] They maintained themselves as an entity independent of the Griquas,[40] but other men moved in to the Griqua orbit, drawn by the prospects of security and land which the Captaincy offered. There they seem to have flourished and to have been considered by Europeans, in a way that is reminiscent of the old Griqua–Bastard dichotomy, to have been the most progressive section of the population.[41] On the other hand they found it difficult to be accepted immediately into full citizenship, and there were periodic complaints, stemming mainly from Titus Klein – the only 'apprentice' ever to gain any position – that they were not receiving the recognition due to them, in terms of office and so forth.[42] At all events, they were an important element in the renaissance of Griqua fortunes.

From around 1868 there were many symptoms that the community was recovering. Adam Kok III himself began to overcome the melancholia which had afflicted him during the previous few years[43] and matured into a well-loved, kindly but very firm old man. The Government was reorganised and became much more bureaucratic, efficient and depersonalised than at the time when Adam 'Eta' Kok had dispensed most of the business 'from the top of a wall, or sitting under the lee side of a house', even if 'with care, promptitude and impartiality'.[44] Economically, the cattle, sheep and herdsmen were becoming accustomed to the peculiarities of the veld, and there were the beginnings of profitable activities beyond the realm of pure agriculture, particularly wood-cutting and transport-riding. It was even felt necessary, in view of the shortage of cash within Nomansland, to issue a paper currency, and 10,000 pound notes were printed, but never issued as the money famine ended.[45] A regular postal service with its own stamp was instituted between Mount Currie and Natal.[46] This period also saw a concerted push to gain some degree of hegemony over the

African tribes among whom the Griquas lived, and thus to fulfil the Griqua dream of being aristocrats above a community of their servants. Finally, in 1872, the old *laager* was finally abandoned and the community as a whole moved down to the new site of Kokstad, on a bluff above the Mzimhlava River.

It was often considered that the resuscitation of Griqua fortunes dated from 1868, in consequence of a spectacularly successful cattle raid conducted under the leadership of 'Gamga' Jan and 'Rooi' Jan Pienaar.[47] This raid, which realised a haul of around 1,700 cattle, 300 horses and 6–8,000 sheep, penetrated into Lesotho as far as the Maletsunyane, within 25 kilometres of Morosi's stronghold, and was successful because the stock had been sent up into the mountains under the protection of small boys, for safety against the Free State commandos then operating. But it cannot have been a turning point in Griqua economic life, for that was based as much on agriculture as on cattle, and, moreover, the two main leaders of the commando were notorious for their later poverty.[48] The causes are wider than a fortuitous haul of cattle and sheep.

A deeper explanation may perhaps be seen when the Commissioners of Enquiry into the Rebellion in Griqualand East, who included Donald Strachan, wrote that after 1869 'matters took a turn for the better. Wheat became an article of regular production; stock seemed to be acclimatised; and the collection of taxes was more systematically arranged.'[49] The Commissioner explained:

> An industrious farmer, like Janse, who began with the spade a few years ago, has become an owner of stock, wagon &c., and is reckoned a well-to-do member of the community. Philander Gous gives the following account of the industrial issues last year 'I sowed 10 muids of wheat, reaping 113, for which I got from 33s. to 40s. per muid. I also reaped 30 bags of mealies, selling them at 12s.; 4 sacks of beans at 3s. the bucket, riding transport as work permits. Besides my riding horse, I have five brood mares, from which I make something. My cattle number about thirty, and I possess a wagon, plough etc. . . . My family does the farm work.'[50]

This wealth was despite a heavy drought in 1878, the year for which he gave his account. Although, no doubt, Janse and Philander Gous were among the most prosperous of the Griquas at that time, so that the commission picked them out for notice, they were not unique. After the 1878 rebellion and the depredations of the Sotho in the Gun War of 1880–1, many individuals claimed well over £100 for lost stock, although, especially on the latter occasion, much stock must have been brought into *laager*, safe from the insurgents.[51] The losses of others show evidence of the beginnings of rural service industries, such as the well-stocked carpenter's shop belonging to Jan Bergover, ex-Treasurer of the Griqua Government,[52] or the forge in possession of Nicholas Pienaar, situated on the

110

Klein Mzimvubu River, well away from the centre of settlement.[53] *Kaptyn*
Nicholas Waterboer, who was an avid carpenter, bewailed the lack of interest in
the craft which he found in Nomansland when he visited it in 1872, but he
seems to have had a certain number of imitators.[54]

The land in Nomansland, on which the prosperity was dependent, was given
out from 1867, although, of course, each Griqua had prospected the land on
which he wished to farm before the main distribution. By right a 3,000 acre farm
was due to any man who had made the trek from Philippolis or to anyone who
might be admitted as a burgher of the Captaincy. An annual quit rent of £2 was
charged. The land registry system was accurate and efficient, duplicates of the
deeds being kept. Adam Kok had had forms printed in Cape Town before any
distribution of farms had been undertaken. They were all headed by a lion
passant and it was hoped they would prevent the chaos which had arisen in
Philippolis in consequence of a much more haphazard system of requests. The
Government employed a surveyor to designate the lands for each farm and
expected Kok to sign the diagrams which he produced, although Kok was not
thereby liable in any way in case of disputes in consequence of faulty surveying.[55]
In fact, the system worked remarkably well. Some 343 land grants were issued
under the Griqua Government, and only three of these had to be cancelled at a
later date, because they overlapped with previous grants, while one more was
withdrawn because the land in question was discovered to be over the border of
the country.[56] The farms were not always occupied in person. Many Griquas
seem to have preferred to extract rent, probably mainly in kind, from an African
population of 'squatters', in an activity which has many parallels throughout
South Africa, particularly in Natal, where it was one of the main sources of
European income at that time.[57] On the other hand, absenteeism was not
allowed. A law passed on 7 December 1870 propounded 'That all proprietors of
farms [*plaatsen*] who are now absent from the country shall before the 1st of
January 1872 personally come to the country to claim their rights. And in case
they do not come within that time, then shall their farms revert to the Government and become government farms.'[58] Notice of this decision was published
and sent to several areas including Griqualand West, to which many Griquas had
returned hoping to benefit from the discovery of diamonds.[59] Moreover, it was
acted upon. Sixteen farms were confiscated under the order, and only one man
known to be away was able to maintain his rights, because he had left one of his
relatives as an agent in the country.[60] The growing agrarian prosperity thus had a
sound basis in legal fact.

The Government had to do more than arrange the system of land rights to
promote the prosperity of the Griqua people. It had to make some provision for
the husbanding of the country's resources. Specifically this meant timber. Away

to the east, towards Riet Vlei and the Mzimkulu River, the wooded valley sides
were covered with large strands of yellow wood and stinkwood. Regulations were
promulgated in 1870 by which the forests could only be exploited under licence
from the *Boschmeester*, Witboi Draai. He was to give a lease on 40 yards radius
of woodland at a rate of 10s. a month, was to charge 6d. a foot for stinkwood and
1s. 6d. a foot for yellow wood, and would take half the proceeds as his salary.
Various parts of the forest were to be left completely uncut, and any saw-pits
left in the bush were to be auctioned off by the Government.[61] During the first
five months of the year, licences were given out to thirteen Griquas, including
several for more than one month and one, to Gert van Rooyen, for a whole year.[62]
This arrangement seems to have worked fairly well, despite complaints that
various individuals were monopolising the forest.[63] Draai himself was a capable
local administrator, for four years later he successfully fulfilled his commission
from the *raad* to prevent the entry of cattle from Natal, and so halted the spread
of Radwater sickness.[64] On some levels the Griquas were able to rule their
country effectively and strictly.

On certain other matters which fell within its competence, the Griqua Government was far less successful. Nomansland's communications remained particularly bad. Mount Currie lies some 150 kilometres from the nearest port at St
John's, which was scarcely in operation before the annexation of the Transkei,
and rather further from Pietermaritzburg and Durban, which were the metrop-
olises to which it looked. Although the country was relatively easy to traverse in
a waggon, being free from deep ravines, the roads were abysmal, merely tracks
through the *veld*, worn down by the passage of wheels. When it rained it was
most profitable to avoid them, but in the dry season they had the advantage of
being free from dust. Still they added considerably to the cost of transport up
from the coast.[65] Perhaps the Griquas had exhausted their energies in building
the great mountain road over Ongeluks Nek, but they scarcely seem to have
improved the transport system of Nomansland at all. Moreover the rivers provided considerable obstacles for transport. There were flat-bottomed ferries set
up on the Mzimkulu and Bisi rivers, and the ferryman at the former, at least, was
a government nominee, but at other rivers, such as the Mzimhlava, the Mzimvubu
and the Kinira, flowing through the centre or west of the country, travellers had
to rely on the traditional fords, or drifts, which could cause them much incon-
venience.[66] The infrastructure of commercialism was slow to appear.

Still, a fair number of trading enterprises did set themselves up in the country.
Some were run by Griquas, several of whom tried to make money riding transport
to Natal, but these enterprises, which were generally undercapitalised and may
well have found difficulty obtaining credit in Pietermaritzburg, came to nought.[67]
Much more of the trade was done by whites who moved up from Natal. They

were subject to licensing by the Griquas, at a rate, after 1870, of £15 *per annum*.[68] In 1872 some twelve licences were issued, while by the next year Balance and Goodliffe were operating three stores, one at Mount Currie and two in the region of Matatiele, among the Sotho, Tlhokwa and Mfengu.[69] This tally excluded the most powerful of the trading interests, namely the firm of Strachan & Co., which, as it included the Secretary to the Government and the magistrate of Umzimkulu district among its partners, was evidently immune from such indignities as licences. It was, however, in a very strong position within the country, holding monopolies for such profitable commodities as guns, gunpowder and shot and maintaining power over the drift in the Mzimkulu River, the only way into Nomansland, to the intense annoyance of its competitors.[70] Such was its power that at least one trader, J. P. Scott, decided to cease operations in the region when he ran foul of Brisley, the Secretary, while trading rivalries were probably of great importance in the expulsion of T. O. Hall by the Griquas in 1872.[71] Such was the power accruing from control over the Griqua polity.

That polity was still in part the same body that had ruled Philippolis, but as its tasks and some of its leading personalities had changed, so had various facets of the way it operated. Moreover, the comparative wealth of evidence that has survived allows a far more detailed picture to be built up. Not only can the workings of various sections of the Government be seen in the records which they left behind but there was, apparently for the first time, a written constitution which gives the rules by which administration was supposed to be carried on.[72]

At the head of the Captaincy, the *Kaptyn*'s power had not diminished. Adam Kok III had grown older and had mellowed, with the earlier impetuosity driven out by the pressures of this thirty-year reign. If somewhat embittered at times, he was still basically a kindly man, who left a good impression on everyone he met.[73] Nevertheless, he maintained a powerful hold over the political life of the community, so that Dower considered the institutions for protest and expression to be but safety valves, behind which Kok operated.[74] After the death of Isaac Read in 1868,[75] the *Kaptyn* seems to have carried on the government much more personally than before, although his cousin, Adam 'Eta' Kok, still occasionally acted as *Provisionaal Kaptyn*, as he had done for some time previously.[76] But there was no rivalry between the two old men, and the power that they exercised over the community can be seen from the decree of 1870 that the *Kaptyn* 'should have the highest power in Griqualand'; have the power to appoint or dismiss officials; and be a necessary signatory to all laws and capital sentences, while being able to diminish or remit any punishments imposed in either criminal or civil cases. Griqualand might be a limited monarchy, but the executive power evidently remained strongly in Adam Kok's hands.

At the centre of government there were two main forces below the *Kaptyn*, namely the Secretary and the various *raaden*. They were, of course, intertwined, as the Secretary had an *ex officio* position on the *raaden*, but they seem to have fulfilled different functions and may be analysed separately. The secretaryship was kept in the hands of an outsider, who could not hope to influence the internal policies of the Captaincy, and thus followed a consistent pattern established at the demise of Hendrick Hendricks. Moreover, the stature of the Secretary was diminished by the appointment of a *raadsclerk*, one Wentzel Heemro, who handled the council minutes and so forth,[77] and by the generally increased literacy among the Griquas.[78] But G. C. Brisley was certainly an important figure in the administration of the Captaincy. His power with regard to his fellow whites was crucial. His role in diplomatic negotiations was of high importance, taking over, as it were, the erstwhile role of the missionaries and conducting the correspondence with the Cape Government, with Natal and with their local officials. He might even, right at the end of the Captaincy, treat with the Cape on behalf of the Griquas, but without any contact with them. Certainly he performed most of the routine tasks of the Captaincy, dealing with both internal and outgoing correspondence, but no direct power can safely be attributed to him.

With the *raaden*, things were rather different. There, at any rate, the apparatus of power was readily apparent. There were, in fact, two distinct if overlapping bodies normally grouped under the head of the Griqua *raad*. In the first place, the *uitvoerende* (executive) *raad* consisted of four members, appointed and chaired by the *Kaptyn*. The powerful men who formed this council, Jan Bergover, Jan Jood, Lucas van der Westhuis, Stoffel Vesasie, were the respected and powerful leaders of the Griqua community. They met irregularly, controlled the finance of the country, and were responsible for carrying out the various decisions which might be taken. They had *ex officio* seats on the other, the *wetgevende* (legislative) *raad*. The rest of this body, whose size and frequency of meeting fluctuated — it normally met every six months and had about six non-official members — was elected by all burghers over the age of twenty.[79] The elections themselves, which occurred every three years, were not conducted by ballot, but rather 'the Field Cornets called all the burghers together on a certain day, and they talked and came to the conclusion that certain individuals would be the best and these were elected'.[80] The participation does not seem to have been very high, but perhaps the mode of procedure explains this. Those who could not agree with the locally dominant party, or could not expect that their voice would be heard in the discussions, may well not have bothered to attend. At any rate, voting figures, which survive only for four of the six wards at but one election, show that the participation ran at about 33 per cent, a low, but not impossible, figure.[81] Thus the systems of election and candidature were weak.

114

On one occasion the *uitvoerende raad* had to cancel the election in two of the six constituencies, in one case because a *veldkornet* had been elected, which was apparently illegal, and in another because the same man had been chosen for two different wards.[82] Significantly, in one of the two districts, the man whom the *raad* suggested should be elected was rejected.[83]

The meetings of the *wetgevende raad* were evidently convivial affairs. The promise of payment for members and the threat of fine for non-attendance would appear not to have been necessary to secure regular attendance, although they might have increased the use of 'substitutes' when absence was unavoidable.[84] The proceedings were opened with a prayer, and then there usually followed a speech from the *Kaptyn*, outlining the business which was to be discussed. A fairly typical example of the matters under consideration may be taken from the meeting in June 1871. It lasted three days, and, after welcoming those two members who had recently been elected, they proceeded to discuss the payment of *raadsmen* who might be absent on Government business, the report of the debt commission — a perennial and unsettled matter which was to leave the Government some £600 in debt in 1874[85] — two applications before the *raad*, one for the payment of debt, which was held over, and one for 'payment' (what for, is unclear), which was refused. There then occurred what must have been a major argument, perhaps explaining why this meeting lasted a day longer than usual, in which it was finally decided that 'the posts of officials who are appointed by the *Kaptyn* or *raad* members are not inheritable, but the post of *Kaptyn* is a heritable post'. This compromise solution, which did not lay down how the succession should be determined, touched on the major arguments within the community at the time, but did not settle them.[86] There then followed various small matters, concerned with the administration of the Africans under Griqua rule, on which the magistrate of Umzimkulu wanted guidance, and with the sale of land from one European to another. The meeting then broke up, not assembling again for four months.

Throughout the meetings, the *raadsmen* were liberally served with tea and coffee, bought on the Government account from the local traders, and not always paid for:[87]

The Deputies were hospitably entertained at Government expense during the session. Its length depended on the size of the animal slaughtered. When the beef gave out, the House rose. No beef, no business, was the unwritten, but standing rule of this Assembly. It was a simpler and more effective extinguisher to Parliamentary oratory than our modern closure. The cooking operations for these '*Achtbare Heeren*' were carried on close to the House of Parliament, and the big pot so placed that members while in session could see the progress of the operations and inhale grateful odours, as an earnest of the coming feast.

Old Piet Draai made frequent visits to the kitchen to light his pipe. He was admitted to be the best judge of the earliest moment when the beef was eatable. When Piet's voice was heard proclaiming the joyful news 'Kerls de kos is gaar', 'Gentlemen the beef is cooked', the house rose with a stampede. These Griqua Parliamentary dinners were held much after the primitive fashion which obtained in England in the days of good King Alfred. The simplicity of manners saved the little state manifold needless costs in the way of crockery, cutlery and napery.[88]

Dower's description of the style of the Griqua parliamentary proceedings may not be totally accurate. If the *raad* had concern only for its stomach, it would never have reduced the frequency of its sittings or the number of its members,[89] nor would it have voted not to pay itself for the emergency session of September 1871.[90] Contrary to Dower's claim, reasonable minutes do survive for the last five years of the Captaincy, and the *raad* could move with considerable speed and efficiency when necessary, as in 1871 when relations with the Bhaca to the west completely broke down, or in 1874 when the British took over the administration of the country. But the atmosphere of the meetings must have been much as Dower described.

What is unfortunately difficult to discover is the relationship of the *raad* members to their constituents, and thus the position of the body within the total framework of Griqua society. Dower considered that

The appearance of political power satisfied the ambitions of the Commons, except in the cases of a few fiery spirits among them. The *Volksraad* gave the opportunity for talk; and talk soothed all grievances and healed nearly all wounds. Kok's policy was to retain the real power in his own hands and he manoeuvred so as to give his policy practical effect. To this task he brought all his exceptional tact, ingenuity and resourcefulness. Occasionally there were storms in the tea-pot, a political crisis, but never a change of ministry.[91]

Perhaps he was right. Perhaps the Griqua *raad* was nothing but a safety valve, to prevent the community blowing itself apart under the pressures of Griqua discontents. Certainly there were enough of these. 'Suspicious, proud and tetchy, a Griqua without a grievance would indeed be an anomaly.'[92] But recent anthropology would seem to suggest that all councils, even those that on the surface seem valueless, mere talk, have important functions, either as a forum for political competition on the local level, or as a means of increasing the feelings of solidarity among its members and the groups they represent. Obviously, councils

116

frequently tend to oscillate between these poles, as their particular tasks differ, and thus there would be a fluctuation between the consensus that could be achieved when it became necessary to present a common face to the subjects of the *raad*, and the wild oppositions that would occur when matters of political importance to the members were under consideration.[93] As the Griqua *raaden* seem to have behaved consistently with such a model, so far as one can judge without detailed analysis of the proceedings, being harsh and united towards Africans, Europeans, or poor, kinless Griquas, but being indecisive and competitive as regards the problems of internal Griqua politics, so it may be assumed that they were more than sops to the sensibilities of important men, but rather were of real importance within the community as a whole.

Below the *Kaptyn* and the *raad* there were a variety of local officials. In Nomansland separation of powers seems to have developed between the leaders of the local community, the *veldkornets*, who were concerned with such matters as the collection of taxes, the administration of African locations, the holding of elections, and the conduct of war, and who were elected by the local community to serve particular and definite districts, and the judicial arm of the Government, the magistrates. These latter were at times concerned with the administration of the outlying districts of the country, only dubiously under Griqua control. Thus Adam 'Eta' Kok and his two sons, Adam 'Muis' and Lodewyk, served in quick succession at Matatiele.[94] On the other hand, at the centres of settlement, at Mount Currie and at Umzimkulu, there were permanent magistrates, whose duties were totally judicial. Thus, when Lodewyk Kok was appointed at Mount Currie in 1870, he was ordered to sit two days a week, to deal with all forms of civil and criminal cases and with the issuing of licences. Witnesses and those who arrested thieves were to be paid costs, and the administration was to be assisted by a clerk and a *Schafmeester*. The running expenses of the magistracy were considerable, but in a period of 10 months a profit of £30 was made, on a turnover of £310.[95]

There was at least one further judicial office. The position of the *vrederegter* (Justice of the Peace) is ambiguous, but it seems to have been a under-magistracy and was, for instance, held by Coenraad Windvogel, previously the Secretary to the Government in Philippolis, at a salary of £50 a year.[96] Similarly, the shadowy *gerigtshof*, which was composed of a *magistraat*, a *veldkornet* and a *vrederegter*,[97] cannot be given a precise place within the legal structure of East Griqualand, although, tentatively, it might be considered to be a substitute for the *raad* in cases of moderate importance in the distant parts of the territory.

In general the courts seem to have been well and fairly conducted, both at the local level and by the *raad*, which was concerned with cases either on appeal or of considerable political importance. Thus they investigated cases of robbery, murder, rape and adultery, without favour, as well as others of lesser importance.

117

They imposed, primarily, fines and corporal punishments, as 'we had a little lock-up, but our prisoners ever ran away'.[98] The great were not spared. 'Rooi' Jan Pienaar, the *veldkommandant*, was once ordered to pay for a horse which he had commandeered on Government business from one of the African chiefs and then lost,[99] while two relatives of the *Kaptyn*, Willem and Jan Kok, were sentenced to three months hard labour in irons and 25 *slagen* (stripes) for the theft of three horses.[100] Marais's summing up of the various court cases, that 'substantial justice seems generally to have been done', remains a very fair assessment of Griqua legal proceedings.

A large part of the work which the judicial and local officials had to do was concerned with the administration of the African population which came under Griqua rule. This had to be undertaken in concert with the task of actually imposing authority over the various African tribes. Initially this was only achieved satisfactorily with regard to the Bhaca and Hlangweni of Umzimkulu and Mount Currie districts and, to a lesser extent, the Sotho around Matatiele. Even in these cases the Griquas were caught in the tangle of African rivalries which stretched back to the Mfecane and lasted until the end of the century. Thus the various interspersed clans of Bhaca and Hlangweni, living mainly in the east of Nomansland and towards Natal, were traditionally at loggerheads. The Griquas found themselves allied to the Hlangweni side of the dispute, primarily because of the long-standing relationship between Smith Pommer, the former Kat River rebel who was managing to insert himself into the ruling clique of the Griquas, and Sidoi, one of the Hlangweni chiefs who had been expelled from Natal in the late 1850s.[101] Moreover, the Griquas could rely on the chief of the other major section of the tribe, Fodo, primarily because they had helped him to defeat a challenge from his brother, Nondabula.[102] These two men remained loyal to the Griquas in virtue of the support which they received which was of vital importance in maintaining their positions within the political systems which were most vital to them.

Achieving a similar relationship with the Bhaca chiefs was considerably more difficult, because the Griquas could not provide sufficient incentives. Basically, therefore, the Griquas attempted to divide and rule, but although the tribe divided frequently this did not make it any more tractable.[103] Rather the leaders of the Bhaca proved a considerable embarassment to the Griquas. Thiba, officially a regent, would not cooperate in the vital matter of paying taxes,[104] and when the Griquas backed his nephew, Nomtsheketshe — who, to complicate matters further, was not even the rightful heir — in his bid to gain control over the tribe, Thiba soon fell so completely foul of the Griqua authorities that he had to flee with all his cattle and followers over the river into Natal. This caused a diplomatic furore, as Natal, not unnaturally, did not view the immigration of a

118

sizeable tribe of Africans into its territory with relish.[105] Nomtsheketshe, however, did not remain quiet, despite the debt which he obviously owed the Griquas.
Rather he was accused of having condoned witchcraft and in consequence was
driven out of Nomansland,[106] for various standards had to be imposed by the
Griquas if they were to give any credibility to their claim to be civilised. Nevertheless, many of the Bhaca who had been among the following of these two
chiefs appear to have remained in Nomansland, as Griqua subjects.[107]

In general, however, the Griquas were able to rule Nomansland with remarkably little difficulty. This was mainly for four reasons. In the first place, they
were obviously more formidable than any African tribe on its own, and the
Transkei was sufficiently split between various factions and subtribes to make
large-scale alliance against the Griquas impossible. Secondly, the Griquas were
moderately astute in their handling of these factional differences, so that some
at least of the African tribes held to the Griquas in order to use them against
other Africans. Thirdly, the Griquas controlled what was by the 1860s the only
unoccupied land in the area, and thus had a valuable asset with which the loyalties of landless men could be secured. Fourthly, the duties which the Griquas
imposed on those who came under their rule were far from heavy, although they
were vital to the Griquas' survival in Nomansland. Thus military service was
scarcely onerous, especially as it was frequently directed against those who were
the enemies of the militia itself. It was perhaps a greater strain on the loyalties of
the Africans when they were forbidden to indulge in what were potentially
highly lucrative cattle raids.[108] Thus the Griquas had little difficulty in compen-
sating for their own lack of numbers, for all that African troops do not seem ever
to have been as effective in the field as the Griquas themselves.

The Griquas also felt a duty to impose a code of laws more in accord with the
ways of the Cape Colony — of Christian civilisation as they saw it — than with
the traditional systems of the tribes they ruled. In part this was to avoid the
taunt of savagery which was being hurled at them by Natalians who coveted
their farms, but as against this the Griquas had a long history of imitating white
ways of government. Adam Kok realised that the imposition of new laws might
strain the legal competence of his state beyond the limit, and initially, virtually
all the judicial functions remained with the chiefs, only gradually moving over to
the courts run by the Griquas at the centre of the Captaincy. It was announced
that murder would be made a capital offence well in advance of the actual
implementation of the promulgation. The major crime that the Griquas were
concerned to stamp out was the practice of 'smelling out' for witchcraft. As this
had been an integral part of the system of social control, such affairs were of
considerable moment.[109] Although large-scale theft was increasingly brought
under the jurisdiction of the Griquas — who had, of course, always been prepared

to bring chiefs to their own justice when they considered it expedient — the routine running of affairs in the locations remained in the hands of Africans. Thus local customs as to marriage, land tenure and so forth (of which the Griquas were ignorant) might be maintained, and the expensive use of interpreters, who were necessary in the Griqua courts, was obviated.[110] Disputes between Griqua and African, however, were always dealt with by the Griqua judiciary. Despite this they by no means invariably resulted in the verdict going to the Griqua party, as the most prominent officials on government business might be arraigned for misuse of their powers.[111] There was even an African chief, Mosi Lipheana, who was dignified by the title of *veldkornet*, primarily because he had among his entourage an Irishman by the name of Paddy O'Reilly, who could conduct the business of that office,[112] but in general the local officials were Griquas who attempted to use the prestige of their rank to maintain order in difficult border areas.[113]

Last and most important, the Africans under Griqua rule were required to pay a hut tax, variously reported as 5s. or 7s. 6d. per hut. By 1874, approximately 43 per cent of Griqua revenue came from this source,[114] enabling any form of Government to be carried on. Indeed the Captaincy's escape from debt, which had been nearly accomplished by the time of the British take-over, was largely in consequence of the hut tax, which might be paid in kind, if no cash was available. For non-payments, individuals might be driven out, but the amount of resistance to the Griqua authorities was small. Only Thiba ever raised major objections and even those were not so much against the principle of paying taxes as against the Government he was paying. Most of the Africans in Nomansland were immigrants, and many must have paid such taxes before, whether in the Cape Colony or in Natal, and so became accustomed to such practices.

The settlements upon which these taxes were levied were almost invariably designated locations, upon which there was a certain amount of pressure from land-hungry Griquas, who may well have hoped to raise income from rents to the same Africans. More than anyone it was the *Kaptyn* himself who contained this pressure,[115] probably because he was more aware of the need for the Griqua nation to placate those among whom they lived than were many of his subjects. Africans who lived on Griqua farms might be expelled by the owner, but interlopers into locations other than their own suffered similarly.[116] Only the Griquas' poverty and their carelessness with regard to the movements of their subjects mitigated a pattern of aristocratic life.[117]

As well as administering the African populations which were already under their control, the Griqua Government was concerned to increase its sway, particularly towards the west. There, in the districts of Mount Fletcher and Mount Frere, there lived a variety of tribes, many of which only moved into the area in

1868, when Sir Peregrine Wodehouse was concerned to reduce the pressure on the Witteberg Reserve in Herschel district on the borders of Lesotho.[118] With these the Griquas had relatively little difficulty, but with the much longer resident Bhaca under Makaula there was frequent trouble, primarily concerned with the theft of stock by and from Griqua subjects who lived on the borders of the two territories. The most notable of these was an Mfengu known as Ncukana.[119] These troubles finally escalated into war during 1871, when the Griqua *raad*, at an emergency session, considered it necessary to declare war on Makaula.[120] The blame for this was, obviously, disclaimed by both sides, and they both managed to persuade their missionaries of the justice of their cause. William Dower wrote that

> A Kaffir tribe lying on our southern border has been making frequent raids into Griqua territory, killing, burning and stealing and, as it turns out now, all with a view to provoke hostilities. Capt. Kok sent once and again a deputation or commission of peace, but without effect. I had hoped that an outbreak might be prevented but all efforts in that direction failed. Capt. Kok did not call out his commando before several of his subjects had been killed and several huts burnt down and a quantity of stock stolen, chiefly belonging to the Basutoo residing under Adam Kok's rule.[121]

Charles White, his opposite number with the Bhaca, thought differently, claiming that 'Makaula says it is because he stopped the stealing of cattle from Natal and sent them back that Adam Kok has sent his army laying his country waste'.[122]

At all events the Griquas were quickly successful. The *raad* had appointed 'Rooi' Jan Pienaar as *kommandant*. He was a veteran of the battles against the Boers in the 1840s and had been one of the leading figures in raids against the Sotho in the early days after the trek, although Dower somewhat scathingly described him as possessing 'all the characteristics of a Griqua – an expert horseman, a crack shot, built in the prodigality of nature, amazingly self-possessed, imperious, haughty, dignified, proud and penniless – "a gentleman of broken means" '.[123] His command, consisting only of those Griqua burghers living in the two westernmost wards and of Sotho and Mfengu auxiliaries from the same area, was soon able to make their considerably superior armaments and mobility tell, and within a week had driven Makaula back to the Tina River in Mpondomise country and captured large quantities of cattle. They burned many Bhaca huts, took many Bhaca prisoner and killed, so they claimed, fifty men for the loss of one Griqua.[124] Makaula was soon suing for peace, which was granted with a few conditions. He applied to become a Griqua subject, as did two of the major chiefs established to the west of Nomansland in Mount Fletcher district.[125] The strength of Griqua arms had been fully demonstrated and the hope of establishing

121

themselves as paramount in the Transkei was evidently more possible, for they had demonstrated their superiority in mobility and firearms, and practice made them militarily, if not numerically, pre-eminent in the region.[126]

The demonstration of the increased strength and confidence of the Griqua community by the early 1870s was the foundation of a town as their capital and the consequent abandonment of the squalid *laager* in which they had lived since their arrival in Nomansland. The site, a very fine one on a bluff overlooking the river Mzimhlava and dominated by the peak of Mount Currie, eight kilometres to the north, was chosen by Adam Kok himself and confirmed by William Dower, who moved down from the *laager* in an attempt to persuade the great body of Griquas to follow him.[127] In the event, the decision was made at a long and exhausting meeting, at which, so Dower relates, the crucial speech was made by 'Gamga' Jan Pienaar.

> He was a typical Griqua, not of mixed parentage, but of the bluest of blue Griqua blood. He was very slightly built, yellow in colour, curly hair and small eyes evidently innocent of work. This man formerly lived in the lap of delights, but now he was in sore straits, vexed with lawyers and harassed with debt, yet he held himself with the air of an aristocrat, was high in the hearts of the people and ranked as a 'groot mensch'. As he spoke, a commetje of tea or coffee was put in his hand, while with the other he gesticulated to give emphasis to his words. He waxed long and eloquent on the merits of the site, and the excellence of the water supply. 'Besides has not this young missionary come on the recommendation of their friend? [Almost certainly Edward Solomon.] Had they not abundance of timber in their own forests, stones in their veld, bricks for making, and grass for cutting? Griquas! think shame of yourselves to hesitate. You are not Kaffirs, you are not children, your blood is not turned to buttermilk; arise and build, possess your heritage, and quit you like men.'
>
> At this final outburst, with an excited gesture, he emptied the contents of the commetje down the neck of another 'groot mensch'.[128]

Despite this, it took firm action by the *Kaptyn* actually to motivate the community to move, but in 1872 the Griquas began to shift down the hill from the *laager* to the new town, named Kokstad in his honour.

The town was originally laid out by the Government Surveyor, an Englishman named Edward Barker, with the assistance and advice of William Dower. Aside from the houses of the burghers, buildings in it were particularly important. The first was the 'Palace', the residence and official building of Adam Kok. This building, which formed the core of the town, was mainly erected and carpentered by Nicholas Waterboer, an obsessive wood-worker who had come from Griqualand

122

West for a few months during the height of the disputes over the ownership of the diamond fields.[129] The second major building was the church, a fine solid building with a tower which still dominates the centre of Kokstad. This was in fact the first building in the town, for its foundations were let in, mainly by voluntary effort, while most of its congregation still lived in the *laager*. By 1879, with the help of the money which the church possessed from the sale of the old land in Philippolis before the trek, it was fully built and furnished, seating 800 people and sporting stained-glass windows.[130]

Most of the houses, however, were much more crudely built, mainly of sod. This material, which was firm, strong and weather-proof when whitewashed and well maintained, also served to enclose the *erven*, at 9d. a yard. Although the *erven* were large, around an acre each, the houses were small and usually fairly scantily furnished. By 1874 there were about fifty of them, and many other men had erected a wagon shed on their *erf*, to house them when they came in for church or to transact whatever business brought them to the town.[131] The furnishings and property can, perhaps, best be seen from the inventory which was made of the possessions of Stoffel Vesasie, one of the richest men among the Griquas and a member of the *raad*, after his house was destroyed in the rebellion of 1878. He claimed that in total they were worth £107 and consisted of his own and his wife's clothing – shirts, trousers, petticoats, skirts and shoes – four chairs, a table, an iron bedstead, a mattress and various chests, nine cups, six plates, knives and forks, five pots, excluding one for making soap, a tripod, a ladle, a cheese-mould, a roasting pan and a tin for baking bread, a water vat and various tools – a broom, two spades, four picks, a chopper and a chopping block, a wagon jack, a vice, a branding iron and a shovel.[132] The furnishings were simple and not luxurious, but suited to a farming existence.

The town itself was laid out in a grid of fairly narrow streets, with a large square in the middle, between Adam Kok's palace and the church complex which included the school and the manse. However, it did not include any public parks or trees. When asked why not, Kok showed that, to his mind at least, the progress which had been made in the last years was by no means complete, although it was substantial and definite. He replied in amazement:

What, General! a *Park* and a *Garden*, like that I saw in Cape Town? General, you don't know this country, nor do you know the weaknesses of our people. Garden! Park! Oh, no; the trees would bring the birds, the birds would eat the ripe corn, and we would have no bread! The shade, too, would be so nice; my people would want to sit under it all day long, instead of cultivating their farms, and by-and-by they would be beggars. No, General! we must 'wacht een beetje' for these nice things.[133]

CHAPTER 9

ANNEXATION, REBELLION AND DISINTEGRATION

In 1925, the resident magistrate of Kokstad described the descendants of the followers of the man after whom his town had been named in these terms:

> They are now town dwellers, and although more tenacious of their town even than they were of their farms, I have no doubt that economic pressure will bring about a steady decrease of such holdings.[1] As a class they are now poverty stricken. Many suffer from malnutrition and often starvation owing to unemployment, drink and generally thriftlessness . . . The men are employed in brick-making, masonry and bricklaying, carpentering, painting, leather-working, gardening and as waiters, shop boys etc. With few exceptions they are unreliable, ever seeking fresh work and new employers . . . Their social life is one of bickering and quarrels and it is impossible to secure a united front with progress and the improvement of their conditions as the object in view . . . This is seen more especially in church affairs, where they divide themselves into three distinct church bodies . . . Apart from the status acquired by local ownership, they do not possess, except in their own imagination, any higher status than the ordinary coloured person. Indeed while a coloured person is not a prohibited person under the liquor laws, the Griqua is.
>
> In conclusion I may say that in my opinion the Griqua as a separate class are doomed to extinction. Melting away of race and dispersion set in many years ago. They will gradually become absorbed into the great coloured class that is ever on the increase in this country.[2]

It was not a happy picture for the half-centenary of the Griquas' town, but it was by and large accurate. True, many of the Griquas who have become dispersed have found niches that suit their historical experience elsewhere. The first leader of the Coloured Representative Council was the great-grandson of a chairman of the Griqua *raad*, but he did not call himself a Griqua.[3] But the community at Kokstad was dead by the 1920s and had been dead for nearly fifty years, ever since the twin blows of the loss of independence in 1874 and the rebellion of 1878 first broke the will and the capacity of the Griquas to resist the pressures

124

of the expanding white society, and then splintered the community when a group attempted, with insubstantial and abortive violence, to challenge it.

At the centre of the Captaincy, Adam Kok was growing old. He passed his sixtieth birthday in 1871 and the weight of thirty-five years rule was affecting him. Moreover, he had no designated successor, for his wife had borne him no children. Her one son and three daughters were by her previous husband, Adam's elder brother Abraham, who had briefly been *Kaptyn* in 1835.[4] Within the Captaincy, then, the various forces began to coalesce in a way which had not happened since that succession crisis thirty years previously in Philippolis. On both occasions the lines of cleavage were remarkably similar. Whereas in the 1830s there had been those who wished to remain cattle raiders, so in the 1870s there were the wild young men, who did not have farms, who appreciated their position as aristocrats in the Transkei and who, in large part, had grown up in East Griqualand, or who had joined the Griquas after the trek. These men looked to Adam 'Muis' Kok, who was a relation — if not very close — of the *Kaptyn*, and might thus make a true hereditary claim. The real standard-bearer, however, was Smith Pommer, one of only two new immigrants who had really forced themselves on the political élite of the captaincy and had gained political office.[5] On the other side were the old men, who ran the Captaincy from their seats on the *raad*, and whose experience at Philippolis had taught them the values of caution, conciliation and the maintenance of a civilised image with the colonial powers. Their candidate was Jan Jood, whose position as a leading *raadsman* was enhanced by his marriage to the eldest of Adam Kok's step-daughters. Attempts were made to secure an alliance with the potent name of Waterboer by marrying Jan Jood's daughter to Nicholas Waterboer's eldest son, but this fell through, apparently in consequence of some dark scandal which Dower does not reveal. The controversy smouldered on. 'Had Adam Kok died suddenly at any time between 1869 and 1874, his death would have been the signal for civil strife and would have led to much bloodshed.'[6]

These problems within the Griqua polity were well known to the colonial officials and formed part of their concern to arrive at a suitable arrangement before Adam Kok died, so that bloodshed did not engulf the area. There were, of course, strong pressures for expansion of European sovereignty into Nomansland. Natalians had never fully acquiesced in the Griqua presence in the area, which they coveted, so that relationships between Kokstad and Pietermaritzburg had always been sour. Natal's rulers continually complained that the chaos beyond its borders, which they tended to exaggerate, endangered the security of their domain. Native administrators and colonial politicians tended to classify the groups with whom they had to deal as 'civilised' or 'barbarous', and considered that the normal canons of non-interference did not apply for the latter class. The

Griquas undoubtedly fell into such a position.[7] The Cape authorities, in contrast, had traditionally thought better of the Griquas. When Sir Peregrine Wodehouse attempted to oil the frictions of the Transkei and simultaneously to settle the mass of tribesmen who had been forced into the overcrowded Witteberg Reserve, in the Herschel district, he was prepared to put them under Griqua authority.[8] Generally there had been little contact between the Griquas and the Cape during the years of their establishment in Nomansland, and that little had been cordial. But the pressures for a more forward policy were growing. The strong lobby of eastern province settlers, with the continual land hunger of their kind, were joined by several of the Cape Liberals from the same area, whose politics were based primarily on their trading relationships with the free peasantries building up throughout the east, and by the military and official interest who saw the danger of further outbreaks of war throughout the Transkei and hoped to avoid it by further annexation.[9] This combination led to the appointment of a Select Committee on Native Affairs which travelled round the Transkei during the course of 1872 and noted with concern the internecine chaos apparently endemic in Nomansland, where the Griquas' attempts to assert their authority had been far from complete.[10] In view of the troubled state of the area and the frequent petitions for British protection by the various chiefs and clans, the commissioners recommended that Nomansland should be subjected to the direct authority of British magistrates.[11] The effect of this report, together with the outbreak of a war between two tribes of the western Transkei, strengthened the hand of the expansionists to such an effect that an arch-expansionist, J. M. Orpen, was appointed as magistrate over the Gatberg and over those tribes who had migrated up from the Witteberg Reserve in 1868, and also as British Resident over the whole of Nomansland.

Orpen himself was determined to bludgeon both his superiors and those with whom he had to deal to accept British authority as widely as possible. He had had long experience on the frontiers of South Africa, initially in the employ of the Orange Free State and then as unofficial ambassador to the court of Moshoeshoe on Thaba Bosigo. In the course of this, he had developed a strong partisanship in favour of the Sotho and against the Griquas, whom he considered to be an effete aristocracy, stupidly imposed on the Transkei, filling the niche that ought to be held by the British themselves.[12] He himself had a farm in the Gatberg, from which he had gained much experience of the area he was to administer, and had been a member of the Legislative Assembly at the time when proposals for the establishment of a Resident in Nomansland were being put through. In fact he was one of the leading advocates of such a forward policy and was appointed primarily in consequence of this.

During the first year he spent in Nomansland, Orpen was concerned with

events further west, as he brought the Mpondomisi into the status of British subjects, and renewed the same status for Lehana, Lebenya, Zibi and the Gatberg
people.[13] In June 1874, however, he turned his attention fully to the Griquas,
whom he considered to have been British subjects ever since the agreement which
they were considered to have made with Sir George Grey allowing them to trek
to Nomansland. The ambiguity of the Griquas' status was thus employed to their
considerable disadvantage.[14] Thus on the 24th of the month, Orpen had a meeting with Kok at which each attempted to discover both what the other was thinking and what the legal situation was. Kok appears on this occasion to have made
the mistake of presuming that the question of his dependence lay with the
British — or, at any rate, Orpen's minute of the meeting claimed that he did. Kok
was worried because it seemed difficult for him to conduct his relations with
African tribes, particularly with the Mpondo, because of the uncertainty as to
whether the treaties he had made with them were held to be valid by the British.
He wished for clarification. If the Government considered the Griquas to be
independent, that should be made clear, but if they were British subjects, that
should also be clear and the advantages that were to be gained from that status
should be defined. He had gathered from the Special Commission of two years
previously that it was likely that in the future the Griqua Captaincy would be
brought under the British, but he had been informed that he would be consulted
in that event. Particularly he was concerned that Griqualand, as it was coming to
be called, should never come under Natal. Orpen, naturally, emphasised the
degree of legal subordination which Kok owed to the Cape Government, detailing
the steps by which Kok had come to gain possession of the country subsequent
to its cession by the Mpondo to the British. Given such a lead, he would not turn
back.[15]

Once this conversation had been reported to Cape Town, the Cape Government and the Governor agreed that the extension of control over the Griquas
should occur speedily. Hence in October 1874 Sir Henry Barkly, the Governor,
arrived in Kokstad with Joseph Orpen and proceeded to shock the Griquas by
announcing that 'The Government of the country will for the future be carried
on under instructions by the British Resident, Joseph Millerd Orpen, Esq.'.
Admittedly they attempted to mollify the Griquas by allowing that all present
laws should remain in force, that all current Government officers should retain
their positions and receive their salaries and that titles to land should remain as
they were. The *Kaptyn*, moreover, was to have a position as President of a
Council with undefined powers as to the administration of the area, and would
receive a salary of £1,000 *per annum* both in respect of these duties and in consideration of past services.[16] The consternation of the Griquas was considerable,
not so much because they disapproved of the fact of annexation — there were

many, particularly the *Kaptyn*, who realised that this was inevitable – but because they had not been consulted. They complained that they had had no time for the long process of discussion which would have been essential for them to become reconciled to the transformation:

> The head and front of the offending lay in this, that they had not been consulted. There had been no 'vergaderings', no 'praat', no treaty, no diplomacy. They had been *'taken over like so many cattle or sheep'*. 'They were not livestock' or 'Kaffirs', or 'onbeschafed', or 'helots', but 'Burghers of a State', 'a people', 'a natie'. To the use of all these lofty titles, which, in the more enlightened, excite a smile, they had become thoroughly accustomed, and felt no incongruity in the use of them.

Certainly the Government had meant well, and annexation opened up many new opportunities for all Griquas, but

> These people were blinded by prejudice, ignorance and pride. For months one heard of nothing but the 'oerneeming'. A failure of crops, an untimely frost, a destructive storm, a sudden death, a maternal disappointment, were all, by some of the more ignorant, attributed to the *'oerneeming'*. Appeals to reason, common-sense, or even a prudent use of satire, were always met by the question, 'How would you like to be treated like beasts, and have to change your allegiance by the stroke of a pen, without being asked by your leave?'.[17]

Administratively, there were few difficulties in the immediate aftermath of the take-over, especially after Brisley and Strachan had been to Cape Town early the next year and smoothed over many of the snags in consultation with the Secretary of Native Affairs.[18] It was the feeling of bitterness consequent upon the manner of the end of Captaincy that was to rankle and fester through the next few years.

The aftermath of the take-over of the Griqua Government was the climax of the Griqua tragedy. Until then, they had managed to contain the forces that threatened to tear their particular view of the world apart and leave them as one of the wrecks in the channels of South African history. They achieved this through a combination of luck – the availability of Nomansland just as the Philippolis community was finally falling apart was nothing but this, and proved their temporary salvation – the astute political manoeuvrings in the chaos of South African politics that had characterised Adam Kok, and a Griqua identity and consciousness that was based upon pride in their nationality and in their consequent superiority over all others whose ancestors had been through the disorientating processes of the Cape Colony and the struggles against the advance of white colonists. The combination of these forces had been sufficient to preserve the unity of the people, and thus to maintain the Griquas in their own image of themselves as respectable, honourable, independent men. After 1874, however, the bases of all three pillars of Griqua survival disappeared and the precariously balanced superstructure fell.

In the break-up which occurred in the years after the take-over, the most crucial event was the death of the *Kaptyn*. On 31 December 1875 he fell from the buggy in which he was travelling, was run over by one of the wheels, and died two hours later, aged 64.[19] Four days afterwards he was buried on the corner of his *erf* in Kokstad, round the corner from the main square, where an exceedingly ugly monument was later erected to his memory. At his death the core of the Griqua political system disappeared, for there was no one of sufficient authority to deal in terms of equality with the new masters of Griqualand. Moreover, the absence of a clear successor meant now not that bloodshed would engulf the Captaincy, but that impotence would cripple whoever might be chosen, for the whole business would seem inconsequential. In the end, an old and respected *raadsman*, Cornelis van der Westhuis was elected, for there was too little passion for politicking to move elsewhere, to the stronger bases of Griqua power. In everyone's eyes, even his own, he was a cipher, and could not hope to mediate, as Adam might have done, between the new administration, harshly and thoughtlessly imposing its will, and a resentful people.[20]

During the same period of time, the Cape Government released the Griquas from the two provisions which Adam Kok had been most concerned to enact, namely the interdicts on the sale of land to foreigners and on liquor. The consequence was that in the first years after 1874 large portions of the territory were sold, both in the form of actual farms and even in claims which those Griquas who had trekked but had not yet received farms had on the Government. Dower, probably exaggerating, reckoned that half the country was sold during the first three years as capital was frittered on conspicuous consumption. No doubt Griquas were affected by the famine of cash that had afflicted Griqualand until 1870 and was now being replaced by temporary surfeit.[21] Certainly land prices were rising and Griquas may have thought it best to realise their assets at a price which they could not hope to see repeated.[22] Moreover, even for those who did not sell, the presence of money-lenders in Kokstad, who charged the customary and exorbitant rates of interest, was an additional temptation, and those who gave their lands as security for a loan were very likely to lose them in consequence.[23] But the deepest cause of the widespread sellings was undoubtedly the malaise of despair that was beginning to affect the Griquas and make them vulnerable to the widespread introduction of *canteens* in the country.

The same phenomena began to affect their political activities as well. The disgruntlement showed first in an *ad hoc* committee, the Committee of Twelve, whose purpose was primarily to air grievances and to talk out the problems of the new situation. But it was considered to be a threat by the Cape Government, which acted on insubstantial rumour. Perhaps in consequence, the officer with the highest reputation, Captain William Blyth, was sent up as Resident in Kokstad to defuse any discontent within the area. He had precisely the opposite effect, for the histrionics that had proved effective in his dealings among the Mfengu served only further to antagonise the Griqua population. His high-handed actions made the Griquas even more aware of their new subordination, and the grievances multiplied and were stifled by his refusal to allow public dissent. Finally, in 1878, the frustration was such that some of the Griquas were driven into opposition by the only means now open to them, armed revolt.[24]

The Griqualand East Rebellion of 1878 was such a complete reversal of previous actions that it demonstrates in a particularly acute way the pressures which had been imposed upon the community by the new political arrangements. The old policy had been clear. One of her daughters wrote to the old *Kaptyn*'s wife that 'the *Kaptyn*'s words were "Never lift a hand against the British Government". He is dead but let his words live'.[25] The reversal came because general dissatisfaction was acted upon by a small clique of leading Griquas who felt themselves to be insulted, considered their ambitions blocked and had strong contacts with the old rebellious tradition which permeated the Transkei. An analysis of the motives of the five rebels who were considered 'groot mensche' shows how this happened. Smith Pommer had been a Kat River rebel, had had various brushes with the Natal administration and could not have relished the prospect of living under British rule, which would curb his extortionate habits. Lodewyk Kok had been away in Griqualand West when the annexation was proclaimed, and when he came back he was shocked at the docility of his fellow Griquas. He had been the most effective and conscientious of the old magistrates and had no wish for the impotence which he saw was to be his role in the new society. Adam 'Muis', his brother, no doubt considered that rebellion was the only way in which the patrimony which he had come to expect after the death of Adam Kok III could be salvaged. Willem, or 'Toll', Kok had also had higher aspirations than expectations, for he was the old *Kaptyn*'s stepson, born to a position which he could never hope to achieve. Lastly, Titus Klein would never have been expected to rebel, for he had been very much of the Government party and as an ex-slave could never have had a great following in the Captaincy. However, he had been roughed up on the orders of Captain Blyth during the first night that Blyth was in the town, and bore a considerable grudge against the British as a consequence.

The rebellion arose from the belief of these men and of those who followed them that they were not being treated fairly by Captain Blyth. Specifically, Lodewyk Kok had been arrested on 20 February, after a brush with one of the white traders over the sale of coffee, and had been sent to the *tronk* for six months on the charge of having used treasonable speech a little while earlier — although this seems to have been untrue. A warrant for his brother's arrest had also been issued, but Adam 'Muis' fled to Pondoland, where he was soon visited by Smith Pommer. There they determined either to clear their names with the magistrate or, by another account, forcibly to free Lodewyk. At all events, Adam 'Muis' returned to the near vicinity of Kokstad on 13 April, with ninety-four Mpondo at his back. He was met by Pommer and they set up camp in the old *laager*, five kilometres north of the town. Meanwhile Pommer had been 'commandeering' men to appear at the meeting, and nearly two hundred arrived. 'The force was armed to promote freedom of discussion, Griquas being thereby put on a level with Captain Blyth.' Nor surprisingly, Blyth took this gathering as a challenge to his authority, and after attempts at parleying, whose main purpose seems to have been to persuade *Kaptyn* Kok's widow to leave the *laager*, he attacked with the forces at his disposal. A dozen Griquas were killed, including Adam 'Muis', and the rest fled, attempting to reach Pondoland, but they were overtaken in the Ingeli mountains where Pommer, two women, and twenty other Griquas, together with eight of the Africans under Blyth's command, were killed. Pommer's head was cut off, so that the soldiers might claim their reward. With the bloodless surrender, a few days later, of a small band who had gone north to the Drakensberg, the rebellion was over, and the prisoners were then shipped off to Cape Town to await trial.[26]

The mass of the rebels came from among the young men of the community, who seem to have seen the possibility of fulfilling their aspirations disappearing under British rule. Many families were split, as fathers remained loyal to the old ideals of the Griqua Captaincy while their sons joined Pommer.[27] Only 25 of the 140 prisoners possessed any landed property,[28] and one loyalist expressed surprise at the presence of Witbooi Draai and a few others among the rebels 'because they had farms'.[29] Another pointed out that only two of the men in the *laager* had ever been members of the *raad*, and that few others had any real influence within the power structure of the community.[30] These young men may have been more willing to attack the British than their seniors, or they may merely have been more impulsive, more willing to take direct action which could be construed as rebellion. Despite the pattern of participation, however, all sections of the community were in some sense implicated. The Commission later blamed the old loyalists, such as Stoffel Vesasie, Adam 'Eta' Kok and Jan Bergover, for not using their influence to moderate the wild young men.[31] This may be an overestimate of the power that these individuals had over the actions of their juniors, but it seems clear that the old loyalists were discontented and merely talked, knowing that at the crisis they would have to side with the British

131

as they had always done, while the younger men, with less to lose in terms of wealth and prestige, were more prepared to take action. The Commission claimed that 'it was when the governing class [of Griquas] realised that the Europeans and others were their equals in law and that the law was in the ascendant, that their minds, losing sight of the benefits of order, became absorbed in the loss of prestige and authority'.[32] However, the perceptions of the equality of the law no doubt differed as between the Commissioners, who were white men assured of wealth, status and political influence, and the Griquas, who saw that they were losing that which they had. Only a demonstration of their power, it seems to have been thought, could balance the inequality that was being seen to favour the colonists.

It is difficult to gauge how far the rebellion was caused by Blyth's belief that one was occurring, and how far there was a premeditated plan to resist him. The only direct evidence is that the Griquas assembled solely to strengthen their hand in negotiation with Blyth. The agents who went round the country persuading men to come armed to the *laager* certainly spread this message.[33] Moreover, the rebels made a crass strategic mistake in encamping in the *laager*, for this left the town of Kokstad between them and Pondoland, their escape.[34] As the Griquas were generally skilled military tacticians, it might be argued that they never intended to fight, and therefore were prepared to acquiesce in what turned out to be a blunder because of the *laager*'s sentimental attractions. On the other hand, the only descriptions of the recruiting techniques obviously comes from other Griquas, who would have been concerned to protect their fellows. Again, if the gathering at the *laager* had merely been to treat with Blyth, then a more favourable response to attempts to arrange parleys might have been expected, but then the terms of these negotiations are not known. An open verdict must therefore be recorded, for although many of the rank and file of the rebellion do not seem to have had any desire to challenge the British, such intentions are far less clear with regard to their leaders.

After the prisoners had been sent to Cape Town, there ensued a long legal battle as to whether they were British subjects, and so could be tried for treason. In the event, it was decided that they could not be, and so they were shipped back to East Griqualand. The legal anomaly was remedied next year when the Cape Government finally annexed East Griqualand — previously they had only taken over the administration of the area — and the independent history of the Griquas came to an end.

Thereafter the community completely fell apart. The cement that had held the families together had been based on their independence, and on the benefits and self-respect that this gave them. When it was gone, they never again had any part to play, and the relevance of the category 'Griqua' became of unimportant

132

sentimental interest, only reviving when A. A. S. le Fleur, whose father had been a Free State burgher of coloured descent who had run a short campaign among the Griquas over their lost land in Philippolis, made use of the label in the early twentieth century.

The true epitaph for the Griquas, however, was given at the crucial moment of their disintegration, namely at the death of *Kaptyn* Adam Kok III. His cousin and colleague in government, Adam 'Eta' Kok, gave an oration at his graveside which, as Dower remembered it thirty years later, sums up the deep tragedy both of the man and of his people. He said:

> We have laid in the grave a man you all knew and loved. He is the last of his race. After him, there will be no coloured king or chief in Colonial South Africa. Of Kaffir tribes, there may still be chiefs; of coloured chiefs he is the last. Take a good look into that grave. You will never look into the grave of another chief of our race. Do you realise that our nationality lies buried there? The deceased was the friend of you all. Did you ever hear of *Adam Kok* making an enemy? Political enemies he had, unfortunately more than his share; private enemies he had none. He had his faults — we all have; but you will all bear me out, he was generous to a fault — too indulgent and gentle and yielding, for a chief. There lie the remains of the one South African chief who never lifted arms nor fired a shot at a British soldier, though sometimes provoked beyond human endurance. There is not a single man here who has not received favours at his hand. If you are ever tempted to forget him, turn to the titles of your properties, and see there his familiar sign manual. I have yielded to the temptation to add this much to what the minister has said because I am his near relative, and he honoured me with his confidence, and occasionally delegated to me his authority . . . Let all questions of politics rest. Let us go home to mourn in secret and in silence, and prepare for the funeral services.[35]

CHAPTER 10

CONCLUSION

With the annexation of Nomansland, the last act of the Griqua tragedy was played out. But the question remains, what sort of tragedy was it? The Griquas had been able to establish control over a large area of southern Africa, and the flocks that it supported had made many of them rich. Their sense of community had developed out of the conflicts with their neighbours, Boer or British, and had been made manifest in their political institutions and their ecclesiastical fellowship. It had been strong enough to maintain them during the crossing of the Drakensberg after they had had to leave Philippolis, and it had enabled them to begin the occupation of Nomansland with success, but with the loss of their independence its basis disappeared and the community disintegrated.

Was this failure the consequence of a tragic flaw in their make-up? In other words, did the style of life that the Griquas had adopted contain within itself contradictions that precluded the realisation of the Griquas' aims, but rather led to the denouement of the 1870s? A very strong case could be made out for this. Permeating Griqua history there was a deep paradox between their individuality and their need for community. They had developed an independent community of men committed to the furtherance of their own individual ends, as capitalist small farmers, and the commercialism of Griqua society meant that many Griquas were prepared to sell the land on which the community depended. In the 'lumping' society by which they were surrounded, the Griquas could not slough off those who failed to live up to the ideals of the community. They could not survive without them, but these men dragged the others down. In a very real sense, the Griquas were as weak as their weakest member. Moreover, a community of men who attempted above all to be recognised and integrated into the colonial economy also required an independent polity, for from their earliest days as a unit only as a community would others take them seriously.

Again it could be argued that the Griquas' rejection of the Africans among whom they lived contributed to their downfall. This rejection showed itself at many levels. Politically, for example, Adam 'Eta' dismissed the 'Kaffir chiefs' as another phenomenon, not comparable in status with his cousin. In terms of behaviour, those Griquas who had the peppercorn hair of their Khoisan forebears

134

always hid it under scarves or hats, while those who had the straight hair of the European displayed it arrogantly.[1] Although they were prepared to admit Africans into the community it was always on the Griquas' own terms. It would not have been within their frame of reference to attempt to build a coalition of tribes similar to that established by Moshoeshoe in the Lesotho. Rather the Griquas relied so greatly on their European frame of reference that they cut themselves off from the Africans among whom they lived. Because they had attempted to dominate, they could not have allies.[2]

Nevertheless, these contradictions only explain the manner in which the Griquas' tragedy was played out, not the broad sweep of the drama. The Griquas' fault, it would seem, was in their stars, not in themselves. Adam 'Eta' was a true prophet. After Adam Kok there was no coloured king or chief in colonial South Africa, and even the Kaffir chiefs he disparaged were in decline. When new chiefs did arise for the 'coloured' people, they were political leaders from Cape Town, not from the rural situation in which the Griquas had operated.[3] By the 1870s, the Griquas were already an anachronism, as the whites were in the process of gaining control of almost all southern Africa. Of modern South Africa, only Pondoland, Zululand and the Venda chieftaincies were still under African rule, and the destruction of the old kingdom of the Zulu was far advanced.

It was not only the independence of the black communities that was being destroyed. Much of the land on which they had lived and farmed was transferred to the whites, and those reserves that were left to the mass of the Africans were entering the cycle of overpopulation, erosion and falling fertility that was to transform them into rural slums, whose purpose was to support the families of a migrant labour force. The common reaction to this cycle of deprivation was to turn to the opiates of the independent churches, which were occasionally also movements of political protest.[4] In this the Griquas shared. In 1898, in the aftermath of the collapse of the Transkeian economy following the Rinderpest epidemic, A. A. S. le Fleur, a Griqua, led one of the widest of the movements of protest in the Eastern Transkei.[5] Nineteen years later his son inspired and organised yet another Griqua trek, as about half the Griquas left in Kokstad in a foolhardy and disastrous move down to the south-west Cape, in an abortive attempt to establish yet another Captaincy, 90 miles north-east of Cape Town. Modern Griquas date the final collapse of their community from this moment.

In that the processes were similar throughout South Africa, it would not appear that the idiosyncratic features of Griqua life were responsible for their failure. Rather it is necessary to examine the tides of South African history and to postulate sequences which explain the Griqua experience. During the course of this book a hypothesis has been presented to try to provide that explanation. In crude terms it ascribes Griqua failure to the spread of the power of the South

African ruling class, to which skin pigmentation was the major criterion for admission. This class was not homogeneous. The cleavages between English and Afrikaners, between easterners and westerners, between the Cape and the Republics or between merchants and farmers remained important, and new ones emerged with the growth of a substantial extractive and industrial sector, with the discovery first of diamonds and then of gold. Nor did it include all those designated as white. There remained many, who were mainly rural, generally Afrikaners and often landless *bywoners* on other mens' farms who were only brought to a status commensurate with their colour during the twentieth century and only after a dispiriting period of poverty, generally by now in the towns. Nevertheless, this class is definitely identifiable and would appear to have been extending its control over South African society throughout the nineteenth century, overrunning all opposition.

This is the view from below at any rate. However, it is necessary to point out that relying on the whites to provide an explanation of the Griquas' failure does not entail a return to an albocentric historiography. Classes only exist in relation to each other, so that an examination of nothing but white history must in itself hide such a development, for it would obscure the relationship of the whites to the rest of South African society. Because a one-class society is a logical impossibility, a study which concerned itself only with that one class could never understand the full workings of the society. The character of the South African ruling class manifested itself only in its dealings with those who were not of itself. In general, the 'poor whites' were succoured, and raised up to a full position within the society. In part this was because they had the vote, but there was a deeper belief that they should be part of respectable society. The Africans, on the other hand, were generally not enabled to hold or to consolidate any gains which they might have made. The legal and the commercial basis of peasant agriculture was always undermined, wherever it began to gain any significant position. Where there had been a certain degree of fluidity, by the late nineteenth century the colour line was hardening, even if it took until the mid-twentieth before the poor whites were fully absorbed into the ruling class. But in the new scheme of things there was no place for such as the Griquas. As the Kat River settlement had folded up, as the Bastards had been driven out of De Tuin, as the peasant societies of the eastern Cape were coming under pressure, as there was never allowed to be any chance for advancement among the Kholwa of Natal and as the cash croppers of the Transvaal were to be eradicated by the 1913 Lands Act, so the society that was dominated by the white farmer, by the merchant and, in time, by the mining capitalist had no place for the Griquas. Without a viable position in the society, this community collapsed.

In this perspective it is surprising that the Griquas survived as long. In part this

was attributable to the fortune and endeavour that enabled them to trek from
Philippolis to Nomansland, and so move into an area where the pressures towards
racial categorisation were less advanced than on the High Veld. In part those
pressures were less uniform and less all-embracing than they subsequently
became. If there had been a division between black and white inherent from the
beginning of South Africa, then the anomaly of a free, independent, 'coloured'
polity, such as the Griqua Captaincies, would not have come into existence, or if
it had it would scarcely have lasted as long as it did. As the correlations between
colour and economic position became more exact, so the outposts across the line
were slowly mopped up, and the Griquas were among the more prominent of
these.

Their legacy to later South Africa has been mixed. They produced no lasting
memorial to their existence, no art, no literature and no legends, but in this they
were not alone. Rather they have provided a sense of history and a tradition
which others of their classification have utilised in an attempt to develop an
identity for themselves. The descendants of Griquas have been remarkably
prominent in recent 'coloured' politics. There is a considerable community in
modern South Africa which calls itself Griqua, but which has few genetic links
with the old Captaincies. Rather it makes use of the symbols which the Griquas
have provided, for any deeper identity is lacking in the general run of the disorientated rural proletariat.[6] They chose the Griquas in part for reasons of
change and background — A. A. S. le Fleur, the founder of the Griqua Refor-
mation movement, had had contact with Kokstad after the British take-over and
his father had led agitation among Griquas in the 1880s[7] — but primarily because
the Captaincies of Philippolis and Kokstad were so much more successful than
other 'coloured' groups in adapting to the pressures of the nineteenth century.
Griquatown went into a long slow stagnation from the 1840s until its catastrophic
crash in the early days of the diamond fields. After the rebellion of 1851, the Kat
River settlement fell apart, and even in the days of its flourishing it had never
been a place to excite the imagination of those who did not live there, for it was
closely under colonial and missionary control. The Namaqualand settlements, in
contrast, never escaped the poverty which their aridity determined. Only
Rehoboth, far from the centre and the consciousness of most 'coloured' men,
survived and developed after its own fashion. Once more the importance of the
Griqua Captaincies within the development of the country is demonstrated.

'Political enemies he had, unfortunately, more than his share.' When Adam
Kok died, his associates recognised the end of their people, an end brought on by
those political enemies and by the new South Africa which they were creating.
The centrifuge had driven the Griquas into the great mass of the 'non-whites',
forcing them to a situation which they, who had been an independent, proud

people, could not relish. A few of them with lighter skins might be accepted surreptitiously into the white group, but most were depressed into the general mass of the coloureds.[8] The *Kaptyn* had been at once the symbol and the leading actor in the preservation of their independence. From then on they could not maintain the struggle against the new social situation which was developing around them, which they had resisted for the past seven years. Although it did not occasion that collapse, Adam Kok III's death marked it. Adam 'Eta' was right and perceptive to notice that the Griquas' nationality lay buried in his cousin's grave. From now on, they had good cause to pray the Griquas' prayer:

> Lord, save thy people. Lord, we are lost unless thou savest us. Lord, this is no work for children. It is not enough this time to send thy son. Lord, thou must come thyself.[9]

APPENDIX 1

GENEALOGY OF THE KOK FAMILY

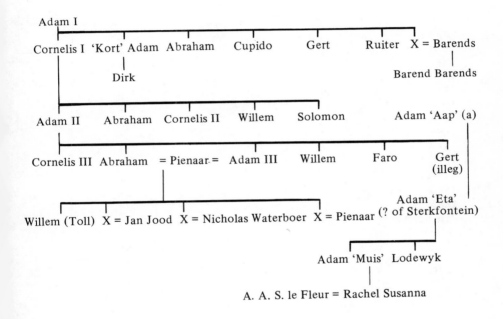

X   indicates a daughter, name unknown.

(a) Adam 'Aap' was of this generation, but his father is unknown.

APPENDIX 2

THE SALE OF FARMS IN THE PHILIPPOLIS CAPTAINCY

	Farms that had been hired	Farms that had never been hired
	No.	No.
1848	1	1
1849	2	0
1850	0	0
1851	1	1
1852	0	1
1853	1	3
1854	38	32
1855	11	17
1856	4	5
1857	4	11
1858	6	10
1859	4	17
1860	2	24
1861	1	37
date unknown	2	4
	77	163

Source: (OVS) AKT volumes 2/1/11, 16, 17, 51, 52, 53, 121, 138

APPENDIX 3

THE GROWTH OF SOUTH AFRICAN EXPORTS AND THE SHIFT TO THE EAST

(All figures in thousands)

Year	Cape Town[a]					Port Elizabeth		
	Wine[b]		Wool		Total	Wool		Total
	gal.	£	lb	£	£	lb	£	£
1838	1088	102	286	16	207	204	10	52
1839	1114	96	377	19	205	208	10	38
1840	969	78	509	24	177	401	21	61
1841[c]	875	67	573	29	178	486	22	58
1842[c]	549	42	519	28	163	853	43	94
1843[c]	534	44	534	27	154	1220	56	110
1844	608	55	936	45	198	1297	67	106
1845	546	52	1109	59	253	2085	114	179
1846	511	40	1082	64	228	2188	113	170
1847	404	39	1135	59	173	2583	132	178
1848	515	49	1590	69	210	2079	86	115
1849	443	41	1567	63	186	3457	136	173
1850	374	35	1589	73	203	4323	212	258
1851	468	49	1777	87	243	3669	194	241
1852	252	24	1848	95	219	5925	309	352
1853	272	26	1703	110	297	6160	390	435
1854	363	40	2008	109	284	6655	337	378
1855	493	61	2326	125	389	9690	508	580
1856	740	85	3026	179	503	11892	651	737

[a] All figures for Cape Town include Simonstown.
[b] These figures amalgamate both the fine Constantia wines and the ordinary vintages, but exclude the dribble which was exported through Port Elizabeth.
[c] In 1841 and 1842 the year of reckoning ended on 10 Oct. as opposed to 5 Jan., the date in all other years. Therefore the figures for 1841 refer only to 9 months and those of 1843 to 15 months.

Source: Cape of Good Hope, *Statistical Blue Books.*

NOTES

Chapter 1

1 Boshof to Grey, 29 Dec. 1855, *SAAR, OVS* II, 340—2. For examples of other characterisations, see G. M. Theal, *History of South Africa since 1795* (5 vols., London 1908), I:406, II:408—33, III:356; Sir G. E. Cory, *The Rise of South Africa* (5 vols., London, 1910—30), II:429—30, 435— 40, IV:271—80, 302—11; W. M. Macmillan, *Bantu, Boer and Briton*, 2nd edn (Oxford, 1963), 57.

2 The most notable exceptions to the general version can be found in P. J. van der Merwe, *Die Noordwaartse Beweging van die Boere voor die Groot Trek* (The Hague, 1937); J. S. Marais, *The Cape Coloured People, 1652— 1937* (reprint, Johannesburg, 1957) and M. C. Legassick, *The Griqua, the Sotho-Tswana and the Missionaries, 1780—1840: the politics of a frontier zone* (Ph.D. thesis, University of California, Los Angeles, 1970, published by University Microfilms, Ann Arbor, 1970).

3 J. Mackenzie, *Ten Years North of the Orange River* (Edinburgh, 1871), 64.

4 H. J. and R. E. Simons, *Class and Colour in South Africa, 1850—1950* (Harmondsworth, 1969), 29.

5 The best syntheses of this process are to be found in two unpublished seminar papers for the Institute of Commonwealth Studies, London, presented in 1974—5, namely J. E. Parkington, 'Recent Development in the Study of Prehistory at the Cape' and R. R. Inskeep, 'The Problem of Bantu Expansion in the Light of Recent Research on the Iron Age in Southern Africa'.

6 This argument is not intended to contradict the strictures on albocentrism first propounded for southern Africa (in the discourse of academic historians at least) by C. W. de Kiewiet in *The Imperial Factor in South Africa* (Cambridge, 1937) and recently reiterated in manifestoes found, for example, in *OHSA*, Preface vii—viii, and Shula Marks, 'African and Afrikaner History', *JAH* XI (1970), 435—71. Rather it hopes to point to an important field of study, as yet neglected, in the social history of the pre-industrial Cape Colony.

7 The debate on this subject is vast. For the most important recent contributions see Pierre L. van den Berghe, *South Africa: a study in conflict*, 2nd edn (Berkeley, 1967), esp. 265—81; Idem, *Race and Racism: a comparative perspective* (New York, 1967), 96—112; Heribert Adam, *Modernising*

Racial Domination: South Africa's political dynamics (Berkeley, 1971) esp. 18–22; Harold Wolpe, 'Industrialism and race in South Africa' in S. Zubaida (ed.), *Race and Racialism* (London, 1970), 156–64; Stanley Trapido, 'South Africa in a comparative study of industrialisation', *Journal of Development Studies* VII (1971), 309–19; Frederick Johnstone, 'White prosperity and white supremacy in South Africa today', *African Affairs* LXIX (1970), 124–40; Idem, 'Class conflict and colour bars in South Africa's gold mining industry, 1910–1926' in *Collected Seminar Papers on the Societies of Southern Africa in the 19th and 20th Centuries* (Institute of Commonwealth Studies, London, 1969–70).

8   E. P. Thompson, *The Making of the English Working Class* (London, 1963), 9–10.

9   M. C. Legassick, 'The frontier tradition in South African historiography' in *Collected Seminar Papers on the Societies of Southern Africa in the Nineteenth and Twentieth Centuries*, Vol. II (Institute of Commonwealth Studies, London, 1970–1), 18, citing S. Patterson, *The Last Trek* (London, 1957), 16.

10 E.g. The mother of the Tswana chief Mothibi was a !Kora. See L.F. Maingard, 'The Brikwa and the ethnic origins of the Batlhaping', *SAJS* XXX (1933), 597–602.

11 For a similar situation, see the analysis presented in Verena Martinez-Alier, *Marriage, Class and Colour in Nineteenth-Century Cuba* (Cambridge, 1974), to which this analysis is indebted, particularly as regards presentation.

12 This discussion simplifies the situation, because there are examples, especially in Latin America, where an individual who is of one race but who displays social signals that pertain to another is treated as a member of the other. In general, however, the distinction holds good, particularly in South Africa. See Michael Banton, *Race Relations* (London, 1967), 54–62.

13 See Robert Ross, 'The "white" population of South Africa in the eighteenth century', *Population Studies* XXIX (1975).

14 The reference is to Thomas Kuhn, *The Structure of Scientific Revolutions* (Chicago, 1962).

15 J. M. Janssens, Proclamation, 20 Feb. 1805, in *BPP* 50 of 1835, 164.

16 W. Blommaert and J. A. Wiid (eds.), *Die Joernaal van Dirk Gysbert van Reenen* (Cape Town, 1937), 23.

17 E. A. Walker, *A History of Southern Africa*, 3rd edn (London, 1963), 23.

18 L. von Rohden, *Geschischte der Rheinischen Missionsgesellschaft* (Barmen, 1868), quoted in Marais, *Cape Coloured People*, 168.

19 R. Godlonton, *Introductory Remarks to a Narrative of the Irruption of the Kaffir Hordes* (Grahamstown, 1835), cited in Tony Kirk, 'Progress and decline in the Kat River settlement', *JAH* XIV (1973), 415.

20 This section is based on Kirk, *ibid.*

21 Shula Marks, *Reluctant Rebellion: Disturbances in Natal, 1906–08* (Oxford, 1970), 119–22.

22 This section is based very heavily on Colin Bundy, 'The emergence and decline of a South African peasantry', *African Affairs* LXXXI (1972), 369–88.

23 Report on Native Location Surveys, CPP, UG42 '22, cited in *OHSA* II:65.

24 See particularly, F. Wilson, 'Farming' in *OHSA* II:127–31.

25 Bundy, 'Emergence and decline', 387.

26 This analysis owes a considerable debt to E. R. Leach, *Political Systems of Highland Burma: a study of Kachin social structure* (London, 1954), esp. 8–10.

27 Legassick, *The Griqua*, chs. 9 and 12, and H. Vedder, *South West Africa in Early Times*, translated by C. G. Hall (London, 1938), esp. 196–219, 243–79, 325–39.

28 It would appear that the Dutch clergymen, who became closely associated with the community in which they ministered, tended increasingly not to baptise those who were of illegitimate birth, which meant primarily those who were coloured. Although there was during the course of the eighteenth century a change from religion to pigmentation as a basis of acceptance, baptism remained of great importance as a symbol of this acceptance. See A. Sparrman, *A Voyage to the Cape of Good Hope 1772–6* (2 Vols., Dublin, 1785), I:203–4.

29 I have adopted this term primarily because the alternatives, 'state' or 'tribe' are basically unsatisfactory, having too many unfortunate connotations. It is intended to act as an abstraction for the various attributes of the Griqua polities, territoriality, ethnicity and governmental institutions, and takes its form from the fact that the title of the head of government among the Griquas, as in all Bastard and many Khoi communities, was *Kaptyn*, or in English Captain. See Robert Ross, 'Griqua Government', *African Studies* XXXIII (1974), 27–8.

30 Cape of Good Hope, *Statistical Blue Book of the Colony for 1842*, 225.

31 Solomon to Freeman, 20 Oct. 1844, LMS 70/1/B; Hendrik Witbooi, *Die Dagboek van Hendrik Witbooi*, foreword by Gustav Voigts (Cape Town, 1929), xiii–xiv.

32 E. D. Genovese, *In Red and Black* (London, 1971), 37, citing M. Harris, *Patterns of Race in the Americas* (New York, 1964), 70. See also W. D. Jordan, 'American Chiaroscuro: the definition of mulattoes in the British colonies', *William and Mary Quarterly*, 3rd Series, XIX (1962), 183–200.

Chapter 2

1 It must be noted that in Dutch 'Bastard' means 'mongrel' as well as 'illegitimate'.

2 J. Campbell, *Travels in South Africa, 1813* (London, 1815), 349.

3 Although in colonial historiography the Griqua tribe is generally known as the Chariguriqua, the prefix 'Chari' (strictly ≠Kari) refers to but one section of the tribe. See R. H. Elphick, *The Cape Khoi and the First Phase of South African Race Relations* (Ph.D. thesis, Yale, 1972, published by University Microfilms, Ann Arbor), 190–1.

4 T. D. Hall, 'South African pastures, retrospective and prospective', *SAJS* XXXI (1934), 57–86.

5 L. Fouche and A. Boeseken (eds.), *The Diary of Adam Tas* (Cape Town, 1970), 111.

6 F. Valentyn, *Description of the Cape of Good Hope with the matters concerning it*, ed. E. H. Raidt (2 vols., Cape Town, 1971–3), II:39.

7 *ibid*. 25.

8 For a description of the relationship, see M. Wilson, 'The hunters and herders' in *OHSA*, I:63; and Elphick, *The Cape Khoi*, ch. 3. On its break up, see G. Harinck, 'Interaction between Xhosa and Khoi: emphasis on the period 1620 to 1750', in L. Thompson (ed.), *African Societies in Southern Africa* (London, 1969), 166–7 citing C. A. Haupt, 'Journal Gehouden . . . op de togt door den Vaandrig August Frederick Beutler (1752)' in E. C. Godée-Molebergen (ed.), *Reizen in Zuid Afrika in de Hollandse Tijd* (4 vols., The Hague, 1916–32), III:292.

9 In fact the choice was not absolute. There is some, albeit tenuous, evidence to suggest that occasionally farm servants passed information to as yet independent groups who proceeded to lift the stock of the informers' master. See N. C. de la Caille, *Journal Historique du Voyage fait au Cap de Bonne Esperance* (Paris, 1776), 329.

10 Sparrman, *Voyage*, I:203. The best description of the process is in Elphick, *The Cape Khoi*, part 2.

11 See the evidence of employers in G. M. Theal (ed.), *Records of the Cape Colony* (36 vols., London, 1899–1905), XXIX:436–86.

12 Sparrman, *Voyage*, II:113–17.

13 L. F. Maingard, 'Studies in Korana history, customs and language', *Bantu Studies* VI (1932), 111.

14 *Ibid*. and H. Vedder, 'The Nama' in H. Vedder (ed.), *The Native Tribes of South West Africa* (Cape Town, 1928), 114–18.

15 This is strongly argued by Legassick, *The Griqua*, 93–100. In particular he cites the description by Maynier of the Bastards as 'such Hottentots, *particularly* of the mixed race, who, possessing some property, were more civilised' (his italics). *RCC*, XXI:394.

16 The Bokkeveld is a plain of good farming land about 120 miles north-east of Cape Town.

17 The Zak River, which is usually dry, 'flows' into the Orange about 200 miles from its mouth. The area in question was almost certainly about 200 miles south of this, where a missionary of the LMS, William Kicherer, founded a short-lived station in 1801.

18 H. Lichtenstein, *Travels in Southern Africa in the years 1803, 1804, 1805*, trans. A. Plumptre (2 vols., Cape Town, 1928–30), II:317.

19 G. Thompson, *Travels and Adventures in Southern Africa* (2 vols., London, 1827), II:84.

20 RLR 12/3, 527.

21 R. Fenton, *Peculiar People in a Pleasant Land: a South African narrative* (Giraud, Kansas, 1905). He appears to have received his information from two leading members of the Griqua state about 1865. One of these was himself a Kok. Although such an alliance is inherently likely, and would

explain much that is puzzling in later history, it is not, to my knowledge, mentioned elsewhere, although good early histories of the Kok family exist, e.g. J. Campbell, *Travels in South Africa . . . being a Narrative of a Second Journey, 1820* (2 vols., London, 1822), II, ch. 22.

22 Lichtenstein, *Travels*, I:316–17.
23 Campbell, *Second Journey*, II:267.
24 See Maingard, 'The Brikwa . . .'
25 Legassick, *The Griqua*, 112–15.
26 Marais, *Cape Coloured People*, 33–5, citing J. Philip, *Researches in South Africa* (2 vols., London, 1828), 56–61. See also R. Moffat, *Missionary Labours and Scenes in Southern Africa* (London, 1842), 194–6, and G. Thompson, *Travels*, I:150.
27 Legassick, *The Griqua*, 181–4.
28 Campbell, *Travels*, 352.
29 S. D. Neumark, *Economic Influences on the South African Frontier, 1652–1836* (Stanford, 1957), 118–22.
30 Alan Smith, 'Delagoa Bay and the Trade of South-Eastern Africa', in R. Gray and D. Birmingham (eds.), *Precolonial African Trade* (London, 1970), 184–6.
31 G. Thompson, *Travels*, I:152. The effectiveness of such warfare was demonstrated at the battle of Kuruman in 1823, when the Griquas inflicted some 500 casualties on marauding Sotho-Tswana without a single life lost themselves. See W. F. Lye, 'The Difaqane: the Mfecane in the Southern Sotho area', *JAH* VIII (1967), 124–6.
32 W. J. Burchell, *Travels in the Interior of South Africa, 1821*, ed. I. Schapera (2 vols., London, 1953), I:112.
33 Evidence of Robert Moffat, 20 April 1824, in BPP 50 of 1835, 128.
34 Campbell, *Second Journey*, II:356–7; Legassick, *The Griqua*, 163–6. See also Plasket to Waterboer, 15 June 1827, GWLC 21.
35 Melvill to Baird (Deputy Landrost, Beaufort West), 12 Sept. 1822, BW 9/27.
36 GLW 166, 160.
37 *Ibid*. 65.
38 A. Smith, *The Diary of Dr Andrew Smith*, ed. P. R. Kirby (2 vols., Cape Town, 1939–40), I:152–3.
39 The ordination of Hans Bezuidenhout, LMS 38/1/C.
40 *Bloemhof Blue Book*, 16.
41 Lichtenstein, *Travels*, II:303–5.
42 R. and M. Moffat, *Apprenticeship at Kuruman: being the journals and letters of Robert and Mary Moffat, 1820–1828*, ed. I. Schapera (London, 1951), 40–1.
43 The Diary of C. F. Wuras, published in the *Missionsbericht* of the Berlin Missionary Society (1843), 24.
44 T. Hahn, *Tsuni-//Goam, the Supreme Being of the Khoi-Khoi* (London, 1881), *passim*, and I. Schapera, *The Khoisan Peoples of South Africa* (London, 1930), 374–89. The only reference to non-Christian practices comes from Donald Strachan, a very close associate of the Griquas in the 1860s and 1870s, who claimed that they still 'give a cow for the maiden-

head and that sort of thing'. *South African Native Affairs Commission; Report 1903–05* (6 vols., Cape Town, 1905), II:1028.

45 Philip to Shaw, LMS Philip Papers, 3/1/C, quoted by Legassick, *The Griqua*, 428. As the report comes from Hendricks via the medium of Philip, and as both these two were notorious exaggerators, it must be treated with scepticism, but the sentiments expressed are feasible and likely.

46 Campbell, *Travels*, 390.

47 Melvill's report of December 1824, in BPP 50 of 1835, 215. Also Stockenström to AS to Governor, 28 Feb. 1828, LG11.

48 Legassick, *The Griqua*, 203. This account follows closely that of Martin Legassick, but is obviously highly abbreviated.

49 See, for example, the comment which Adam Kok II made about him to Andrew Smith: 'He was without experience, headstrong and fiery to the extreme . . . wherever he thought blame lay he punished without enquiry just on mere belief.' Smith, *Diary*, I:199–200.

50 Moffat, *Apprenticeship*, 278–9.

51 Legassick, *The Griqua*, 301–2.

Chapter 3

1 Cited in van der Merwe, *Noordwaartse Beweging*, 195.

2 Actual figures for the relevant area include:
Philippolis   415.7 mm p.a.
Fauresmith   386.6 mm p.a.
Trompsburg   391.4 mm p.a.
Source: Union of South Africa, Weather Bureau, *Climate of South Africa* (Pretoria, 1960), part 9.

3 R. A. Alexander, 'Horse sickness', *Farming in South Africa* IX (1934), 336, 346.

4 J. P. H. Acocks, *Veld Types in South Africa* (Pretoria, 1953).

5 On these see C. G. and M. Sampson, *Riversmead Shelter: Excavation and Analysis*, Memoir No. 5, National Museum, Bloemfontein, 1967; *Idem*, 'Excavations at Zaayfontein Shelter, Norvalspont, Northern Cape', 'Excavations at Glen Elliot Shelter, Colesberg District, Northern Cape', 'A later Stone Age open site near Venterstad, Cape', *Researches of the National Museum, Bloemfontein* II, parts 4, 5 and 6 respectively (1967); T. M. O'C. Maggs, 'Pastoral settlements on the Riet River', *South African Archaeological Bulletin* XXVI (1971), 37–61; A. J. B. Humphreys, 'Comments on the raw material usage in the later Stone Age of the middle Orange River area' *South African Archaeological Society, Goodwin Series* I (1972).

6 W. M. Macmillan, *The Cape Coloured Question*, 128–32; Melvill to Plasket, 5 Sept. 1825, BPP 50 of 1835, 224; London Missionary Society, *A Register of Missionaries, Deputations etc. from 1796–1923*, ed. James Sibree, 4th edn (London, 1923), 9–10.

7 Macmillan, *Bantu, Boer and Briton*, 57.

8 Philip, *Researches*, II:90, 97–8.

9 Miles to Directors, 10 Jan. 1827, LMS 10/1/C. These were marauding bands of Africans, displaced by the Mfecane. This group was probably Moletsane's Taung. See D. F. Ellenberger, *History of the Basuto, Ancient and Modern*, translated by J. C. MacGregor (London, 1912), 174–5, and also Moletzane's statement in LG 9.

10 Melvill to Directors, 2 Apr. 1827, LMS 10/2/B.

11 Clark to Stockenström, 6 Feb. 1827, GR 10/6.

12 Kolbe to Directors, 9 Oct. 1834, LMS 13/14/A.

13 Melvill to van Ryneveld, 28 Mar. 1828, GR 10/8.

14 Melvill to Stockenström, GR 10/6; Melvill's Journal for 21 Feb. 1827, in LMS South Africa Journals, 4/92; Goeyman to Philip, 15 Jan. 1825, Philip Papers (Rhodes House), 431.

15 Statement of Johannes Coetzee, 1 Mar. 1830, LG 9.

16 The Griquas' attitude to the San was finally shown by the Bushman law passed by the *raad* on 8 Oct. 1846, whereby Kok would only allow into his territory those San who were either under mission influence or under contract with a Boer or a Griqua, and registered as such with the British Resident or with Kok. See (OVS) GS 1388.

17 On the !Kora, see, above all, J. A. Engelbrecht, *The Korana* (Cape Town, 1936) and Maingard, 'Studies'. Also important are R. Broom, 'Bushmen, Korannas and Hottentots', *Annals of the Transvaal Museum* (1948); P. V. Tobias, 'Physical Anthropology and the Somatic Origins of the Hottentots', *African Studies*, XIV (1955), C. S. Grobbelaar, 'The Physical Characteristics of the Korana', *SAJS* LIII (1956); D. N. Beach, *The Phonetics of the Hottentot Language* (Cambridge, 1938).

18 For a fuller analysis of this episode, see Legassick, *The Griqua*, 426–31, and W. F. Lye, 'The Ndebele kingdom south of the Limpopo River', *JAH* X (1969), 91–5.

19 Maingard, 'Studies', 127–30.

20 Melvill to Miles, 29 Oct. 1829, LMS 11/4/A; A. Smith, *Diary*, I:193.

21 See the Journal of Andrew Smith, South African Museum.

22 A. Smith, *Diary*, II:185.

23 H. T. Wangemann, *Die Berliner Mission im Koranna-lande* (Berlin, 1873), 30.

24 *Ibid*. 49.

25 Englebrecht, *The Korana*, 53–7; *Berliner Missionsbericht* (1841), 175–7; P. Sanders, 'Sekonyela and Moshoeshoe', *JAH* X (1969), 416.

26 Wangemann, *Die Berliner Mission*.

27 Grobbelaar, 'Characteristics', 100.

28 Legassick, *The Griqua*, 485–501.

29 See note 18 above.

30 Kirk, 'Progress and decline', 417.

31 This Nguni word, which means 'time of killing', has generally been translated into the Sotho-Tswana 'Difaqane' when referring to events west of the Drakensberg.

32 These groups have often and erroneously been known as Mantatees, a name

which derives from Mma-Ntatisi of the Tlokwa. For them, see Lye, 'The Difaqane', 126 ff. On the Ndebele, see Lye, 'The Ndebele kingdom' 88–93.

33   On this period, see W. F. Lye, 'The Distribution of the Sotho peoples after the Difaqane' in *African Societies in Southern Africa*, ed. L. Thompson (London, 1969), 191–206.

34   For example, Atkinson to Ellis, 14 Nov. 1836, LMS 15/1/E; Atkinson to Rawstorne, 10 May 1844, CBG 4/1/6; Solomon to Tidman, 1 July 1853, LMS 28/1/A; Kok to Tidman, 15 June 1859, LMS 31/3/A.

35   For the early history of the Bethulie mission, see S. H. Pelissier, *Jean Pierre Pelissier van Bethulie* (Pretoria, 1956), ch. 14.

36   Pelissier to PEMS, 15 Feb. 1839, quoted in *ibid*. 290.

37   Pelissier to LG, 7 Sept. 1841, LG 509; Rawstorne to ASLG, 25 Sept. 1841, LG 197.

38   Theophilus Jousse, *La Mission Française Evangelique au Sud de l'Afrique* (2 vols., Paris, 1889), I:216–22.

39   Pelissier's biographer implies otherwise, but there is no evidence in the files of the Colesberg magistracy to suggest that he did exert any pressure, while the letter, quoted in the same book, from Philip to the Griquas in December 1840, shows that he strongly supported Pelissier's incumbency. There is neither evidence nor reason to think that this was false, or that he changed his mind in the succeeding months. On the contrary his concern to bolster Moshoeshoe, which was as strong as his hopes for the Griquas, would have prevented him from risking any breach with the PEMS. See Pelissier, 305, 319–20. For Philip's own reply, which makes this point more strongly, see Philip to Freeman, 30 Mar. 1840, Philip Papers (Rhodes House), 1154.

40   Hudson to Rawstorne, 9 Sept. 1841, LG 655; Rawstorne to ASLG, 2 Oct. 1841, LG 197.

41   See e.g. J. Barrow, *An Account of Travels into the Interior of Southern Africa* (2 vols., London, 1801–4), II:401–4, Sparrman, *Voyage*, II:122.

42   Barrow, *ibid*.

43   This is argued in Neumark, *Economic influences, passim*.

44   The importance of the frontier situation in determining the racial attitudes of the Afrikaner community was stressed by I. D. MacCrone, *Race Attitudes in South Africa* (London, 1937), particularly 89–125. This has been challenged, effectively, by Legassick in 'The frontier tradition'.

45   On this, see particularly Barrow, *Travels*, I:247–50. A full analysis of the process is given by van der Merwe, *Noordwaartse Beweging*.

46   By far the best analyses of this process are to be found in two works by P. J. van der Merwe. For the period before about 1800, see *Die Trekboer in die Geskiedenis van die Kaap Kolonie* (Cape Town, 1938), and for the later period see *Noordwaartse Beweging*.

47   G. M. Theal (ed.), *Basutoland Records* (3 vols., Cape Town, 1883) (hereafter *Bas. Rec.*), II:424.

48   Stockenström to Col. Sec., 11 June 1827, cited in van der Merwe, *Noordwaartse Beweging*, 220.

49   Bell to CC, GR, 10 Apr. 1829, GR 8/19. See also the Journal of Charl

Celliers, in J. Bird (ed.), *The Annals of Natal: 1495 to 1845* (2 vols, Pieter-maritzburg, 1888), 252.

50 See the land grant cited in Macmillan, *Bantu, Boer and Briton*, 61.

51 As a draft of the petition was found in the Philip Papers, in Rhodes House, it may be assumed that the move was suggested by him as part of his attempts to improve the legal position of the 'coloured' people.

52 The accusations are to be found in the volume in the Cape Archives LG 9, and reported in Sir Andries Stockenström, *Autobiography of Sir Andries Stockenström*, edited by C. W. Hutton (2 vols., Cape Town, 1887), I:272–92.

53 *Ibid*. 272.

54 In 1834, 225 such deprived men signed a petition to D'Urban, hoping that the colony might be extended to provide suitable land: van der Merwe, *Noordwaartse Beweging*, 329–31.

55 *Ibid*. 309–11.

56 Andrew Smith's Journal in the South African Museum. See also Kok to Philip, 30 May 1831, Philip Papers, 587.

57 Kok to van Ryneveld, 7 Feb. 1831, GR 10/35; van Ryneveld to Kok and van Ryneveld to van Schallwyk, both 16 Feb. 1831, GR 16/49; Kok to van Ryneveld, 4 Jan. 1835, GR 10/18.

58 For the form of the hiring, see, e.g., Statement of Solomon Kok in van Ryneveld to Bell, 10 Feb. 1836, GR 10/54. The farm itself was an area of supposedly 6,000 acres, which was considered to be the acreage necessary to support a Boer family. Whether it did so or not depended primarily on the availability of water.

   The legal consequences of hiring farms, under the accepted customary law of the Griquas, is difficult to discover, but see the evidence of Jan Bloem, much later: 'I am living at Holdam; have done so for 13 years. Other persons occupied it before me. If these persons were to return, they could not dispossess me, because I have lived permanently there and made permanent improvements. If even these improvements were to cease to exist, and I were to leave the place, anyone might go and live there, but would have to give way on my return. I made a dam, enclosed lands (16 yards); no house, but stone kraals. This was formerly the law among the Philippolis Griquas.' (GLW 166, 263).

59 Stockenström to Hare, 14 May 1845, in Hare to Maitland, 28 May 1845, GH 8/14.

60 See van der Merwe, *Noordwaartse Beweging*, 342–57, for an elaboration of this theme.

61 These papers are to be found enclosed in Hare to Napier, 22 Aug. 1842, GH 8/10.

62 He was generally known as Cornelis III. See the genealogy in Appendix 1.

63 Melvill, LMS South African Journals, 4/92.

64 Melvill to Secs., 1 Jan 1829, LMS 11/3/A.

65 Only in this context. The appelation 'Griqua', in this sense, although wide-spread, is almost never used except in contradistinction to 'Bastards'.

66 A third son, Gert, who was illegitimate, was canvassed by Hendricks a year

before, but never seems to have had any serious support. Philip to D'Urban, 16 July 1835, BPP 538 of 1836, 620.

67 A. Smith, *Diary*, I:72.
68 Cf. J. R. Goody, 'Introduction', to J. R. Goody (ed.), *Literacy in Traditional Societies* (Cambridge, 1969), 10. The difference between this situation and those described by Goody is that no caste of *literati* could emerge in the fluid and temporarily uneven distribution of literacy among the Griquas, so that literacy became but one resource among many in political competition.
69 A. Smith, *Diary*, I:80.
70 R. and M. Moffat, *Apprenticeship*, 284.
71 Legassick, *The Griqua*, 303.
72 Melvill to Miles, 29 Oct. 1829, LMS 11/4/A.
73 A. Smith, *Diary*, I:73.
74 *Ibid*. 81–2.
75 CMK 1/140.
76 Read to Stockenström, 11 June 1817, GR 10/35.
77 Evidence of Nicholas Kruger, *Bloemhof Blue Book*, 8.
78 Deposition of D. A. Pienaar, GR 18/24.
79 Andrew Smith's Journal in the South African Museum.
80 Memorial of Adam Kok, 26 Aug. 1835, GH 19/4.
81 This is argued by Legassick, *The Griqua*, 476–7.
82 Philip to Wade, 10 Oct. 1833, printed in BPP 425 of 1837, 143–51.
83 *Ibid*.; also Kolbe to van Ryneveld, 7 Oct. 1832, GR 10/35; A. Smith, *Diary*, I:76–7.
84 Kolbe to Berrange, 7 Oct. 1831, GR 10/35.
85 Philip to Wade, 10 Oct, 1833, BPP 425 of 1837, 144; Kolbe to van Ryneveld, 7 Oct. 1832, GR 10/25.
86 Probably Hendrick Hendricks.
87 Kolbe, LMS, South African Journals, 4/108.
88 See the letter to Kolbe (author not recorded), 24 Dec. 1832, Philip Papers (Rhodes House), 622.
89 Kolbe, LMS, South African Journals, 4/108; Bernhard Kruger, *The Pear Tree Blossoms; a history of the Moravian mission stations in South Africa* (Genadendaal, 1966), 172.
90 Philip to D'Urban, 4 July [1834], in BPP 538 of 1836, 620.
91 BPP 252 of 1835, 114–17; Macmillan, *Cape Coloured Question*, 174.
92 Aberdeen to D'Urban, 11 Apr. 1835, in BPP 252 or 1835, 117.
93 Cf. J. S. Galbraith, 'The "Turbulent Frontier" as a Factor in British Expansion', *Comparative Studies in Society and History*, II (1959–60), 165–8.
94 Minutes of a meeting at Philippolis, 26 Jan. 1836, GR 10/35; van Ryneveld to Bell, 10 Feb. 1836, GR 10/35.
95 A. Smith, *Diary*, I:73.
96 Van Ryneveld to Bell, 10 Feb. 1836, GR 10/35.
97 Hudson to Rawstorne, 9 Jan. 1837, CBG 4/1/1.
98 A translation of the treaty is published in David Arnot and F. H. S. Orpen,

The Land Question in Griqualand West; an inquiry into the various claims to land in that territory (Cape Town, 1875), 191–4.

99 Wright to Stockenström, 1 March 1837, LG 495.
100 Wright to Philip, 1 Feb. 1837, LMS 15/3/A. On Wiese, see van Ryneveld to Bell, 16 July 1831, GR 16/50, and the diary of Gregorowski in *Missionsbericht* of the Berlin Missionary Society (1836), 28.
101 Atkinson to Philip, 24 Jan. 1837, LMS 15/3/A.
102 Atkinson to Stockenström, 28 June 1837, LG 495; Wright to Stockenström, 6 Aug. 1837, LG 495.
103 Atkinson to Directors, 25 Dec. 1837, LMS 15/4/B; Lucas to Stockenström, as reported in the register to LG 493. (The original letter is missing).
104 Rawstorne to Hudson, 19 Feb. 1838, LG 194.
105 Henceforth known as Adam Kok III.

Chapter 4

1 This was the term by which those Boers who had migrated over the Orange River, whether as part of the Great Trek or not, were known.
2 A. Smith, *Diary*, I:73.
3 The laws are contained in GO 2.
4 A. Smith, *Diary*, I:80; J. Backhouse, *Narrative of a Visit to Mauritius and South Africa* (London, 1884), 349–50; Schreiner to Freeman, 8 August 1841, LMS 18/2/A.
5 R. G. Cumming, *Five Years of a Hunter's Life in the Far Interior of South Africa* (2 vols., London, 1856), I:140.
6 For instance, in 1840 there were two large and several small hat manufacturies in Graaff Reinet, two in Cradock and four in Colesberg, and no other manufactures in any of the three divisions. See Cape of Good Hope *Statistical Blue Book* for 1840, 300.
7 Schedule by Kolbe, 4 Dec. 1834, LMS 14/1/E.
8 Cape of Good Hope *Statistical Blue Book* for 1842, 225.
9 See chapter 5 below.
10 According to Wright there were seven brandy shops within an hour of Philippolis. Wright to Freeman, 25 Oct. 1842, LMS 18/3/B. See also Schreiner to Freeman, 8 Aug. 1841, LMS 18/2/A and 24 Dec. 1841, LMS 18/2/C.
11 The figure is taken from Kok's lists of farms leased for less than 40 years. GH 10/4/B.
12 Schreiner to Ellis, 28 Dec. 1840, LMS 17/3/C.
13 Van der Merwe, *Noordwaartse Beweging*, 309–11.
14 Schreiner to Freeman, 8 Aug. 1841, LMS 18/2/A, Wright to Philip, 19 Sept. 1842, LMS 19/1/B.
15 Macmillan, *Bantu, Boer and Briton*, 245.
16 Schedule by Kolbe, 4 Dec. 1834, LMS 14/2/E.
17 Buck Adams, *The Narrative of Private Buck Adams, 7th (Princess Royal's) Dragoon Guards on the Eastern Frontier of the Cape of Good Hope, 1843–1848*, ed. A. Gordon-Brown (Cape Town, 1941), 65–6.

18 George Nicholson, *The Cape and its Colonists . . . with hints to prospective emigrants* (London, 1848), 89–90. See also Solomon to Read, 25 Feb. 1843, enclosed in Philip to Tidman, 29 May 1843, LMS 19/2/A.

19 J. S. Galbraith, *Reluctant Empire: British policy on the South African frontier, 1834–54* (Berkeley, 1963), 84.

20 Robert Moffat, *Missionary Scenes*, 200.

21 C. Gray, *Life of Robert Gray, Bishop of Cape Town and Metropolitan of Africa* (2 vols., London, 1876), I:190.

22 Macmillan, *Bantu, Boer and Briton*, 66.

23 In his evidence before the Select Committee on Aborigines, BPP 538 of 1836, 184–5.

24 Melvill to Miles, 29 Oct. 1829, LMS 11/4/A.

25 The terms of his appointment are in BPP 252 of 1835, 116–17.

26 Wright was Philip's closest ally in ecclesiastical politics. The appointment was made after Philip had been on a long tour of the interior. See Macmillan, *Bantu, Boer and Briton*, 216–38.

27 On Imperial Policy, see Galbraith, *Reluctant Empire*, and C. F. J. Muller, *Die Britse Owerheid en die Groot Trek*, 2nd edn (Johannesburg, 1963).

28 Earl Grey, *The Colonial Policy of Lord John Russell's Administration*, 2nd edn (2 vols., London, 1853), II:248.

29 The exceptions were the Earl of Caledon, who held office from 1807 to 1811, and Sir Henry Pottinger, whose tenure of office lasted 10 months during 1847. For a general analysis of the military mind and the consequent effects on Imperial policy, see J. S. Galbraith, 'The "Turbulent Frontier" ', 150–68.

30 Galbraith, *Reluctant Empire*, ch. 4.

31 *Ibid*.

32 Herman B. Giliomee, 'The Cape Eastern Frontier, 1775–1812', unpublished seminar Paper of the Institute of Commonwealth Studies, London, 1973.

33 The only possible exception to this generalisation might have been the Zulu kingdom at its zenith under Shaka, whose military machine, if well led, might have posed problems for even the finest European troops. Even the Sotho fortress of Thaba Bosio must have been vulnerable to the concerted attack of British regiments.

34 On this, see L. Thompson, 'Co-operation and conflict: the High Veld' in *OHSA*, I:441–2.

35 This argument, and the description of the colonists, comes from Ronald Robinson, 'Non-European foundations of European imperialism: sketch for a theory of collaboration' in Roger Owen and Bob Sutcliffe (eds.) *Studies in the Theory of Imperialism* (London, 1972), 124–6. For an example of this use of the threat of British power, see Jean van der Poel, 'Basutoland as a factor in South African politics (1852–1870)', *AYB for SAH* (1941) I, 180–1.

36 Grey to Hogge, 15 Dec. 1851, cited in Galbraith, *Reluctant Empire*, 258–9.

37 The best general survey of these events is still E. A. Walker, *The Great Trek*, 2nd edn (London, 1936).

38 The Act is known as the *Cape of Good Hope Punishment Act*, (Cap. No.

57 of 6 & 7 William IV.). For a discussion of it and its precedents, see Galbraith, *Reluctant Empire*, 183, and Muller, *Britse Owerheid*, 111–13, 258–9.

39   See Napier's proclamation of 7 Sept. 1842, in *Cape of Good Hope Government Gazette*, 9 Sept. 1842.

40   Kok to Rawstorne, 20 Oct. 1842, in Wright to Philip, 27 Oct. 1842, LMS 19/1/B.

41   Kok to Mocke, 23 Oct. 1842, in *ibid*.

42   A full account of the meeting is to be found in Cory, *The Rise of South Africa*, IV:287–92.

43   M. C. E. van Schoor, 'Politieke Groepering in Transgariep', *AYB for SAH* (1950, II) 15–16.

44   Wright to Rawstorne, in Rawstorne to ASLG, 29 Nov. 1842, LG 199.

45   The report is to be found in the *South African Commercial Advertiser*, 19 Nov. 1842. The comment the paper made was that 'the reply of the Griqua chief rings like metal. It will remind the scholar of the Tuscan or Germanic harangues recorded by Livy or Tacitus, full of ancient faith and resounding with barbaric virtue.' This is quaint, but unlikely. For the provenance of the report, see Fairbairn to Moore Craig, 22 Nov. 1842, enclosed in Napier to Hare, 25 Nov. 1842, LG 65. Fairbairn, the editor of this notoriously liberal newspaper, claimed the original, from which he translated it, was as written down by the Griquas (presumably Hendricks) under the authority of Kok.

46   E.g. Rawstorne to ASLG, 3 Dec. 1842, LG 199.

47   Wright to Philip, 6 Jan. 1843, LMS 19/1/B.

48   Minute of meeting, 29 Dec. 1842, LG 605.

49   In fact, of course, it was not against the Boers that Lepui had been protected, but against the Griquas. See ch. 3 above.

50   Minute of meeting, 2 Jan. 1843, LG 605.

51   Wright to Philip, 20 Dec. 1842, LMS 19/1/B.

52   Macmillan, *Bantu, Boer and Briton*, 245.

53   Solomon to Freeman, 14 May 1843, LMS 19/1/A.

54   Elders and Deacons of Philippolis to James Read Snr., 17 Apr. 1843, in Philip to Tidman, 8 May 1843, LMS 19/1/D; Kok and Council to Read, in *ibid*.

55   Macmillan, *Bantu, Boer and Briton*, 246.

56   The treaty is printed in BPP 424 of 1851, 214–15.

57   *Grahamstown Journal*, 28 Dec. 1843, LMS 20/3/C.

58   Thomson to Tidman, 10 Nov. 1844. Also Read to Philip, in Philip to Directors, 2 Apr. 1844, LMS 20/1/D.

59   Hughes to Freeman, 20 July 1844, LMS 20/1/B.

60   Kok to Hare, 9 Feb. 1844, in Hare to Napier, 16 Feb. 1844, GH 8/13. See also *Grahamstown Journal*, 12 Feb. 1844.

61   Proclamation of 16 Oct. 1843, GO 2.

62   See P. Bonner, 'The relations between internal and external politics in Swaziland and the eastern Transvaal in the mid-19th century' in *Collected Seminar Papers on the Societies of Southern Africa in the 19th and 20th*

Centuries (University of London, Institute of Commonwealth Studies, 1970–1), 35–44; Walker, *Great Trek*, 328–33.

63 Walker, *Great Trek*, 332, 346; van Schoor, 'Politieke Groepering', 14.
64 Rawstorne to ASLG, 8 June 1844, LG 203.
65 The quotation is actually from Hare to Maitland, 11 Apr. 1844, GH 8/13. The same sentiment is expressed in Montague (Secretary to Governor) to LG, 28 June 1844, LG 81.
66 Van Schoor, 'Politieke Groepering', 15–17.
67 Rawstorne to ASLG, 25 Nov. 1844, LG 203.
68 Rawstorne to ASLG, 21 Dec. 1844, LG 203.
69 The document was copied and translated by Thomson and then sent to Philip. See Thomson to Philip, 25 Dec. 1844, LMS 21/2/A.
70 *Ibid.*
71 Rawstorne to ASLG, 17 Mar. 1845, and 22 Mar. 1845, LG 204.
72 Maitland to Hare, 11 Apr. 1845, LG 68.
73 Rawstorne to ASLG, 15 Apr. 1845, enclosed in Hare to Maitland, 24 Apr. 1845, GH 8/10.
74 *Grahamstown Journal*, 24 Apr. 1845.
75 Rawstorne to ASLG, 26 Apr. 1845, LG 373.
76 *Ibid.*
77 Richardson to O'Reilly, 1 May 1845, in Hare to Maitland, 9 May 1845, GH 8/14.
78 Rawstorne to ASLG, 8 May 1845, LG 373.
79 *Idem* to *idem*, 23 May 1845, LG 373.
80 Maitland to Stanley, 1 Aug. 1845, *Bas. Rec.*, I:93.
81 Thompson to Philip, 17 Oct. 1844, in Philip to Secs., 10 Feb. 1845, LMS 21/2/A.
82 Maitland to Stanley, 1 Aug. 1845, *Bas. Rec.*, I:96–8.
83 *Ibid.* 95.
84 Rev. B. Maitland to Kok, 25 June 1845, LMS 21/2/C.
85 Kok to Maitland, 26 June 1845, LMS 21/2/C.
86 Rev. B. Maitland to Kok, 29 June 1845, LMS 21/3/C.
87 Kok to Maitland, 30 June 1845, LMS 21/2/C.
88 *Ibid.*
89 Rev. B. Maitland to Kok, 25 June 1845, LMS 21/2/C. It is incorporated word for word in the final treaty.
90 Kok to Maitland, 30 June 1845, LMS 21/2/C.
91 These figures are gleaned from the land registers of the Orange Free State, (OVS) AKT 2/1/12, 2/1/51, 2/1/52, 2/1/121 and 2/1/138, from the registers of the 'Forty Years Money', CMK 1/140, and from Kok's lists of farms leased for less than 40 years, GH 10/4/B.
92 A copy of the final treaty is to be found in G. W. Eybers, *Select Constitutional Documents Illustrating South African History (1795–1910)* (London, 1918).
93 Solomon to Tidman, 7 June 1846, LMS 22/1/C.
94 Court of the Special Magistrate, 22 Dec. 1845, GH 10/1.
95 *Ibid.*

96   *Ibid.* for 8 Jan. 1846.

97   Warden to Rev. B. Maitland, 16 June 1846, CM 10/1.

98   Galbraith, *Reluctant Empire*, 228–9.

99   Maitland to Stanley, 1 Aug. 1845, *Bas. Rec.*, I:95.

100   Smith to Grey, 3 Feb. 1848, in BPP 969 of 1847–8, 61.

101   Smith's proclamation is in *ibid.* 63–4.

102   Minutes of Conference of 27 Jan. 1848, *Bas. Rec.*, I:158–9.

103   Statement by Kok, n.d., LMS South Africa Odds, 2. For a debate on whether Smith actually threatened the Griqua, in which the weight of the evidence would seem to be that he did, see *Friend*, 8 Mar. 1852 and 20 Mar. 1852.

104   See, e.g., his statement before the Commission of Enquiry into the Affairs of Griqualand East, CPP G37 '76, 188.

105   The agreement between Smith and Kok is printed in BPP 969 or 1847–8, 62.

106   Kok to Uithaalder, 27 Aug. 1851, enclosed in Warden to Garrock, 31 Aug. 1851, (OVS) HC 1/1/3.

107   Warden to Montague, 29 Feb. 1848, (OVS) BR 2/1.

Chapter 5

1   See D. Hobart Houghton and J. Dagut, *Source Material on the South African Economy* (3 vols., Cape Town, 1972–3) I:14–19.

2   See, e.g., W. S. van Ryneveld, *Aanmerking over de Verbetering van het Vee aan de Kaap de Goede Hope*, ed. H. B. Thom (Cape Town, 1942), *passim*.

3   Barrow, *Travels*, II:394–410.

4   Theal, *RCC*, XXV:95–6, and XXVII:499.

5   Neumark, *Economic Influences*, 135–7.

6   'Report of the Commissioners of Inquiry upon the Trade of the Cape of Good Hope, the Navigation of the Coast and the improvement of the Harbours of that Colony', Theal, *RCC*, XXXV:229–87.

7   Nicholson, *The Cape*, 15.

8   Theal, *RCC*, XXXV:235.

9   See appendix 3.

10   This is the burden of the argument propounded by Neumark, *Economic Influences*. See especially p. 4. For a trenchant criticism of that work see W. K. Hancock 'Trek', *EcHR* 2nd Series, X (1956–7).

11   H. B. Thom, *Die Geskiedenis van Skaapboerdery in Suid-Afrika* (Amsterdam, 1936), Deel III, *passim*. The first merinos were introduced among the Colesberg flocks in 1842: *ibid.*, 316.

12   Cape of Good Hope, *Statistical Blue Book* for 1856, 597.

13   D. Hobart Houghton, 'Economic Development, 1865–1965' in *OHSA*, II:4.

14   On these towns, see the reports of the various magistrates in Cape of Good Hope, *Statistical Blue Books* from 1856 onwards.

15   *Friend*, 6 Dec. 1861.

16   Sir George Clerk to Newcastle, 8 Oct. 1853, (OVS) SC 2/2.

17 W. W. Collins, *Free Statia: reminiscences of a lifetime in the Orange Free State* (Cape Town, 1965), 84–5.

18 *SAAR, OVS*, II, facing page 264.

19 J. F. Midgley, 'The Orange River Sovereignty (1848–1854)', *AYB for SAH* (1949, II), 293.

20 Neumark, *Economic Influences*, 121–3; Lichtenstein, *Travels*, II:325; Burchell, *Travels*, I:112.

21 A. Smith, *Diary*, I:382; Legassick, *The Griqua*, 426–31; Lye, 'The Ndebele Kingdom', 91–5.

22 For the career of this man, see D. Livingstone, *Family Letters, 1841–1856*, ed. I. Schapera (2 vols., London, 1959), I:148, 179, II:14; R. Moffat, *The Matabele Journals of Robert Moffat*, ed. J. P. R. Wallis (2 vols., London, 1945), I:195, 216, II:31; Mary Moffat to R. Moffat, 12 June 1854, in the Moffat Papers in the Rhodesian National Archives. (My thanks are due to Miss Moira Botha of the University of Cape Town for procuring me a copy of this last letter.)

23 Livingstone, *Family Letters*, I:221, II:125.

24 Solomon to Tidman, 30 May 1860, LMS 25/1/C.

25 Livingstone, *Family Letters*, II:147, and at many other points in his writings on the subject.

26 *Ibid*. II:151.

27 J. Chapman, *Travels in the Interior of South Africa* (2 vols., London, 1868), I:194–5.

28 *Ibid*. 43–4.

29 CMK 1/140.

30 D. Livingstone, *Missionary Correspondence, 1841–1856*, ed. I. Schapera (London, 1961), 174.

31 W. B. Boyce, *Notes on South African Affairs*, (London, 1839), 155–6.

32 Cumming, *Five Years*, I:138–9; James Read Snr. to Tidman, 6 Feb. 1850, LMS 25/2/B.

33 Livingstone, *Family Letters*, I:172–3.

34 Kok asked for cash with which to purchase ammunition on the grounds that there was none in Philippolis. This may have been false, but was sufficiently plausible to convince the Civil Commissioner of Colesberg. See Rawstorne to ASLG, 10 Dec. 1844, LG 199.

35 Kok to Wodehouse, 28 Mar. 1862, in CPP G53 '62, 18.

36 Thomson to Tidman, 30 Dec. 1847, LMS 23/1/B; van der Schalk to Cameron, 1 Sept. 1849, LMS South African Odds, 3/5/C.

37 Read to Tidman, 6 Feb. 1850, LMS 25/2/B.

38 Freeman's evidence in BPP 635 of 1851, 40.

39 Solomon to Thompson, 1 Oct. 1850, LMS 25/1/E.

40 Solomon in LMS *Annual Report* for 1852.

41 *Ibid*.

42 *Ibid*.

43 Solomon in *ibid*. for 1854.

44 Nicholson, *The Cape*, 64.

45 *Friend*, 3 Mar. 1855.

46 I argued this point with considerably more vigour in a paper entitled 'Griqua power and wealth; an analysis of the paradoxes of their inter-relationship', *Collected Seminar Papers of the Institute of Commonwealth Studies, London, Southern Africa* IV (1973). I now consider that I gave too much weight to this factor: although the general course of events outlined there would still seem to be true, the motor for the model which I presented there would appear to be far too simple for a highly complex reality.

47 See above and Thom, *Skaapboerdery*, 150–1.

48 Solomon to Tidman, 10 Apr. 1856, LMS 30/1/A.

49 Solomon to Tidman, 22 Dec. 1856, LMS 30/1/A. My insertion was due to a hole in the manuscript.

50 Solomon to Tidman, Mar. 1857, LMS 30/3/A.

51 The photograph, which must have been taken between 1857, when W. B. Philip arrived in Philippolis, and 1861, is to be found in the W. B. Philip collection, in the Jagger library of the University of Cape Town.

52 These papers are to be found in GWLC 28, folder C4.

53 *Friend*, 6 Dec. 1861.

54 'The Griquas and their exodus', *Cape Monthly Magazine* (December 1872). W. B. Philip may be presumed to be the author of this anonymous article.

55 See D. Roy Briggs and Joseph Wing, *The Harvest and the Hope: the story of Congregationalism in South Africa* (Pretoria, 1970), 102–9.

56 Christie for Philip to Freeman, n.d. [1849], LMS South African Odds, 4/1/B.

57 See J. J. Freeman, *A Tour in South Africa* (London, 1851), 5; van der Schalk to Freeman, 1 Sept. 1849, LMS South African Odds, 3/5/C; James Read Snr. to Freeman, 24 Dec. 1849, LMS South African Odds, 4/1/A.

58 On the origins of this remarkable family, see W. E. G. Solomon, *Saul Solomon; THE member for Cape Town* (Cape Town, 1948), 4–7.

59 Edward Solomon to Ellis, 6 June 1855, LMS South African Odds, 7/4/A.

60 Church and Deacons of Philippolis to Tidman, 9 Nov. 1855, LMS South African Odds, 7/3/B.

61 Hendricks and Pienaar to Freeman, 12 Aug. 1849, LMS South African Odds, 3/3/A.

62 W. B. Philip to Tidman, 10 Feb. 1858, and 11 Feb. 1858, LMS 31/2/B; *idem* to *idem*, 15 Feb. 1861, LMS 32/3/A.

63 W. B. Philip to Grey, 5 May 1859, GH 14/3.

64 'The Griquas and their exodus', 334–5.

65 Edward Solomon, *Two lectures on the Native Tribes of the Interior, delivered before the Mechanics Institute, Cape Town* (Cape Town, 1858) 19–21.

Chapter 6

1 Figure gleaned from CMK 4/16.

2 Kok and Council to Smith, 22 Feb. 1848, GH 22/3.

3 See (OVS) GS 1390 and (OVS) AKT 2/1/16 & 17, *passim*.

4   See below, pp. 90–2.

5   Smith to Grey, 20 Jan. 1851, printed in BPP [1360] of 1851, 81–5.

6   See Stockenström's letter in *Cape of Good Hope Observer*, 28 Aug. 1849. See also Midgley 'The Orange River Sovereignty', 247; A. H. Duminy, 'The Role of Sir Andries Stockenström in Cape Politics' *AYB for SAH* (1960, II), 100.

7   See Kok to Philip and Fairbairn, 22 Jan. 1849, and Kok and Hendricks to Philip, 9 Feb. 1849, both in LMS 24/4/A.

8   See Freeman to Grey, 20 Aug. 1850, in BPP [1360] of 1851, 95–6; Smith to Grey, 20 Jan. 1851, in *ibid*. 81–5. See also Freeman's evidence before the Select Committee on Kafir tribes, BPP 635 of 1851, 31–42.

9   Clerk to Newcastle, 25 Aug. 1853, (OVS) SC 2/2. Also *idem* to *idem*, 8 Oct. 1853 and 10 Nov. 1853, *ibid.*; Galbraith, *Reluctant Empire*, 271.

10 Even as early as 1849 it would be written that 'land is rapidly advancing in value — 100% since my arrival'. Stuart (magistrate at Bloemfontein) to Southey, GH 10/3. He had been there for six months.

11 Warden to Southey, 17 June 1848, GH 10/2.

12 Kok to Warden, 3 Dec. 1848, (OVS) HC 1/1/1.

13 Midgley, 'The Orange River Sovereignty', 252–3.

14 Van der Schalk to Freeman, 14 May 1850, LMS 25/1/B.

15 Kok to Freeman (translated by van der Schalk), 9 July 1850, LMS 25/1/C; Warden to Garrock (Secretary to Governor), 3 Aug. 1850, (OVS) GS 1390.

16 See, e.g., John Campbell (Acting Civil Commissioner of Colesberg) to Southey, 21 June 1848, Southey Papers, Cape Archives.

17 Warden to Garrock, 31 June 1850, (OVS) BR 2/1. Hendricks excepted Gideon Joubert, the old *veldkommandant* of the northern Cape frontier, from his condemnation.

18 *Ibid.*

19 *Friend*, 6 May 1854.

20 Sir Charles Warren, *On the Veldt in the Seventies* (London 1902), 272.

21 Viljoen to Januarie, 11 June 1852, LMS South African Odds, 12/2/C. In fact, Januarie, who was always nicknamed Apé, seems to have carried out his commission. See James Chapman, *Travels in the Interior of South Africa, 1849–1863: hunting and trading journeys from Natal to Walvis Bay and visits to Lake Ngami and Victoria Falls*, ed. E. C. Tabler, 2 vols (Cape Town, 1971), I:50.

22 *SAAR, Transvaal* I:5–6. For similar examples, see *ibid.*, 65, and *SAAR, Transvaal* II:190, 476. See also M. C. E. van Schoor, 'Die Nasionale en Politieke Bewuswording van die Afrikaner en sy Ontluiking in Transgariep tot 1854', *AYB for SAH* (1963, II), 69, 80.

23 Cf. Solomon to Thompson, 28 Sept. 1853, LMS 25/3/B. In this Solomon considered that the only possibilities for the Griquas were: (1) to stick to the Maitland Treaty and to call for the aid of the British Government in the event of a clash, when it would be unlikely to come; (2) to abandon the treaty and ally with the other blacks, which would be very dangerous, as the Griquas were surrounded by whites, comparatively weak in number and with few arms; (3) to attempt to create an alliance with the Free State

Boers, which would be unlikely to last; (4) to sell up and leave, if they could find space, as the east was too thickly populated as it was and, if they went to Namaqualand, they would all become freebooters.

It may, perhaps, be as well to give a few details of the later career of that remarkable man Hendrick Hendricks. He lived until 1881, remaining in Griqualand West when the main body of the Philippolis Griquas trekked over the Drakensberg (CMK 4/16), but apart from owning an *erf* in Philippolis around 1859 he seems to have played little part in the politics of the area. There are two exceptions to this. Either he or a man of the same name signed the 'Hottentot League of Nations', a treaty between the various Khoikhoin and Oorlam groups in Namaqualand in 1859 (see CPP UG41 '26, 71), and in the early 1860s he vented what remained of his considerable spleen against Andries Waterboer by giving a highly biased and misleading account of early Griqua history to the Orange Free State (see (OVS) GS 1389).

24 Midgley, 'The Orange River Sovereignty', 121.
25 *Ibid*. 131.
26 Government Notice, 20 Aug. 1848, *Bas. Rec.*, I:177. But see also Sir H. G. W. Smith, *The Autobiography of Sir Harry Smith*, ed. G. C. Moore Smith (2 vols., London, 1903), II:244. The description of the battle of Boomplaats was taken from the diary of Lt. Howdich, Sir Harry's ADC.
27 Legassick, *The Griqua*, ch. 10.
28 Minutes of the meeting at Viervoet, 29 June 1851, *Bas. Rec.*, I:419. For a full-scale analysis of this campaign, see Midgley, 'The Orange River Sovereignty', chs. 9 and 14.
29 Warden to Garrock, 14 July 1851, *Bas. Rec.*, I:428.
30 See Galbraith, *Reluctant Empire*, ch. 1; C. W. de Kiewiet, *British Colonial Policy and the South African Republics 1848–1872* (London, 1929), ch. 5.
31 Quoted in de Kiewiet, *British Colonial Policy*, 60.
32 Galbraith, *Reluctant Empire*, 252.
33 The Sand River Convention was signed on 16 January 1852.
34 Grey to Smith, 14 Jan. 1852, BPP 1428,of 1852. Of course the sovereignty was not the only reason for the dismissal of Sir Harry. The war on the eastern frontier was, if anything, more important.
35 Clerk to Newcastle, 25 Aug. and 3 Nov. 1853, 18/2/53, (OVS) SC 2/2.
36 When he went out, the policy of the British Government towards the territory had not been finalised, but Clerk's dispatches soon settled the matter.
37 The draft agreement is in CPP A118 '61, 1.
38 Kok to Clerk, 7 Mar. 1854, in *ibid*. 1–3; *Friend*, 26 Feb. 1854. Clerk had claimed in the *Friend* that Kok had broken the treaty by allowing the sale of land, which Kok emphatically denied.
39 Solomon to Thompson, 22 Sept. 1853, LMS 28/3/B.
40 If Sir Harry Smith had bothered to promulgate the Letters Patent establishing the Orange River Sovereignty Government, then it would have been necessary to have passed an Act of Parliament before the Sovereignty could have been abandoned. As it was the papers were left in a drawer in his

office, and so the legal formalities were much easier. See de Kiewiet, *British Colonial Policy*, 70—1.

41 Solomon to Thompson, 18 Mar. 1854, quoted in W. Thompson, *The Griquas* (Cape Town, 1854), 7.

42 Green's speech of 15 Mar. 1854, as recorded in Clerk to Kok, 1 Apr. 1854, in CPP A118 '61, 6—7.

43 Kok to Clerk, 12 July 1854, in *ibid.* 8; Clerk to Kok, 3 Aug. 1854, in *ibid.* 9.

44 For this figure see Solomon to Thompson, 24 Mar. 1854, quoted in Thompson, *Griquas*, 10.

45 Stander was one of the leading republicans who had been a close associate of Pretorius and had been in Colesberg gaol after the battle of Zwartkoppies.

46 Thembu, in modern orthography. This incident occurred in 1847, in the aftermath of the War of the Axe.

47 Thompson, *Griquas*, 11.

48 See paper on Griqualand question drawn up by J. N. Orpen for the Assembly of Delegates, Orpen papers, Cory Library, Grhamstown, no. 1241.

49 Vesasie to Clerk, 24 June 1854, (OVS) SC 1/1; Vesasie to Grey, 17 Aug. 1857, GH 10/4.

50 Memorial of Draay, n.d., GH 10/6.

51 See CMK 4/16; Kok's lists in GH 10/4/B.

52 For instance, the piece of ground known as Blaauwbosch Leegte was given out to Petrus Pienaar on the 22 Dec. 1859 and sold by him to M. A. Theunissen for £25 seven days later. See (OVS) AKT 2/1/52.

53 Of the 32 farms sold in 1854, which had been previously hired, and for which the month of sale is known, only four were sold before June and only four in the months of November and December.

54 Kok to Hoffman, 30 May 1854, and Hamelberg to Kok, 3 June 1854, both in (OVS) SC 3/5.

55 Thompson to Solomon, 3 June 1854, LMS 29/2/A.

56 E.g. Hutton to Staat Secretaris, 12 Sept. 1854, (OVS) GS 338; Christian Bock to Hoffman, 17 Oct. 1854, (OVS) GS 1388.

57 Kok to Grey, 28 Apr. 1856, GH 10/4, Solomon to Grey, 11 May 1855, GH 14/2. Solomon made sure that Grey realised the advantages which the Griquas possessed, by adding that he might be reached at the office of Saul Solomon, proprietor of the *South African Commercial Advertiser* and Member of the Assembly for Cape Town. Saul Solomon was one of the most powerful politicians in South Africa at the time, a liberal by conviction and Edward Solomon's brother. He did from time to time exert his influence on behalf of the Griquas. See, e.g., *South African Commercial Advertiser*, 8 May 1856, reporting the House of Assembly debate of 29 April and pp. 100—1 below.

58 Boshof to Grey, 29 Dec. 1855, *SAAR, OVS*, II:340—2.

59 Declaration of J. P. Straus, 16 April 1856, (OVS) GS 340. It may be, of course, that the rumour was fabricated by those who thereby hoped to have an excuse not to go on commando against Witsie.

Chapter 7

1   This is the estimate of William Dower, *The Early Annals of Kokstad and Griqualand East* (Port Elizabeth, 1902), 13. Kok himself claimed that 1,500 families trekked, almost certainly an exaggeration. See Kok to Wodehouse, 28 Mar. 1862, CPP G53 '62, 18. The census of 1878 gave a minimum total of 2,150, but by then it would have been considerably affected by immigration and emigration from the community. Also the territorial cover of this census is not certain. See CPP G17 '78, 73.
2   See Faku and Mqikela to Grey (written by Thomas Jenkins), 25 Dec. 1860, CPP A118 '61, 23.
3   See Lindsay Young, 'The native policy of Benjamine Pine in Natal, 1850–1855', *AYB for SAH* (1951, II), 304–16.
4   See Sir George Grey to Newcastle, 19 Feb. 1861, in CPP A118 '61, 19–22.
5   Mackenzie, *Ten Years*, 64–5.
6   For complaints, see *Friend*, 1 Aug. 1857.
7   For these articles, see CPP A118 '61, 13–14.
8   Clerk to Merivale, 8 June 1859, A118 '61, 17–19.
9   'The Griquas and their exodus', 332–3. W. B. Philip, the anonymous author of this article, was in Philippolis at the time and recorded this, but no actual case can be found in the archives. For the official position, see the treaty of 15 July 1857, GWLC 22, exhibit 407.
10   Dower, *Early Annals*, 10.
11   Adam Kok (*Provisionaal Kaptyn*) to *Staats President*, n.d. (1858), (OVS) GS 1388.
12   *SAAR, OVS*, III:79.
13   Statement of Adam Kok, 1 Oct. 1875, CPP G37 '76, 191–3.
14   Philip, 'The Griquas and their exodus', 333.
15   R. Richards 'Pommer and Sidoi', *Natal Magazine* (1879), 322. See also J. B. Wright, *Bushman Raiders of the Drakensberg* (Pietermaritzburg, 1971), 131–2. By then it was estimated that there were about 400 'coloured' rebels and deserters in Nomansland. See Theal, *History*, III:445.
16   *Friend*, 8 July 1859. By August they do not appear to have arrived. See *Natal Mercury*, 25 Aug. 1859.
17   This account is taken from 'The Griquas and their exodus', 333–4. Philip must have heard the reports which they made to the rest of the community, and so may be trusted.
18   *Friend*, 16 Dec. 1859.
19   For the description of this complicated move, see C. F. Goodfellow, *Great Britain and South African Confederation, 1870–1881* (Cape Town, 1966), 15–21; de Kiewiet, *British Colonial Policy*, chs. 7 and 8.
20   On this episode, see, *inter alia*, E. M. Attree, 'The Closer Union Movement between the Orange Free State, South African Republic and Cape Colony (1838–1863)', *AYB for SAH* (1949, I), 352–66.
21   Grey to Lytton, 12 Jan. 1859, GH 23/27.
22   'The Griquas and their exodus', 334.
23   D. Voortman to Government Secretaris, 16 Oct. 1861, GS 349.

24 See H. J. van Aswegen, 'Die verhouding tussen blanken en nie-blanken in die Oranje Vrystaat, 1854–1902', D.Phil, UOVS (1968), 116–18.

25 Vedder, *South West Africa in Early Times*, 338–9.

26 In CMK 5/16, there is a list of the residences in 1888 of the 40 years money holders (the descendants of those Griquas who had leased farms in the alienable territory of Philippolis for more than 40 years). About half were in Griqualand West.

27 Many of the farms were resold within a year, often for 50 per cent more than the Griqua owner had received. See (OVS) AKT volumes, *passim*.

28 Minutes of Conference, 11 Feb. 1862, between Moshoeshoe and J. Burnet and J. M. Orpen. *Bas. Rec.*, III:48.

29 *Friend*, 16 Apr. 1860; Agreement between Adam Kok and M. W. Pretorius, 15 Mar. 1860, (OVS) GS 1588.

30 *Friend*, 6 June and 13 June 1860.

31 On Arnot, see J. J. Oberholster, 'Die Anneksasie van Griekwaland Wes', *AYB for SAH* (1945), 58–60. See also Kok's notice of 14 July 1860 in *Friend*, 17 Aug. 1860.

32 On Harvey, see *Friend*, 30 Jan. 1858. For power of attorney, see GWLC 23, Exhibit 503. No record of his bankrupcy exists in either the Free State or the Cape Archives, but there is a gap in about the right place in the 'H' volume of (OVS) IB 611, which may well have accounted for this. For attestation of his bankruptcy, see Dower, *Early Annals*, and in CMK 1/140.

33 On Solomon's career, see Solomon, *Saul Solomon, passim*. Much material on his relations with the Griquas exists in the Solomon papers, Johannesburg Public Library, in which see Arnot to Solomon, 31 Aug. 1861.

34 The Rev. Edward Solomon to Saul Solomon, 23 Jan. 1861. Solomon papers.

35 D. Hobart Houghton, 'Economic Development', *OHSA*, II:9. On the buoyancy of the market see *Friend*, 11 May 1860 and 20 Apr. 1860, in which it is written that 'In the Brak river ward [near Cradock] nearly 50 farmers have come to the conclusion of migration to the Orange Free State, in consequence of troubles with their black servants.' Most of the purchasers of Griqua land seem to have come up from the Cape.

36 'The Griquas and their exodus', 335.

37 See table in appendix 2.

38 There were six stores in Philippolis, and merchants were said to be taking up to £15–20 a day. *Friend*, 6 Dec. 1861.

39 See Young, 'Native policy', 301–2; J. B. Wright, *Bushman Raiders*, ch. 5.

40 For a description of the negotiations, which is particularly full on the Natal side, see B. A. le Cordeur, 'The relations between the Cape and Natal', *AYB for SAH* (1965, I), 94–109.

41 J. Rutherford, *Sir George Grey, a study in colonial government*, (London, 1961), 451.

42 Grey to Newcastle, 19 Feb. 1861, CPP A118 '61, 19–22.

43 *Ibid.*; Solomon to Kok, 12 Mar. 1861, Solomon Papers.

44 This became a matter of controversy after the Griqualand East Rebellion of 1879. See CPP G58 '79, 12–14, 1B, 180.

45 Arnot to Solomon, 31 Aug. 1860, Solomon Papers.

46 See, e.g., Wodehouse to Granville, 23 Oct. 1869, GH 23/30.
47 See ch. 9 below.
48 CPP G58 '79, 51—2, 149.
49 'The Griquas and their exodus', 335.
50 See Orange Vrij Staat, *Volksraad Notulen*, 22 Feb. 1861.
51 Act of M. W. Pretorius, 26 Dec. 1861, (OVS) GS 1390.
52 Minute Book of the Philippolis Nederduitsche Gereformeerde Kerk, 12 July 1863. There seems to have been some controversy over the price obtainable, and in consequence W. B. Philip did not trek all the way, as he had planned to do. See Dower, *Early Annals*, 21—2.
53 See Cape of Good Hope, *Statistical Blue Books*, 1858 to 1863. In 1857, the average price of draught oxen in the Colesberg division was £4 10s. It rose to £8 10s. in 1859 and to a peak of £12 in 1861, before falling to £8 in 1862. Only in 1861 was the Colesberg price higher than the average for the eastern Province. See also 'The Griquas and their exodus', 335.
54 W. B. Philip to Solomon, 23 May 1862, Solomon Papers.
55 'The Griquas and their exodus', 336.
56 *Ibid.*
57 R. Germond, *Chronicles of Basutoland* (Morija, 1967), 299.
58 Philip to Solomon, 23 May 1862, Solomon Papers; Scott to Newcastle, 3 Jan. 1863, (Natal) GH 1213.
59 Dower, *Early Annals*, 13. This picture goes some way towards dispelling the normal stereotype of Griqua laziness. Rather, like the trekboers, their beliefs in the value of independence kept them from work as servants, or in jobs which servants did. Cf. van der Merwe, *Die Trekboer*, ch. 8.
60 Dower, *Early Annals*, 13.

Chapter 8

1 Alan Paton, *Cry the Beloved Country* (Penguin edition, Harmondsworth, 1958), 8. The titihoya is the black-winged plover (*Stephanibyx melanopterus*).
2 Much of the information contained in this paragraph was obtained in March 1972 from various farmers in East Griqualand, to whom I am most grateful. See also P. L. Carter, 'Late Stone Age exploitation patterns in southern Natal', *South African Archaeological Bulletin*, XXV (1970), 55—7; Solomon and Read to Tidman, 30 June 1966, LMS 34/1/A.
3 A. F. Hattersley (ed.), *Later Annals of Natal* (London, 1938), 23.
4 See Payne Mss., 12 July 1866, KCL Durban.
5 Solomon and Read to Tidman, 30 June 1866, LMS 34/1/A.
6 Fenton, *Peculiar People*, 212—15; Dower, *Early Annals*, 80.
7 Fenton, *Peculiar People*, 213.
8 This information was gleaned from an analysis of the books of land grants in East Griqualand, GO 10 & 11. See also CPP G58 '79, 137—8.
9 See E. Rosenthal, *Southern African Dictionary of National Biography* (London, 1966), 365.
10 CPP G58 '79, 28.
11 When he died in 1897 he was worth £20,000, all in land. (See Register of

Wills, Cape Archives.) See also G. P. Stafford and Darby & Tyrell to Special Commissioners, 27 Oct. 1875, in CPP G37 '76, 97–8.

12 See Dower, *Early Annals*, 40; Turner Papers, *passim* (microfilm in Library of University of Cape Town).

13 Griffith, Ayliff and Grant to Col. Sec., 14 May 1871, CPP SC12 '73, 114–17, Scott Mss., KCL Durban.

14 Scott Mss., KCL Durban.

15 *Ibid.*

16 Dower, *Early Annals*, 21.

17 Twells diary, USPG archives, E.26, 1279–80.

18 *Ibid.*

19 Solomon to Tidman, 6 June 1866, LMS 34/2/A.

20 Twells diary, USPG archives. E.26, 1290.

21 Solomon and Read to Tidman, 30 June 1866, LMS 34/1/A.

22 See marriage records in the Griqua National Church in Kokstad.

23 Jenkins to Secs., 22 Dec. 1865, WMMS SA box XV.

24 Ordination of Johannes Bezuidenhout, LMS 38/1/C.

25 S. J. Halford, *The Griquas of Griqualand* (Cape Town, n.d. [1949]), 111.

26 See n 22.

27 Jean van der Poel, 'Basutoland as a factor in South African Politics', 184–5.

28 Currie to Grey, 29 June 1861, enclosed in Grey to Newcastle, 12 July 1861, GH 28/76.

29 Memorandum of J. M. Orpen, 26 June 1861, *Bas. Rec.*, II:588–93.

30 Statement of Nehemiah, CPP G37 '76, 138.

31 *Ibid.* 135.

32 Special Commissioners to Col. Sec., 25 Oct. 1875, printed in CPP G16 '76, 96–7.

33 *Ibid.* See also Rolland to Wodehouse, 20 June 1863, GH 18/4.

34 Statement of Kok, CPP G37 '76, 204; Statement of Nehemiah, *ibid.* 141.

35 Statement of Kok, *ibid.* 201–2; Fenton, *Peculiar People*, 213.

36 S. Mlamleli to Orpen, 29 Mar. 1906. Orpen Papers, Cory Library, Grahamstown.

37 On the Kat River, see above all Marais, *Cape Coloured People*, 216–45; Donovan Williams, *When Races Meet* (Johannesburg, 1967), 154–96; Kirk, 'Progress and decline', 411–27.

38 On Pommer, see Richards, 'Pommer and Sidoï'.

39 Census of Jan. 1874, in CPP G27 '74, 56. Also memorandum by J. M. Orpen, CPP SC12 '73, 30; Griffith, Ayliff and Grant to Col. Sec., 18 May 1871, in *ibid.* 127; Dower to Mullens, 29 Aug. 1874, LMS 37/4/A.

40 On the attempt of the Griquas to take over, and the political situation generally, see Nicholas Waterboer's journal in GWLC 33.

41 See, e.g., Griffith, Ayliff and Grant to Col. Sec., 14 May 1871, CPP SC12 '73, 111.

42 Dower, *Early Annals*, 19.

43 He testified to this himself. See Kok to Commissioners, n.d. in CPP G37 '76, 76.

44 Fenton, *Peculiar People*, 212–13.

45 These were stashed away in the magistrate's office at Umzimkulu, until finally one was bound into every copy of the Dower's Book. See CPP G58 '79, 52.
46 See Dower, *Early Annals*, 40.
47 E.g. CPP G58 '79, 51. See also the Statement of Lehana, in CPP G37 '76, 119; Thomas Jenkins to Secs., 27 Dec. 1865, WMMS, SA box XX.
48 Dower, *Early Annals*, 43; Dodgshun Papers, South Africa Public Library.
49 CPP G58 '79, 52.
50 *Ibid.* 2–3.
51 CPP G74 '80, *passim*; CMK 5/8, *passim*.
52 CPP G74 '80, 35–6.
53 CMK 5/8.
54 See his journal in GWLC 33. His interest in carpentry may well have been stimulated by a gift of tools from Sir Benjamin D'Urban when he visited Cape Town with his father to sign a treaty in 1834.
55 These books are at GO 10 & 11. On the business of land and its surveying, see the evidence of G. C. Brisley in CPP G4 '83, 511; the instructions for giving out land, GO1, 7 Mar. 1867; and the appointment of Edward Barker as surveyor, GO6, 10 Feb. 1868.
56 CPP G37 '76, 84–7, 270–5.
57 GO, 20 Mar. 1872; Molefe, census officer, in CPP G21 '75, 116–17. Cf. Henry Slater's description of Natal in 'The Natal Land and Colonisation Company, 1860–1948', *Collected Seminar Papers of the Institute of Commonwealth Studies, London, Southern Africa* IV (1973).
58 GO1, 7 Dec. 1870.
59 This notice is kept in GWLC 33.
60 See CPP G37 '76, 84–7; David Isaak to Abel Pienaar, 19 Nov. 1871 in Pienaar Papers, Macgregor Memorial Museum, Kimberley.
61 See Strachan to Brisley, 27 May 1871, GO6.
62 Gleaned from the records in the loose folder in GO6.
63 Strachan to Brisley, 27 May 1871, GO5.
64 GO3, 4 Feb. and 4 May 1874.
65 E.g. G. St. V. Cripps, 'Highlands and lowlands of Kaffraria', *Cape Monthly Magazine* (1877), 327; M. S. Benham, *Henry Callaway M.D. D.D.; First Bishop of Kaffraria* (London, 1896), 192–3.
66 See CPP G21 '75, 87, and, on the appointment of J. C. Barker as Ferryman, GO3, 8 Dec. 1870.
67 CPP G58 '79, 50.
68 GO3, 14 July 1874.
69 GO3, Licences folder.
70 G. P. Stafford and Darby and Tyrell to Special Commissioners, 27 Oct. 1875, in CPP G37 '76, 97–8.
71 See Scott Diary, Durban; Griffith, Ayliff and Grant to Col. Sec., 14 May 1871, CPP SC12 '73, 1/4–17.
72 The original is found GO2, 35–8, and, rendered into English with one significant mistranslation, in CPP G58 '79.
73 See particularly the glowing record of him in Dower, *Early Annals*, 78–82,

but also Sir Arthur Cunynghame, *My Command in South Africa, 1874–8* (London, 1879), 152–3, and Cripps, 'Highlands and Lowlands', 327.

74 Dower, *Early Annals*, 17.
75 CMK 4/16, Records of the 40 Years money, Griqualand East.
76 Dower, *Early Annals*, 77.
77 GO2, 10 Nov. 1865.
78 Between 1874 and 1876 there were 134 people married in the Griqua church of whom 47 per cent (63) were able to sign their names. Many of those who were illiterate were of Sotho extraction, so far as can be told by their names.
79 CPP G58 '79, 60; GO2, Law of 5 Oct. 1858.
80 Evidence of G. C. Brisley, CPP G4 '83, 512.
81 The voting figures are in GO5, and the population figures are based on the censuses in CPP G17 '78, 73 and G21 '75, 120. For a contrary interpretation of the same material, see Marais, *Cape Coloured People*, 65.
82 GO5, 16 Aug. 1870.
83 GO5, 7 Sept. 1870.
84 Constitution, GO2, 37.
85 Memorandum of G. C. Brisley, CPP G21 '75, 72.
86 GO1, 6–8 June 1871.
87 See the disparaging remarks of both the Commission of Enquiry into the Rebellion in Griqualand East, CPP G58 '79, 50, and the Select Committee on Native Affairs, CPP SC12 '73, 111.
88 Dower, *Early Annals*, 18.
89 GO1, 7 March 1872.
90 GO1, 6 Sept. 1871.
91 Dower, *Early Annals*, 17.
92 CPP G58 '79, 8.
93 In this analysis I follow F. G. Bailey, 'Decisions by consensus in councils and committees', Association of Social Anthropologists Monographs II, *Political Systems and the Distribution of Power* (London, 1965), 13, and Adam Kuper, 'Council structure and decision making' in A. Richards and A. Kuper (eds.), *Councils in Action* (Cambridge, 1971).
94 CPP G58 '79, 50.
95 On his appointment, see GO1, 102–5. On the profits of office, see GO1, 7 Dec. 1869, and GO3, 10 Dec. 1870.
96 GO2, 8 Dec. 1864.
97 Unpublished 1870 Constitution, GO2, 37–8.
98 Evidence of G. C. Brisley, CPP G4 '83, 510.
99 GO1, 8 Dec. 1868.
100 GO1, 19 Oct. 1864.
101 On this see David Welsh, *The Roots of Segregation* (Cape Town, 1972) 112, 120–1; A. T. Bryant, *Olden Times in Zululand and Natal*, (London, 1929), 351–2; Richards, 'Pommer and Sidoi', 317–24; Hulley Papers, KCL, sec. 3.
102 See E. Stafford to Henrique Shepstone (magistrate of Alfred County), n.d. [7 Mar. 1871], and Henrique Shepstone to Secretary of Native Affairs,

Natal, 9 Mar. 1871, both enclosed in Keate to Barkly, 10 Aug. 1871, GH 9/9. See also L. Pretorius and J. Smith to Govt Sec., 7 Mar. 1871, GO5.

103 As it happened, they were greatly aided by the exceptionally complicated dynastic situation among the Bhaca. Of this, it is important, for our present purposes, to distinguish the Bhaca of Makaula, the largest group who lived in Mount Frere, from those who followed Cijisiwe, Thiba and Nomtsheketshe, who lived in Umzimkulu district. For further explanation see W. D. Hammond-Tooke, *The Tribes of Mount Frere District* (Pretoria, 1956).

104 He 'did not like paying Hottentots'. Statement of Duta and Mehlwana, 14 Mar. 1865, enclosed in Maclean to Wodehouse, 28 Mar. 1865, GH 9/6.

105 There is a voluminous correspondence on this episode in GH 9/8.

106 Hammond-Tooke, *Mount Frere District.*

107 See Hulley Papers (KCL) and R. K. Hulley to Resident Magistrate, Umzimkulu, 28 Mar. 1956 (Courtesy of Professor W. D. Hammond-Tooke).

108 Kok to Letuka Morosi, Stephanus Lepheane, Lebu Lepheane and Mosi Lepheane, 30 Jan. 1867, in GO1.

109 This section follows the evidence of G. C. Brisley to the Commission on Native Laws and Customs, CPP G4 '83, 510–12, and is confirmed by the records of the case of Monjonjo's murder, GO4, 15 July 1871.

110 Brisley, see n 109 above.

111 Sidoi v. 'Rooi' Jan Pienaar, GO1, 8 Sept. 1866.

112 GO9, Hut tax record for 1867. Paddy O'Reilly's 'real' name was Murphy. See Strachan, *Kokstad Advertiser*, 19 Dec. 1902.

113 CPP G58 '79, 50.

114 Memorandum of G. C. Brisley, 15 Oct. 1875, CPP G21 '75, 72.

115 Special Commissioners to Col. Sec., Cape Town, 25 Oct. 1872, in CPP G16 '76, 99.

116 See complaints of Jacobus de Vries and Sakopula, GO3, 5 Sept. 1872.

117 See book of passes in GO9. They were only necessary for those Africans who wished to travel to the Cape Colony or Natal.

118 These were the Tlhokwa under Lebenya and two groups of Hlubi, one under Ludidi and the other under Zibi. See Memorandum of J. M. Orpen, CPP SC12 '73, 20.

119 Gedye to Shepstone, 23 Sept. 1871, enclosed in Keate to Barkly, 7 Oct. 1871, GH 9/9.

120 GO1, 5 Sept. 1871.

121 Dower to Mullen, 12 Oct. 1871, LMS 35/5/B.

122 White to Shepstone, 29 Sept. 1871, in Keate to Barkly, 7 Oct. 1871, GH 9/9.

123 Dower, *Early Annals*, 43. For his previous career see F. W. Rawstorne to ASLG, 9 Apr. 1845, LG 204 and for his appointment see GO1, 5 Sept. 1871.

124 Dower to Mullen, 12 Oct. 1871, LMS 35/5/B; also Gedye to Boyce, 2 Oct. 1871, WMMS Box XV; Gedye to Shepstone, 7 Oct. 1871, and White to Shepstone, 7 Oct. 1871, both in (Natal) SNA 1/1/21.

125 GO1, 19 Dec. 1871.

126 Dower, *Early Annals*, 43. Cf. Shula Marks and Anthony Atmore, 'Firearms in Southern Africa: a survey', *JAH* XII (1971), 519.
127 See Dower, *Early Annals*, 30–4; [Strachan], *Kokstad Advertiser*, 19 Dec. 1902.
128 This is found in the manuscript biography of Dower by Margaret Dodgshun in the South African Public Library.
129 Dower, *Early Annals*, 38–9. A stool made by Nicholas Waterboer for Wesleyan missionary, John Ayliffe, is in the Killie Campbell Museum, Durban.
130 See Dower, *Early Annals*, 22, 36; CPP G58 '79, 5.
131 CPP G58 '79, 5.
132 CPP G74 '80, 60–2.
133 Dower, *Early Annals*, 50.

Chapter 9

1 In fact, Griquas remained in possession of many of the *erven* in Kokstad until 1970, when they were forced to move to three streets on the edge of the town, in consequence of the application of the Group Areas Act.
2 CPP UG41 '26, 24.
3 I owe this information and much else to J. J. Leeuwenburg of the University of Cape Town.
4 See CPP G58 '79, 46; Dower, *Early Annals*, 57.
5 See Dower, *Early Annals*, 33, 59. The other man was Titus Klein, an old slave who became one of Kok's councillors; *ibid*. 88. On Muis's descent, see Clark papers, KCL Durban.
6 Dower, *Early Annals*, 45–6.
7 See e.g., Shepstone to Lieutenant Governor, n.d. enclosed in Keate to Wodehouse, 24 Oct. 1868, GH 9/8.
8 CPP G37 '76: statement of Lehana, 131.
9 For the political position and economic base of the eastern Province Cape Liberals, see Stanley Trapido, 'Liberalism in the Cape in the 19th and 20th centuries', *Collected Seminar Papers of the Institute of Commonwealth Studies, London, Southern Africa* IV (1972–3).
10 See Griffith, Ayliff and Grant to Col. Sec., 10 May 1871, CPP SC12 '73, 112.
11 W. B. Campbell, 'The South African frontier, 1865–85; a study in expansion', *AYB for SAH* (1959, I), 113.
12 Orpen's report, March 1874, CPP G27 '74, 50.
13 Orpen to Brownlee, 10 Sept. 1873, CPP G27 '74, 79.
14 See ch. 7 above.
15 See CPP G21 '75, 67 Kok to Commissioners, 30 Aug. 1875; CPP G37 '76, 76–8, gives a rather different account of the meeting, stressing that Kok only wished for clarification of his position.
16 Memorandum of Sir H. Barkly to Kok, CPP G21 '75, 73; Orpen to Secretary of Native Affairs, 7 Nov. 1874, CPP G21 '75, 76.
17 Dower, *Early Annals*, 53.

18   The details of these negotiations are published in CPP G21 '75, 74—8.
19   Dower, *Early Annals*, 75—6.
20   *Ibid*. 82.
21   CPP G58 '79, 50.
22   Evidence of Brisley, CPP G58 '79, 171.
23   Evidence of Dower, *ibid*. 213.
24   Campbell, 'The South African Frontier', esp. 122—4, gives an account of Blyth's career before he reached Griqualand.
25   CPP G58 '79, 412—13.
26   For a more detailed narrative of the rebellion and for an analysis of the motives of many of those involved in it, see CPP G58 '79, 6—7.
27   *Ibid*. 41.
28   See tables in CPP A51 '78, 58.
29   Evidence of Philander Gous, CPP G58 '79, 191.
30   Evidence of Jan Jood, *ibid*. 113.
31   *Ibid*. 41.
32   *Ibid*. 21.
33   See the evidence of Lawrence, *ibid*. 102.
34   This point is made by the Commission of Enquiry, *ibid*. 45.
35   Dower, *Early Annals*, 77.

Chapter 10

1   Gilbert Gilkes, *Extracts from Letters Written at Ikwesi Lamaci* (London, 1896), 14—15.
2   A similar pattern was frequently the case in the New World, among the structurally similar group of Free Coloureds. See David W. Cohen and Jack P. Greene, *Neither Slave nor Free: the freedman of African descent in the slave societies of the New World* (Baltimore, 1972), 13—14.
3   For the origins of this, see Stanley Trapido, 'The origin and development of the African political organisation' in *Collected Seminar Papers on the Societies of Southern Africa in the 19th and 20th Centuries* (Institute of Commonwealth Studies, London, 1969—70).
4   See Bob Edgar, 'Garveyism in Africa: Dr Wellington and the "American Movement" in the Transkei, 1925—30' in *Collected Seminar Papers on the Societies of Southern Africa in the 19th and 20th Centuries*. (Institute of Commonwealth Studies, London, 1974—5).
5   On this, see C. van Onselen, 'Reactions to rinderpest in southern Africa', *JAH* XIII (1972), 976—9.
6   This analysis owes a great deal to long conversations with J. J. Leeuwenburg of the University of Cape Town, and relies to a large extent on his unpublished research material.
7   On Le Fleur and the 40 Years money, see particularly William Dower, 'A History of the 40 Years Money', manuscript in CMK 1/140.
8   Although the nature of the phenomenon is such that hard data are impossible to come by, it is reasonably certain that various of the descendants of the Griquas are by now classified as 'white'. Gossip around

Kokstad and Kimberley will reveal names. For a similar process in the urban environment of Cape Town, see Graham Watson, *Passing for White: A study of racial assimilation in a South African School* (London, 1970), *passim*.

9 Quoted in W. K. Hancock, *Smuts, I. The Sanguine Years* (Cambridge, 1962), 521.

NOTE ON SOURCES

This study is based almost entirely on written sources, apart from occasional snatches of description of the modern situation, which I owe mainly to the anthropological investigations of J. J. Leeuwenburg. Pilot studies in and around Kokstad showed quickly that there was no great depth of tradition of the independent Captaincies remaining among the Griquas. It would not have been worth the time and the money necessary to collect what does survive, for insofar as it can be judged, this would only have substantiated in minor details the picture presented by archival and other records. Though annoying, this is in itself not surprising, for the Griquas were always a literate people, and never had any institutionalised medium for the preservation and transmission of unwritten historical material. They seem to base their knowledge of their past on the books written about them, even if they claim that those books are as false as they are undoubtedly patronising.

Such a lacuna would be fatal to the study of the history of many African societies. For the Griquas, however, there exists a plethora of written sources, both published and unpublished. These records fall into four main categories. First there are the records of travellers, who from time to time met the Griquas and wrote of their impressions. The main difficulty with these fairly numerous sources is that their writers tend to impose stereotypes – frequently those of Boer or British settlers to the south, or of British philanthropists stirred up by mission propagandists – upon the Griqua scene. Moreover, they scarcely ever stayed long enough to gain first-hand experience of the political processes at work within the Griqua Captaincies. An honourable exception to this is Dr Andrew Smith who made a long trip north of the Orange in 1834–5 and whose diaries and journals are very valuable. Primarily, however, the use of this type of material is in providing local colour, for information on the detailed development of Griqua life is best gained elsewhere.

Secondly, there are the reports that the various missionaries sent back to their employers in Europe. Of these, the records of the London Missionary Society, the Wesleyan Methodist Missionary Society and the United Society for the Propagation of the Gospel have been studied in the original, while only the

172

published reports of the Paris Evangelical Missionary Society and the Berlin Missionary Society have been read. All except the LMS are essentially peripheral to the Griquas. Only the agents of the London Society ever ministered in Philippolis or Kokstad. Even the letters of these men, however, must be used with caution. They were often concerned to mould the political life of the society in which they worked, and to provide a good report for their financial backers, or to exaggerate difficulties in times of failure. Nevertheless, these men were often confidantes and advisors of the *Kaptyns* and were participant observers in the processes of Griqua life, so that their observations may be relied on, to a fair degree. Similar strictures apply, more forcibly, to the agents of other societies, but some of them, notably the Wesleyans who had a long tradition of feud with the Congregational London society, exacerbated by the psychological pressures prevalent on the frontier of 'civilisation', provide evidence of the concerns and actions of those with whom the Griquas were competing.

Thirdly, there are those records collected by the Cape colonial Government and the Governments of the Orange Free State and Natal. These were studied in South Africa, in the archives at Cape Town, Bloemfontein and Pietermaritzburg, for they were fullest there, rather than in the Public Record Office in London, for much that is of interest to the historian of the local scene would have been filtered out before it reached Britain. These records have the obvious disadvantages of partisanship and selective ignorance. Virtually all the Griquas' political ideas are relayed through them, and so only such thoughts and statements as the Griquas wanted the various white Governments to receive have been preserved. On the other hand, the British in the Cape and the Boers in the Free State were such important actors in the Griqua drama that the fullness of the archives more than compensates for their deficiencies. Particularly useful were the letters of Fleetwood Rawstorne, for long Civil Commissioner at Colesberg on the northern border of the Cape Colony.

All the sources so far discussed have a common disadvantage. They are all external to the Griqua situation, merely records of Griqua dealings with non-Griquas, primarily whites. Although it is impossible to eliminate completely such bias, it is most fortunate that, uniquely for so-called 'non-Europeans' in South Africa at such a date, there exists a fair amount of material of purely Griqua origin. Some is scattered in unlikely places in South Africa. The papers of the last Secretary to Government in Philippolis and other similar documents were produced as evidence in the Griqualand West Land Court and in various other legal wrangles over the Diamond Fields. The papers that Kok left with his agent to cope with business in the Free State after the Griquas had left it were found in the Albany Museum in Grahamstown. A few registers still exist in the Griqua National Independent Church in Kokstad. By far the most valuable, however, are the records of the Griqua Government itself, although unfortunately these only exist from the time of the trek to East Griqualand. Only the law book survived the crossing of the Drakensberg, when the other records of the Philippolis Government were lost in a flood. Moreover, they are fullest only for the last four years of the Griquas' independence, when they were organised by G. C. Brisley, an Englishman who was the Government Secretary, and do not contain much information on the workings of the various subordinate officials. There is, for instance, no mention of the outlawry of Cornelis van Wyk in the judicial reports, nor of the *cause célèbre* when Nicholas van der Westhuis fined Harry Escombe, later Prime Minister of Natal, five pounds for contempt of court. In general, however, they contain a remarkable quantity of valuable material.

SELECT BIBLIOGRAPHY

MANUSCRIPT MATERIAL

Cape Arvhices: Files in the following series: Beaufort West (BW), Colesberg (CBG), Kokstad (CMK), Colonial Office (CO), Government House (GH), Griqualand West (GLW), Griqualand Government, Griqualand East (GO), Graaff-Reinet (GR), Griqualand West Land Court (GWLC), Lieutenant Governor of the Eastern Province (LG), Native Affairs Department (NA), Receiver of Land Revenue (RLR), Verbatim Copies (VC).

Archives of the Orange Free State, Bloemfontein: Files in the following series: Assistant Commissioners (AC), Registrateur van Aktes (AKT), British Resident (BR), Goewerment Secretaris (GS), High Commissioner (HC), Insolvende Boedels (IB), Steytler Collection (SC), Volksraad (VR).

Natal Archives, Pietermaritzburg: Files in the following series: Hawkins Papers (GH), Parliamentary Papers (PP), Secretary of Native Affairs (SNA).

Cory Library of Historical Research, Grahamstown : Orpen Papers.

Griqua National Independent Church, Kokstad: Church Registers.

Jagger Library, University of Cape Town: W.B. Philip collection.

Johannesburg Public Library: Solomon Papers.

Killie Campbell Library, Durban: The papers collected from the following Natal families proved valuable: Clark, Hulley, Payne, Scott, Stafford.

London Missionary Society (now the archives of the Congregational Council for World Missions, housed in the School of Oriental and African Studies. London): South African In Letters, South African Odds, South African Journals.

Macgregor Memorial Museum, Kimberley: Pienaar Papers.

Nederduitsche Gereformeerde Kerk, Philippolis: Minute Books.

Rhodes House, Oxford: The Philip Papers of Professor W. M. Macmillan.

South African Museum, Cape Town: Andrew Smith Papers.

South African Public Library, Cape Town: Dodgshun Papers.

United Society for the Propagation of the Gospel: South African volumes.

Wesleyan Methodist Missionary Society: South African Boxes.

OFFICIAL PUBLICATIONS

Cape Colony or Union of South Africa Parliamentary Papers
These are designated in the footnotes by 'CPP'

Bibliography

Published by order of the Cape House of Assembly
A118 '61   *Correspondence relative to the Occupation of Nomansland by Captain Adam Kok and the Griquas, 1861*
A51 '78   *Papers relative to the Griqualand East Rebellion, 1878*
A23 '80   *Copy of a letter of Adam Kok to Government, 4 October, 1861*

Published by Order of the Cape Government
G53 '62   *Correspondence relative to the Settlement of the Country between the Bashee and the Western Border of Natal, 1862*
G27 '74   *Bluebook on Native Affairs, 1874*
G21 '75   *Bluebook on Native Affairs, 1875*
G16 '76   *Bluebook on Native Affairs, 1876*
G52 '76   *Appendix to Bluebook on Native Affairs, 1876*
G37 '76   *Report of a Commission to inquire into the affairs of the Territory of Griqualand East, 1876*
G12 '77   *Bluebook on Native Affairs, 1877*
G17 '78   *Bluebook on Native Affairs, 1878*
G33 '79   *Bluebook on Native Affairs, 1879*
G43 '79   *Appendix to Blue Book on Native Affairs, 1879*
G58 '79   *Report of a Commission to Enquire into the causes of the recent outbreak in Griqualand East: and further into the Justice of the demands of certain residents of the said territory for compensation for alleged losses therefrom, 1878*
G74 '80   *Second Part of the Report of the Commission to Enquire into the Outbreak in Griqualand East, 1878*
G4 '83   *Report of the Commission on Native Laws and Customs, 1883*
G2 '84   *Report of the Land Commission to Griqualand East, 1884*
            (This is often referred to as the 'Vacant Land Commission')
G2 '85   *Blue Book on Native Affairs, 1885*

Report of a Select Committee of the Cape House of Assembly
SC12 '73   *Report of a Select Committee on Native Affairs, 1873*

Published By Order of the Union Government
UG41 '26   *Report of the Rehoboth Commission, 1926*

Miscellaneous
The Bloemhof Blue Book
(This elusive but very valuable document is strictly 'Evidence taken at Bloemhof before the Commission appointed to investigate the claims of the South African Republic, Chief N. Waterboer, chief of West Griqualand, and certain other native chiefs, to portions of territory on the Vaal River, now known as the Diamond Fields.' It is Annexure 74 of 1872 to the Cape House of Assembly. The archival copy can thus be found in the Cape Archives, in volume HA 89, although other copies exist in a variety of places.)
Cape of Good Hope, *South African Native Affairs Commission: Report, 1903–1905* (6 vols., Cape Town, 1905).

Other South African Official Publications
Cape of Good Hope, *Statistical Blue Book of the Colony, 1825–1863*
Orange Vrij Staat, *Volksraad Notulen, 1860–3*
Union of South Africa, Archives Commission, *South African Archival Records, Natal*, I–IV, *Transvaal*, I, II, *Orange Free State*, I–IV
Union of South Africa, Weather Bureau, *Climate of South Africa* (23 parts, Pretoria, 1960)

British Parliamentary Papers
(In the footnotes these are designated by 'BPP', followed by the command number and the session date. In this list, the Roman numeral refers to the volume number in the standard binding.)
1835, 50, 252, XXXIX, *Papers regarding the condition and treatment of the Native Inhabitants of Southern Africa within the Colony of the Cape of Good Hope or beyond the Frontier of the Colony*
1836, 538, VII. *Report of the Select Committee on Aborigines (British Settlements) with Minutes of Evidence*
1836, 279, XXXIX. *Papers relative to the late Caffre War and the death of Hintsa*
1837, 425, VII, *Appendix to the Report of Select Committee on Aborigines (British Settlements)*
1837, 503, XLIII, *Correspondence with the Governor of the Cape of Good Hope relative to the late Caffre War*
1847, 786, XXXVIII, *Correspondence with the Governor of the Cape of Good Hope relative to the State of the Kafir tribes*
1847–8, 912, 969, XLIII, *Correspondence with the Governor of the Cape of Good Hope relative to the state of the Kafir tribes on the Eastern Frontier of the Colony*
1849, 1056, XXVI, *Correspondence with the Governor of the Cape of Good Hope relative to the State of the Kafir tribes on the Eastern Frontier of the Colony*
1849, 1059, XXXVI, *Correspondence relative to the Establishment of the Settlement of Natal and the Recent Rebellion of the Boers*
1850, 1288, XXXVIII, *Correspondence with the Governor of the Cape of Good Hope relative to the Kafir tribes on the Eastern Frontier of the Colony*
1851, 424, XXXVIII, *Copies or Extracts of Correspondence relative to the Kafir tribes between the years 1837 to 1845*
1851, 1334, 1352, 1380, XXXVIII, *Correspondence with the Governor of the Cape of Good Hope relative to the State of the Kafir tribes and to the recent outbreak on the Eastern frontier of the Colony*
1851, 635, XIV, *Report of the Select Committee on the Kafir tribes*
1851, 1360, XXXVII, *Correspondence with the Governor of the Cape of Good Hope relative to the Assumption of Sovereignty over the Territory between the Vaal and Orange Rivers*
1852, 1428, XXXIII, *Correspondence with the Governor of the Cape of Good*

Hope relative to the State of the Kafir tribes and to the recent outbreak on the Eastern Frontier of the Colony

1852–3, 1646, LXVI, *Further Correspondence relative to the State of the Orange River Territory*

1854, 1758, XLIII, *Further Correspondence relative to the state of the Orange River Territory*

1860, 216, 357, XLV, *Copies or Extracts of all Correspondence which has taken place between the Colonial Office and Governor Sir George Grey respecting his recall from the Cape of Good Hope and his subsequent re-appointment to the Government of that Colony*

BOOKS

Acocks, J. P. H. *Veld Types of South Africa* (Pretoria, 1953)

Adam, Heribert *Modernising Racial Domination: South Africa's political dynamics* (Berkeley, 1971)

Adams, Buck *The Narrative of Private Buck Adams, 7th (Princess Royal's) Dragoon Guards on the Eastern Frontier of the Cape of Good Hope 1843–1848*, ed. A. Gordon-Brown (Cape Town, 1941)

Agar-Hamilton, J. A. I. *The Native Policy of the Voortrekkers: an essay on the history of the interior of South Africa, 1836–1858* (Cape Town, 1928)

Arbousset, T. *Voyage d'exploration au nord-est de la Colonie du Cap de Bonne Esperance* (Paris, 1842)

Arnot, D. and Orpen, F. H. S. *The Land Question of Griqualand West: an inquiry into the various claims to land in that territory; together with a brief history of the Griqua Nation* (Cape Town, 1875)

Backhouse, J. *Narrative of a visit to Mauritius and South Africa* (London, 1884)

Banton, M. *Race Relations* (London, 1967)

Barrow, Sir J. *An Account of Travels into the interior of southern Africa* (2 vols., London, 1801–4)

Beach, D. M. *The Phonetics of the Hottentot Language* (Cambridge, 1938)

Benham, Marian S. *Henry Callaway, M.D. D.D.: First Bishop of Kaffraria* (London, 1896)

Bird, J. (ed.) *Annals of Natal: 1495 to 1845*, 2 vols. (Pietermaritzburg, 1888)

Blommaert, W. and Wiid, J. A. (eds.) *Die Joernaal van Dirk Gysbert van Reenen* (Cape Town, 1937)

Borcherds, P. B. *An Autobiographical Memoir* (Cape Town, 1861)

Bosch, J. A. *Eufeesgedenkboek van die N.G. Gemeente Philippolis 1802–1962* (n.p. 1962)

Boyce, William B. *Notes on South African Affairs* (London, 1839)

Briggs, D. Roy, and Wing, Joseph *The Harvest and the Hope: the story of Congregationalism in South Africa* (Pretoria, 1970)

Bryant, A. T. *Olden Times in Zululand and Natal* (London, 1929)

Burchell, W. J. *Travels in the Interior of South Africa, 1822*, ed. I. Schapera (2 vols., London, 1953)

Bibliography

Campbell, J. *Travels in South Africa, 1813* (London, 1815)
    Travels in South Africa . . . being a Narrative of a Second Journey, 1820,
    2 vols. (London, 1822)
Carstens, W. P. *The Social Structure of a Cape Coloured Reserve* (Cape Town,
    1966)
Chapman, J. *Travels in the Interior of South Africa*, 2 vols. (London, 1868)
    *Travels in the Interior of South Africa, 1849–63: hunting and trading
    journeys from Natal to Walvis Bay and visits to Lake Ngami and Victoria
    Falls*, ed. E. C. Tabler (2 vols., Cape Town, 1971)
Chase, J. C. *Natal Papers* (Cape Town, 1843)
    The Cape of Good Hope and the Eastern Province of Algoa Bay, (Cape
    Town, 1843)
Cohen, David W. and Greene, Jack P. *Neither Slave nor Free: the freedman of
    African descent in the slave societies of the New World* (Baltimore,
    1972)
Collins, W. W. *Free Statia: reminiscences of a lifetime in the Orange Free
    State* (Cape Town, 1965)
Cory, Sir George E. *The Rise of South Africa* (5 vols., London, 1910–30)
Cumming, R. G. *Five Years of a Hunter's Life in the Far Interior of South
    Africa* (2 vols., London, 1856)
Cunynghame, Sir Arthur *My Command in South Africa, 1874–8* (London,
    1879)
de Bruin, C. G. *Early History of Adam Kok and East Griqualand* (n.p., n.d.)
de Kiewiet, C. W. *British Colonial Policy and the South African Republics
    1848–1872* (London, 1929)
    The Imperial Factor in South Africa: a study in politics and economics
    (Cambridge, 1937)
    A History of South Africa: social and economic (London, 1941)
de la Caille, N. C. *Journal Historique du Voyage fait au Cap de Bonne
    Esperance* (Paris, 1776)
Derricourt, R. and Saunders, C. C. (eds.) *Beyond the Cape Frontier, studies
    in the history of the Transkei and Ciskei* (Cape Town, 1974)
Dobie, J. S. *John Shedden Dobie's South African Journal, 1862–1866*, ed.
    A. F. Maltersley (Cape Town, 1945)
Dover, C. *Half-Caste* (London, 1937)
Dower, William *Vriendelijk Raad aan Een Verlegen Volk: zijnde een brief van
    Eerwd. W. Dower aan de Griquas* (King Williams Town, 1876)
    The Early Annals of Kokstad and Griqualand East (Port Elizabeth, 1902)
du Plessis, J. A. *A History of Christian Missions in South Africa* (London,
    1911)
Edwards, J. *Reminiscences of the Early Life and Missionary Labours of the
    Rev. John Edwards*, 2nd edn (London, 1886)
Ellenberger, D. F. *History of the Basuto, Ancient and Modern*, trans. J. C.
    MacGregor (London, 1912)
Elphick, R. H. *The Cape Khoi and the First Phase of South African Race
    Relations* (Ph.D. thesis, Yale, 1972, published by University Microfilms,
    Ann Arbor)

179

Engelbrecht, J. A. *The Korana: an account of their customs and their history* (Cape Town, 1936)

Eybers, G. W. *Select Constitutional Documents illustrating South African History 1795–1910* (London, 1918)

Fawcett, J. *Account of an Eighteen Month Residence at the Cape of Good Hope in 1835–6* (Cape Town, 1836)

Fenton, Reginald *Peculiar People in a pleasant land: a South African narrative* (Giraud, Kansas, 1905)

Fischer, E. *Die Rehobother Bastards und das Bastardierungsproblem beim Menschen* (Jena, 1913)

Fouche, L. and Boeseken, A. (eds.) *The Diary of Adam Tas* (Cape Town, 1970)

Freeman, J. J. *A Tour in South Africa* (London, 1851)

Frye, John (ed.) *The War of the Axe and the Xhosa Bible: the Journal of the Rev. J. W. Appleyard* (Cape Town, 1871)

Galbraith, J. S. *Reluctant Empire: British policy on the South African frontier, 1834–54* (Berkeley, 1963)

Genovese, E. D. *In Red and Black* (London, 1971)

Gerdener, G. B. A. *Bouwstoffen vir die Geskiedenis van die Nederduitsche Gereformeerde Kerk in die Transgariep* (Cape Town, 1930)

Germond, R. *Chronicles of Basutoland* (Morija, 1967)

Gilkes, Gilbert *Extracts from Letters written at Ikwesi Lamaci* (London, 1896)

Goodfellow, C. F. *Great Britain and South African Confederation, 1870–1881* (Cape Town, 1966)

Goody, J. R. (ed.) *Literacy in Traditional Societies* (Cambridge, 1969)

Gray, C. *The Life of Robert Gray, Bishop of Cape Town and Metropolitan of Africa* (2 vols., London, 1876)

Gray, Richard, and Birmingham, David (eds.) *Precolonial African Trade* (London, 1970)

Grey, H. G. 3rd Earl *The Colonial Policy of Lord John Russell's Administration*, 2nd edn (2 vols., London, 1853)

Gutsche, Thelma *The Microcosm* (Cape Town, 1968)

Hahn, T. *Tsuni-//Goam, The Supreme Being of the Khoi-Khoi* (London, 1881)

Halford, S. J. *The Griquas of Griqualand* (Cape Town, n.d. [1949])

Hancock, W. K. *Smuts: 1, The Sanguine Years 1870–1919* (Cambridge, 1962) *Smuts: 2, The Fields of Force 1919–1950* (Cambridge, 1968)

Hamelberg, H. A. L. *Die Dagboek van H. A. L. Hamelberg*, ed. F. J. du T. Spies (Cape Town, 1952)

Hammond-Tooke, W. D. *The Tribes of Mount Frere District* (Pretoria, 1956) *Bhaca Society* (London, 1962)

Harris, W. C. *The Wild Sports of Southern Africa* (London, 1839)

Hattersley, A. F. (ed.) *More Annals of Natal* (London, 1936) (ed.) *Later Annals of Natal* (London, 1938)

Herman, Louis *A History of the Jews in Southern Africa from the earliest times to 1895* (London, 1930)

Hodgson, T. *The Memoirs of the Rev. Thomas Hodgson, Wesleyan Missionary in South Africa*, ed. T. Smith (London, 1854)

Bibliography

Holden, W. C. *History of the Colony of Natal, South Africa: to which is added an appendix containing a brief history of the Orange River Sovereignty and of the various races inhabiting it, the Great Lake Ngami, Commandos of the Dutch Boers etc. etc.* (London, 1855)
   A brief History of Methodism and of the Methodist Mission in South Africa (London, 1877)
Houghton, D. Hobart and Dagut, J. *Source Material on the South African Economy* (3 vols., Cape Town, 1972–3)
Hunter, M. *Reaction to Conquest* (London, 1936)
Jousse, T. *La Mission Française Evangelique au sud de l'Afrique: son origine et son dévelopment jusqu'a nos jours* (2 vols., Paris, 1889)
Kay, S. *Travels and Researches in Caffraria* (London, 1834)
Kirby, P. R. *Sir Andrew Smith: his life and works* (Cape Town, 1965)
Kotze, D. M. (ed.) *Letters of the American Missionaries* (Cape Town, 1950)
Kruger, B. *The Pear Tree Blossoms: a history of the Moravian mission stations in South Africa* (Genadendaal, 1966)
Kuhn, T. S. *The Structure of Scientific Revolutions* (Chicago, 1962)
Leach, E. R. *Political Systems of Highland Burma: a study of Kachin social structure* (London, 1954)
Legassick, M. C. *The Griqua, the Sotho-Tswana and the Missionaries, 1780– 1840: the politics of a frontier zone* (Ph.D. thesis; University of California, Los Angeles, 1970, published by University Microfilms, Ann Arbor, 1970)
Leyland, J. *Adventures in the Far Interior of South Africa* (London, 1866)
Lichtenstein, H. *Travels in Southern Africa, 1803, 1804, 1805*, trans. A. Plumptre (2 vols., Cape Town, 1928–30)
Lindley, A. F. *Adamantia: the truth about the South African diamond fields: or a vindication of the right of the Orange Free State to that territory* (London, 1873)
Livingstone, D. *Family Letters, 1841–1856*, ed. I. Schapera (2 vols., London, 1959)
   Missionary Correspondence, 1841–1856, ed. I. Schapera (London, 1961)
   Missionary Travels and Researches (London, 1857)
   Private Journals, ed. I. Schapera (Berkeley, 1960)
Livingstone, D. and C. *Narrative of an Expedition to the Zambesi and its Tributaries* (New York, 1866)
London Missionary Society *A register of missionaries, deputations etc. from 1796 to 1923*, prepared by James Sibree, 4th edn (London, 1923)
Lovett, R. *History of the London Missionary Society, 1795–1895* (London, 1899)
MacCrone, I. D. *Race Attitudes in South Africa: historical, experimental and psychological studies* (London, 1937)
   Group Conflicts and Race Prejudice, Hoernle Memorial Lecture (Johannesburg, 1947)
McKenzie, John *Ten Years North of the Orange River* (Edinburgh, 1871)
MacMillan, Mona *Sir Henry Barkly: mediator and moderator 1815 to 1895* (Cape Town, 1970)

181

MacMillan, W.M. *The Cape Coloured Question: a historical survey* (London, 1927)
   Bantu, Boer and Briton, 2nd edn (Oxford, 1963)
Majeke, N. *The role of the Missionaries in Conquest* (Johannesburg, 1952)
Marais, J. S. *Maynier and the first Boer Republics* (Cape Town, 1944)
   The Cape Coloured People, 1652–1937 (reprint, Johannesburg, 1957)
Marks, Shula *Reluctant Rebellion: Disturbances in Natal, 1906–08* (Oxford, 1970)
Martinez-Alier, Verena *Marriage, Class and Colour in Nineteenth-Century Cuba: a study of racial attitudes and sexual values in a slave society* (Cambridge, 1974)
Mentzel, O. F. *A Geographical and Topographical Description of the Cape of Good Hope (1787)*, translated by G. V. Marais and J. Hoge, revised and edited by H. J. Mandelbrote (3 vols., Cape Town, 1921, 1924, 1944)
Meredith, D. (ed.) *The Grasses and Pastures of South Africa* (Cape Town, 1955)
Merriman. N. J. *The Kafir, the Hottentot and the Frontier Farmer* (London, 1853)
   Cape Journals of Archdeacon N. J. Merriman, 1848–1855, ed. D. H. Varley and H. M. Matthew (Cape Town, 1957)
Methuen, H. H. *Life in the Wilderness: or wanderings in South Africa* (London, 1846)
Moffat, J. S. *A Life of Robert and Mary Moffat* (London, 1885)
Moffat, R. *Missionary Labours and Scenes in Southern Africa* (London, 1842)
   The Matabele Journals of Robert Moffat, ed. J. P. B. Wallis (2 vols., London, 1945)
Moffat, R. and M. *Apprenticeship at Kuruman: being the journals and letters of Robert and Mary Moffat, 1820–1828*, ed. I. Schapera (London, 1951)
Molesworth, Sir W. C. *Materials for a speech in defence of the policy of abandoning the Orange River Territory* (London, 1854)
Moodie, D. *The Record: or a series of official papers relative to the condition and treatment of the native tribes of South Africa* (Cape Town, 1838–42)
Muller, C. F. J. *Die Britse Owerheid en die Groot Trek*, 2nd edn, revised (Johannesburg, 1963)
Neumark, S. D. *Economic Influences on the South African Frontier, 1652–1836* (Stanford, 1957)
Nicholson, G. *The Cape and its Colonists . . . with hints to prospective emigrants* (London, 1848)
Omer-Cooper, J. D. *The Zulu Aftermath* (London, 1966)
Orpen, J. M. *Reminiscences of Life in South Africa from 1846 to the Present Day* (Cape Town, 1904)
Patterson, Sheila *Colour and Culture in South Africa: a study of the status of the Cape coloured people within the social structure of the Union of South Africa* (London, 1953)
   The Last Trek (London, 1957)
Pelissier, S. H. *Jean Pierre Pelissier van Bethulie* (Pretoria, 1956)

Bibliography

Philip, J. *Researches in South Africa* (2 vols., London, 1828)

Powell, F. W. *Hancock's Drift: the story of the great wagon road* (Pietermaritz-burg, 1960)

Read, James (Jnr.) *The Kat River Settlement in 1851* (Cape Town, 1852)

Richter, J. *Geschichte der Berliner Mission* (Berlin, 1924)

Ridsdale, Benjamin *Scenes and Adventures in Namaqualand* (Cape Town, 1883)

Rosenthal, E. *Southern African Dictionary of National Biography* (London, 1966)

Rouillard, Nancy *Matabele Thompson: an autobiography* (London, 1936)

Rutherford, J. *Sir George Grey, a study in colonial government* (London, 1961)

Sampson, C. G. and M. *Riversmead Shelter: excavations and analysis* Memoir no. 5, National Museum Bloemfontein (1967)

Schapera, I. *The Khoisan Peoples of South Africa* (London, 1930)
Government and Politics in Tribal Societies (London, 1956)

Selous, F. C. *A Hunter's Wanderings in Africa* (London, 1881)

Shaw, Barnabas *Memorials of Southern Africa* (London, 1841)

Shaw, W. E. (ed.) *Memoirs of Mrs. Anne Hodgson . . . compiled from Materials furnished by her husband, the Rev. T. L. Hodgson, comprising also an Account of the Commencement and Progress of the Wesleyan Mission amongst the Griqua and Bechuana tribes of Southern Africa* (London, 1836)
The Story of My Mission in South Eastern Africa (London, 1865)

Sillery, A. *Sechele* (Oxford, 1954)

Simons, H. J. and R. E. *Class and Colour in South Africa, 1850–1950* (Harmondsworth, 1969)

Smith, Andrew *The Diary of Dr. Andrew Smith*, ed. P. R. Kirby (2 vols., Cape Town, 1939–40)

Smith, Sir H. G. W. *The Autobiography of Sir Harry Smith*, ed. G. C. Moore Smith (2 vols., London, 1903)

Solomon, E. *Two Lectures on the Native Tribes of the Interior, delivered before the Mechanics Institute, Cape Town* (Cape Town, 1858)

Solomon, W. E. G. *Saul Solomon: THE Member for Cape Town* (Cape Town, 1948)

Sparrman, A. *A Voyage to the Cape of Good Hope, 1772–6* (2 vols., Dublin, 1785)

Spoelstra, C. *Bouwstoffen voor de Geschiedenis der Nederduitsch Gerefor-meerde Kerken in Zuid-Afrika* (2 vols., Amsterdam, 1906–7)

Stanford, Sir Walter *The Reminiscences of Sir Walter Stanford*, ed. J. W. MacQuarrie (2 vols., Cape Town, 1958, 1962)

Stedman, A. *Wanderings and Adventures in the Interior of Southern Africa* (London, 1835)

Stockenström, Sir Andries *The Autobiography of Sir Andries Stockenström* ed. C. W. Hutton (2 vols., Cape Town, 1887)

Stow, G. W. *The Native Races of South Africa* (London, 1905)

Tabler, E. C. *The Far Interior (1847–99)* (Cape Town, 1955)

Theal, G. M. (ed.) *Basutoland Records* (3 vols., Cape Town, 1883)
    History of South Africa since 1795 (5 vols., London, 1908)
    Records of the Cape Colony (36 vols., London, 1899—1905)
Thom, H. B. *Die Geskiedenis van Skaapboerdery in Suid-Afrika* (Amsterdam, 1936)
Thompson, E. P. *The Making of the English Working Class* (London, 1963)
Thompson, G. *Travels and Adventures in Southern Africa* (2 vols., London, 1827)
Thompson, W. *A Word on Behalf of the Downtrodden* (Cape Town, 1854)
    The Griquas (Cape Town, 1854)
Thunberg, C. B. *Travels in Europe, Africa and Asia made between the years 1770 and 1779* (4 vols., London, 1795)
Tindall, Rev. H. *Two Lectures on Great Namaqualand and its Inhabitants* (Cape Town, 1856)
Valentyn, F. *Description of the Cape of Good Hope with the matters concerning it*, ed. E. H. Raidt (2 vols., Cape Town, 1971—3)
van den Berghe, P. L. *South Africa: a study in conflict*, 2nd edn (Berkeley, 1967)
    Race and Racism: a comparative perspective (New York, 1967)
van der Merwe, P. J. *Die Noordwaartse Beweging van die Boere voor die Groot Trek* (The Hague, 1937)
    Die Trekboer in Die Geskiedenis van die Kaap Kolonie (Cape Town, 1938)
    Trek, Studies oor die Mobiliteit van die Pioneersbevolking aan die Kaap (Cape Town, 1945)
van Ryneveld, W. S. *Aanmerking over de Verbetering van het Vee aan de Kaap de Goede Hope*, ed. H. B. Thom (Cape Town, 1942)
Vedder, H. H. (ed.) *The Native Tribes of South West Africa* (Cape Town, 1928)
    South West Africa in Early Times, trans. C. G. Hall (London, 1938)
Walker, E. A. *The Frontier Tradition in South Africa* (Oxford, 1930)
    The Great Trek, 2nd edn (London, 1936)
    W. P. Schreiner: a South African (London, 1937)
    A History of Southern Africa, 3rd edn (London, 1963)
Wallis, J. P. R. *Thomas Baines of King's Lynn: explorer and artist (1820—1875)* (London, 1941)
Wangemann, H. T. *Die Berliner Mission im Koranna-lande* (Berlin, 1873)
Warren, Sir C. *On the Veldt in the Seventies* (London, 1902)
Watson, G. *Passing for White: a study of racial assimilation in a South African school* (London, 1970)
Welsh, D. *The Roots of Segregation* (Cape Town, 1972)
Williams, Donovan *When Races Meet: the life and times of William Ritchie Thompson* (Johannesburg, 1967)
Wilson, M. and Thompson, L. M. (eds.) *The Oxford History of South Africa* (2 vols., Oxford, 1969, 1971)
Witbooi, H. *Die Dagboek van Hendrik Witbooi* (Cape Town, 1929)
Wright, J. B. *Bushman Raiders in the Drakensberg* (Pietermaritzburg, 1971)

ARTICLES

Alexander, R. A. 'Horse sickness', *Farming in South Africa* IX (1934)

Anon. 'A run to Nomansland', *Cape Monthly Magazine* (1876–7)

Atmore, Anthony 'The passing of Sotho independence, 1865–1870' in *African Societies in Southern Africa*, ed. L. Thompson (London, 1969)

Atmore, Anthony, Chirenje, J. M., and Mudenge, S. I. 'Firearms in Central Africa', *Journal of African History* XII (1971)

Atmore, Anthony, and Sanders, Peter 'Sotho arms and ammunition in the nineteenth century', *Journal of African History* XII (1971)

Attree, Eileen M. 'The Closer Union Movement between the Orange Free State, South African Republic and Cape Colony (1838–1863)', *Archives Year Book for South African History* (1949, I)

Bailey, F. G. 'Decisions by consensus in councils and committees' in Association of Social Anthropologists Monographs II, *Political Systems and the Distribution of Power* (London, 1965)

Barnard, B. J. 'n'Levensbeskrywing van Major Henry Douglas Warden', *Archives Year Book for South African History* (1948, I)

Bonner, P. 'The relations between internal and external politics in Swaziland and the eastern Transvaal in the mid-19th century', in *Collected Seminar Papers on the Societies of Southern Africa in the 19th and 20th Centuries*. Vol. II (University of London, Institute of Commonwealth Studies, 1970–1)

Broom, R. 'Bushmen, Korannas and Hottentots', *Annals of the Transvaal Museum* XX (1948)

Bundy, Colin, 'The emergence and decline of a South African peasantry', *African Affairs* LXXXI (1972)

Campbell, W. B. 'The South African frontier, 1865–85: a study in expansion', *Archives Year Book for South African History* (1959, I)

Carter, P. L. 'Late Stone Age exploitation patterns in southern Natal', *South African Archaeological Bulletin* XXV (1970)

Cripps, G. St. V. 'Highlands and Lowlands of Kaffraria', *Cape Monthly Magazine* (1877)

Duminy, A. H. 'The role of Sir Andries Stockenström in Cape Politics', *Archives Year Book for South African History* (1960, II)

du Toit, A. E. 'The Cape frontier: a study of Native Policy with special reference to the years 1847–1866', *Archives Year Book for South African History* (1951, I)

Edgar, Bob. 'Garveyism in Africa: Dr Wellington and the "American Movement" in the Transkei, 1925–30' in *Collected Seminar Papers on the Societies of Southern Africa in the 19th and 20th Centuries*. Vol. VI (Institute of Commonwealth Studies, London, 1974–5)

Freund, William 'Race relations in southern Africa at the turn of the nineteenth century; the Cape Colony in the Batavian era', in *Collected Seminar Papers on the Societies of Southern Africa in the 19th and 20th centuries*. Vol. I (Institute of Commonwealth Studies, London, 1969–70)

Gahey, H. H. 'John Philip's role in Hottentot emancipation', *Journal of African History* III (1962)

Galbraith, J. S. 'The "Turbulent Frontier" as a factor in British Expansion', *Comparative Studies in Society and History* II (1959–60)

Grobbelaar, C. S. 'The physical characteristics of the Korana', *South African Journal of Science* LIII (1956)

Grobelaar, J. J. G. 'Die Vrystaatse Republiek en die Basoetoe Vraagstuk', *Archives Year Book for South African History* (1939, II)

Hall, T. D. 'South African pastures, retrospective and prospective', *South African Journal of Science* XXXI (1934)

Hancock, W. K. 'Trek', *Economic History Review*, 2nd Series, X (1956–7)

Harinck, Gerrit 'Interaction between Xhosa and Khoi: emphasis on the period 1620–1750' in *African Societies in Southern Africa*, ed. L. Thompson (London, 1969)

Humphries, A. J. B. 'Comments on the raw material usage in the later Stone Age of the middle Orange River area', *South African Archaeological Society, Goodwin Series* I (1972)

Johnstone, Frederick 'Class conflict and colour bars in South Africa's gold mining industry, 1910–1926' in *Collected Seminar Papers on the Societies of Southern Africa in the 19th and 20th centuries*. Vol. I (Institute of Commonwealth Studies, London, 1969–70)
    'White prosperity and white supremacy in South Africa today', *African Affairs* LXIX (1970)

Jordan, W. D. 'American Chiaroscuro: the definition of mulattoes in the British colonies', *William and Mary Quarterly*, 3rd Series, XIX (1962)

Kirk, Tony 'Progress and Decline in the Kat River settlement', *Journal of African History* XIV (1973)

Kuper, Adam 'Council structure and decision making', in *Councils in Action*, ed. Audrey Richards and Adam Kuper (Cambridge, 1971)

Le Cordeur, B. A. 'The relations between the Cape and Natal', *Archives Year Book for South African History* (1965, I)

Legassick, M. C. 'The frontier tradition in South African historiography', in *Collected Seminar Papers on the Societies of Southern Africa in the 19th and 20th centuries*. Vol. II (Institute of Commonwealth Studies, London, 1970–1)

Lye, W. F. 'The Difaqane: the Mfecane in the southern Sotho area', *Journal of African History* VIII (1967)
    'The distribution of the Sotho peoples after the Difaqane', in *African Societies in Southern Africa*, ed. L. Thompson (London, 1969)
    'The Ndebele kingdom south of the Limpopo River', *Journal of African History* X (1969)

Maggs, T. M. O'C. 'Pastoral settlements on the Riet River', *South African Archaeological Bulletin* XXVI (1971)

Maingard, L. F. 'The lost tribes of the Cape', *South African Journal of Science* XXVIII (1931)
    'Studies in Korana history, customs and language', *Bantu Studies* VI (1932)

'The Brikwa and the ethnic origins of the Bathlaping', *South African Journal of Science* XXX (1933)

Marks, Shula 'African and Afrikaner History', *Journal of African History* XI (1970)

'Khoisan resistance to the Dutch in the seventeenth and eighteenth centuries', *Journal of African History* XIII (1972)

Marks, Shula, and Atmore, Anthony 'Firearms in southern Africa: a survey', *Journal of African History* XII (1971)

May, I. R. 'Locusts and/or grasshoppers' *Optima* XIX (1969)

Midgley, J. F. 'The Orange River Sovereignty (1848–1854)', *Archives Year Book for South African History* (1949, II)

Moffat, R. (Jnr) 'Journey from Colesberg to Steinkopf, 1854–5', *Journal of the Royal Geographical Society* XXVIII (1858)

Oberholster, J. J. 'Die Anneksasie van Griekwaland Wes', *Archives Year Book for South African History* (1945)

Parsons, H. A. 'The Coinage of Griqualand', *Numismatic Calendar* XXXV (1927)

[Philip, W. B.] 'The Griquas and their exodus', *Cape Monthly Magazine* (December 1872)

Richards, R. 'Pommer and Sidoi', *Natal Magazine* (1879)

Robertson, H. M. '150 Years of Economic Conflict between White and Black', *South African Journal of Economics* II (1934)

Robinson, R. E., 'Non-European foundations of European imperialism: sketch for a theory of collaboration' in Roger Owen and Bob Sutcliffe (eds.) *Studies in the Theory of Imperialism* (London, 1972)

Ross, R. 'Griqua power and wealth; an analysis of the paradoxes of their inter-relationship' in *Collected Seminar Papers of the Institute of Commonwealth Studies, London, Southern Africa* IV (1973)

'Griqua Government', *African Studies* XXXIII (1974)

'The "white" population of South Africa in the eighteenth century', *Population Studies* XXIX (1975)

Sampson, C. G. and M. 'Excavations at Zaayfontein Shelter, Norvalspont, Northern Cape', *Researches of the National Museum, Bloemfontein*, II (1967)

'Excavations at Glen Elliot Shelter, Colesberg District, Northern Cape', *Researches of the National Museum, Bloemfontein*, II (1967)

'A later Stone Age open site near Venterstad, Cape', *Researches of the National Museum, Bloemfontein*, II (1967)

Sanders, Peter 'Sekonyela and Moshoeshoe', *Journal of African History* X (1969)

Sanderson, J. 'Memoranda of a trading trip into the Orange River Free State and country of the Transvaal Boers, 1851–2', *Journal of the Royal Geographical Society* XXX (1860)

Saunders, C. C. 'Early knowledge of the Sotho', *Quarterly Bulletin of the South African Library* CCXCIII (1966)

Scholtz, P. L. 'Die Historiese Ontwikkeling van die Onder Oliphants Rivier', *Archives Year Book for South African History* (1966, I)

Schutte, C. E. G. 'Dr. John Philip's observations regarding the Hottentots',

Archives Year Book for South African History (1940)

Silberbauer, G. B., and Kuper, Adam 'Kgalagadi masters and Bushman serfs: some observations', *African Studies* XXV (1966)

Slater, Henry 'The Natal Land and Colonisation Company, 1860–1948', *Collected Seminar Papers of the Institute of Commonwealth Studies, London, Southern Africa* IV (1973)

Smith, Alan 'Delagoa Bay and South-Eastern Africa' in *Precolonial African Trade*, ed. R. Gray and David Birmingham (London, 1970)

Sutherland-Harris, N. 'Trade and the Rozwi Mambo', in *Precolonial African Trade*, ed. R. Gray and David Birmingham (London, 1970)

Tabler, E. C. 'Non-Europeans as Interior Men', *Africana Notes and News* XIII (1959)

Tobias, P. V. 'Physical Anthropology and the Somatic Origins of the Hottentots', *African Studies* XIV (1955)

Trapido, Stanley 'The origin and development of the African political organisation' in *Collected Seminar Papers on the Societies of Southern Africa in the 19th and 20th Centuries*. Vol. I (Institute of Commonwealth Studies, London, 1969–1970)

'South Africa in a comparative study of industrialisation', *Journal of Development Studies* VII (1971)

'Liberalism at the Cape in the 19th and 20th centuries', *Collected Seminar Papers of the Institute of Commonwealth Studies, London, Southern Africa* IV (1972–3)

Tylden, G. 'The Cape Coloured Regiments, 1793–1870', *Africana Notes and News* VII (1950)

'The development of the commando system in South Africa, 1715–1922', *Africana Notes and News* XIII (1959)

'The commando system in South Africa, 1795–1881', *Africana Notes and News* VII (1950)

Tyler, W. B. 'Sir George Grey, South Africa and the Imperial Military Burden', *Historical Journal* XIV (1971)

van der Poel, Jean 'Basutoland as a factor in South African politics (1852–1870)', *Archives Year Book for South African History* (1941, I)

van Onselen, Charles 'Reactions to rinderpest in southern Africa, 1896–7', *Journal of African History* XIII (1972)

van Schoor, M. C. E. 'Politieke Groepering in Transgariep', *Archives Year Book for South African History* (1950, II)

'Die Nasionale en Politieke Bewuswording van die Afrikaner en sy Ontluiking in Transgariep tot 1854', *Archives Year Book for South African History* (1963, II)

Wilcox, A. 'Sheep and sheepherders in South Africa', *Africa* XXXVI (1966)

Wolpe, Harold 'Industrialism and race in South Africa' in *Race and Racialism*, ed. S. Zubaida (London, 1970)

Wuras, C. G. 'An account of the Korana', *Bantu Studies* III (1927–9)

Young, Lindsay 'The native policy of Benjamine Pine in Natal, 1850–1855', *Archives Year Book for South African History* (1951, II)

THESES AND OTHER UNPUBLISHED WORKS

Cragg, D. G. L. 'The Relations of the Amampondo and the Colonial Authorities', D.Phil., Oxon., 1959

Giliomee, H. B. 'The Cape Eastern Frontier, 1775–1812', unpublished Seminar Paper, Institute of Commonwealth Studies, London (1973)

Inskeep, R. R. 'The Problem of Bantu Expansion in the light of recent research on the Iron Age of Southern Africa', unpublished Seminar Paper, Institute of Commonwealth Studies, London (1975)

Parkington, J. E. 'Recent Developments in the Study of Prehistory at the Cape', unpublished Seminar Paper, Institute of Commonwealth Studies, London, (1974)

Saunders, C. C. 'The annexation of the Transkeian Territories (1872–1895) with special reference to British and Cape Policy', D.Phil., Oxon., 1972

van Aswegen, H. J. 'Die verhouding tussen blanken en nie-blanken in die Oranje Vrystaat, 1854–1902', D.Phil, University of the Orange Free State, 1968.

NEWSPAPERS

South African Commercial Advertiser, 1830–1854
Grahamstown Journal, 1838–1854
Friend of the Sovereignty (after March 1854 *Friend of the Free State*), 1850–1862
Kokstad Advertiser, odd numbers
Natal Witness, 1859–1879
Natal Mercury, 1859–1879

PERIODICALS

Missionsberichte of the Gesellschaft zur Beforderung der Evangelischen Missionen unter den Heiden (*Berliner Missionsbericht*), 1833–1860

INDEX

Index